THE
forever
staircase

A MEMOIR

Kate McIver

ISBN-13: 978-1-95756-628-3
Cover and Interior Design by Scot McDonald
Cover images: clouds © Atstock Productions/iStock; toys © Elena/ Adobe Stock; staricase © spline_x/ Adobe Stock
LCCN: 2025910136

Printed in the United States of America
1 2 3 4 5 6 7 8 9 10 Printing/Year 28 27 26 25 24

Table Of Contents

Introduction

As a compulsive diarist, notetaker, and unofficial family historian, I had always planned to write a memoir but was never quite sure what its focus should be. Should I write about being a preacher's kid? About coming of age in Dallas, Texas, during the 1960s? Should I perhaps publish my ninth-grade diary, which is quirky enough to stand on its own?

Or maybe I could continue the legacy of my father, a gifted storyteller who found real-life events far more interesting than any fiction. Before his death in 2001, Dad wrote several books that portrayed the humorous, touching, and sometimes strange events he had encountered as both a minister and a father. Still, there were many stories he never got around to recounting, and I toyed with the idea of composing a sequel to his own books.

While the latter remains a future option, my primary impulse was to write a more personal autobiography. I made several false starts on the memoir but always ran into the same problem: I was devoting an inordinate amount of time and space to my early childhood—so much so that my first seven years could have become a separate book.

The main reason for this was that my birth mother died shortly after my fourth birthday . . . and this loss remains the most seminal event of my life. It cleaved my world disproportionately, with my first four years carrying as much weight as the next sixty-six. Each time I tried to tackle a memoir, those early years refused to be skimmed over or treated as mere background information.

I finally decided to give them the attention they needed and deserved. Thus, *The Forever Staircase* primarily concerns the time before Mother's death, and the subsequent three years of adjustment for Daddy and myself.

My memory has always been especially good, and it served me well as I re-created those distant eras. I suppose that most people envision their early childhood as a long, fog-shrouded road where occasional images break through, blurring together without much context. My situation was somewhat different. Since our family moved several times during my preschool years, it was easy to correlate an event with a location and thus pinpoint my age. If a particular memory came from our orange duplex in Dallas, I knew that I was at least four years old. Recollections from a white house in Lubbock marked my age at two or three. And if I recalled something from a blue house in San Marcos, Texas, then I must have been under two years old.

In portraying "The World as It Was" before Mother's death, I relied not only upon personal memories but also upon a rich trove of family history, stories, and written records. And I will always be grateful for the two calfskin-bound volumes that my father passed down to me, each filled with hundreds of sympathy letters, cards, and telegrams. Together, these missives provide a panoramic view of my mother's personality and are a testament to her positive influence during her thirty years on earth.

While I wrote *The Forever Staircase* to relate my own life story, I also wanted to depict a fuller portrait of my birth mother. My parents and I moved to Dallas in the summer of 1956. There, we joined Wilshire Baptist Church (of which my father later became pastor). Only a handful of members knew my mother, from their years at Baylor University. She became ill and died three weeks later—before most other members had been able to meet her or form friendships.

Even after Daddy became pastor, everyone knew that he had lost his first wife. But he rarely mentioned this tragedy from the pulpit, or even in social circumstances. He remarried in 1960. And as the years passed, my birth mother became a ghostly memory to fewer and fewer people. In 1990, my father—for the first time—wrote about his wife's death in his book *Stories I Couldn't Tell While I Was a Pastor*. I had not realized how meaningful it would be to me to simply have her life affirmed and acknowledged.

In *The Forever Staircase*, I provide even more details about Jean McIver's background, life, and passing. Thus, the following pages are in part an elegy to my mother. But they also chronicle my own experience with grief. The topic is unavoidably sad for readers but is, I trust, balanced by light-hearted moments and even humor.

And while I faced many emotional challenges throughout my youth and adulthood, I finally arrived at a place of peace and resolution. Today, I can gratefully declare:

> The lines are fallen unto me in pleasant places; yea, I have a
> goodly heritage. (Psalm 16:6, KJV)

I

The World As
It Was

1

Return To San Marcos

As a preacher's daughter, I think it's fitting that one of my earliest memories took hold beneath a steeple.

I was only a year old at the time, too young to have much awareness of any world beyond playpens and backyard fences. I didn't realize that my family lived in San Marcos, a pretty college town meandering up one flank of the Texas Hill Country. Nor did I grasp that my father was an ordained minister who, instead of pastoring his own congregation, taught Bible classes and directed Baptist student activities at Southwest Texas State Teachers College. I *was* quite aware that my parents and I frequently spent time at a church but didn't know that its name was "First Baptist," or that I was a member of its Cradle Roll Department. Nevertheless, it was in that place that my one-year-old mind latched onto a scene so vivid and recurrent that I still recall it with ease:

It is a Sunday morning, probably in 1953. A worship service has just ended, and my mother is fetching me from the church nursery where, true to form, I have been acting quite immature for my age. Although I have learned to walk, I refuse to play on the floor with the other toddlers. The boys are too rough, shoving girl babies onto their diapered bottoms or clonking them over the head with wooden blocks. As usual, I have signaled to the teacher that I want to be safely stowed in a special crib: the one with a colorful cradle gym strung across its rails. I have a similar toy at home, but mine is not nearly as fancy as this one. The church's model has a greater array of wooden dowels, plastic rings, and jingly bells. But best of all, its blue/red/yellow color scheme has been expanded with . . . purple! It is this marvelous grapey hue that draws me to a particular crib week after week, where I spend my Sunday school hours batting at an infant toy while my peers develop their social skills on a nearby floor.

The nursery is located off the sanctuary's foyer. My mother is the church organist, and it is possible that I catch strains of her music vibrating through the walls. If I imagine my father's role at all, I probably picture him singing congregational hymns as I conceive them: "Jesus Loves Me," "Three Blind Mice," or maybe a rollicking "Rig-a-Jig-Jig" or "Away We Go," which Daddy sometimes warbles off-key while swinging me around our living room as best as his lame hip will allow.

When the church service ends, I am boosted through the top half of the nursery's Dutch door and passed to my mother, who then mingles in the foyer with other congregants. The men wear suits, and the ladies' hands are gloved. Glass-eyed weasels drape the bosoms of older matrons; younger women sport small flat hats above their Mamie Eisenhower bangs. Everyone is properly attired for Sunday-morning worship in the 1950s. Among the parishioners are quite a few of Daddy's students, and I recognize several faces that float in and out of my life at social gatherings, campus events, and here at church. Even now, a sea of hands reaches toward me, crowding close. Everyone, it seems, wants to pat my dimples or finger the lace on my butter-yellow coat and bonnet, both handmade by Grandmother Withers.

Craning my head around fur collars and hat nettings, I peer into the sanctuary and study its stained glass windows. Although I hunt in vain for purple, I am enthralled by the other rainbow colors: apple reds, Easter-chick yellows, lily-pad greens, and cobalt hues so dazzling they might be gemstones set into Old King Cole's crown.

* * *

On a spring day several decades later, my father and I once again stood in that San Marcos sanctuary, now empty except for the two of us and the church's young minister. At the time, I was living 130 miles east in College Station. Dad had long resided in Dallas, where our family had moved (after a stint in Lubbock) shortly before Mother's unexpected death in 1956. For thirty years, my father had shepherded the large flock of Dallas's Wilshire Baptist Church, where he currently served as pastor emeritus.

I'm not sure what triggered my hankering to revisit my birthplace, but a few days earlier I had phoned Dad to ask if he would go with me. I reminded him that we had moved to Lubbock right after my second birthday and that I had no memories of revisiting San Marcos. "I can recall a house and rooms and a yard," I told him, "but have no idea what the town itself looked like."

Agreeing to serve as tour guide, Dad had driven down to College Station for an overnight visit. The next morning, we motored two hours west toward the Hill Country. I had invited Lawanna, my longtime "second mother," to come with us, but she had graciously declined, saying that this was a journey Daddy and I needed to make by ourselves.

Numerous hip, spine, and heart surgeries had scarred my father's body. His sideburns had whitened, and he walked with a cane. But he was still fairly active and had easily steered his Camry through Central Texas, past meadows frothy with bluebonnets and Indian paintbrush. "You know," he mused as each mile carried us further back in time, "Jean and I didn't have much money, but those years in San Marcos were some of the happiest I've ever known." He and my birth mother had been young newlyweds in the early 1950s, their lives as yet untouched by major stresses. I had glimpsed this more carefree world through old black-and-white photos of my parents joining college students for songfests, Valentine banquets, or weenie roasts on the banks of the Guadalupe River.

By the time we reached Interstate 35—the main corridor between Austin and San Antonio—the weight of decades seemed to have fallen from Dad's shoulders. His spirits were buoyant when, a half hour later, we eased up the Balcones Escarpment and into San Marcos. Having always pictured the town as being flat and scrub-brushy, I was surprised to find a steep, leafy terrain. In fact, were it not for the limestone cliffs peeking through foliage and small cactus plants ornamenting a few front yards, we might have been in the Blue Ridge foothills of my father's native North Carolina.

We crossed a river whose cypress-shaded waters I vaguely recalled and made our initial stop at the First Baptist Church. Moments later, I stood near the Lord's Supper table, half listening as Dad and the church's younger pastor discussed denominational politics and various challenges of the ministry. But the bulk of my attention was on the sanctuary itself . . . and the realization that I had once laid infant eyes on this very room. Undoubtedly, the decor had changed multiple times. The hymnbooks had passed through several revisions, and the organ and baby grand piano had been updated or replaced.

But those windows! They were original. Tall and rectangular, their stained glass formed abstract patterns that seemed more modern than medieval. The colors were both familiar and elusive, like long-buried dreams: happy reds—cheery as the nose on my roly-poly clown, the cherries painted on our kitchen dishes, or the polish on Mother's softly rounded fingernails.

A few feet away, the men had segued into anecdote-swapping. Leaning on his cane, Dad launched into a tale about the time our Dallas church needed to raise emergency hurricane-relief funds for a sister congregation in the Caribbean. "We got the request early on a Sunday morning," he told the pastor. "I normally didn't twist arms for money—I didn't even like to *talk* about it—but I had personally promised our missionary liaison that a specific amount would be wired that afternoon."

Having heard the story many times, I continued to study the windows' palette: honeybee golds; mossy, sun-splashed greens; blues so deep that one might drown in them.

"Now mind you," Dad was saying, "this was right in the middle of football season back in the '70s, when the Cowboys were in their glory days. At any rate, just before the benediction at the eleven o'clock service, I explained the situation to the congregation and told them how much money was needed. I said, 'Okay, folks, here's what's going to happen. I've instructed the ushers to *lock* all of the sanctuary doors, and we're going to pass the offering plates. The Cowboys are scheduled to kick off at one o'clock, and it's now . . . let's see . . . 12:04.'"

Even as I joined in on the chuckles, my mind was still far across the room. Of all the windows' colors, it was that unique shade of blue that tugged at some deep place, causing my throat to tighten with an almost primal longing. I had visited cathedrals in England and many churches throughout America. But I was certain that I had seen that peculiar cobalt shade in only one place—here in this room.

My father's voice seemed to come from a distant tunnel: "So a few minutes later we counted the contributions, and I went back to the microphone and said, 'Folks, you've done a great job. But we're still a bit short of the amount needed. So we're going to pass the plates one more time. It's now 12:14, and I remind you—the Cowboys are *still* kicking off at one o'clock!'"

Drawn by the Old King Cole blue, I felt myself suddenly whooshed back in time, as if through a cosmic vacuum. In an instant, it was once again 1953. No one had ever heard of Sputnik or Elvis Presley. *Captain Kangaroo,* Hula-Hoops, and Disneyland were still in the future. John F. Kennedy was just a senator, and Vietnam a little-known country.

Nothing was yet "Blowin' in the Wind," and The Beatles had never existed. Nor had hippies, Woodstock, jumbo jets, or space shuttles. And the Dallas Cowboys were not even a pipe dream.

"So did you raise the funds, Bruce?" asked the pastor.

"Every penny," laughed Dad. "You've never seen such a scramble for wallets and checkbooks!"

I waited until the men's chuckles died down and then softly spoke: "The nursery was over there."

"Huh?"

"The nursery. It was just off the foyer, over on the left."

Dad looked in the direction I was pointing. "You know," he said, "I believe you're right. It *was* over there."

"You can remember that far back?" asked the pastor.

"Yes," Daddy attested. "She can."

* * *

After leaving the church, my father drove the two of us toward the college that had been renamed "Southwest Texas State University." Near the campus, he paused at a large stone manor—now a fraternity house—that had once been the Old Soldiers and Sailors Memorial Hospital. It was there that I had been born on Easter Sunday of 1952. Because I had not been due for another two weeks, Dad had accepted a preaching engagement in Corsicana, almost two hundred miles away. According to family lore, Mother went out with girlfriends on Saturday night and gorged on pizza, which threw her into a pepperoni-induced labor. Upon getting an unexpected wake-up call on Sunday morning, Daddy had raced back to San Marcos as fast as possible on the pre-interstate roads. I beat him to the hospital, arriving shortly after 9 a.m. (In those days, of course, fathers were not allowed in the delivery room, and their wives were usually knocked out cold for the birth itself. In one surviving letter, my mother effused to a friend: "I like my doctor so much. He didn't let me know a *thing!*")

Continuing on to the campus, Dad and I next stopped at the Baptist Student Union, a low-slung modern structure built during my father's tenure as BSU director. A pillared mansion had previously occupied the site, and it was there that Lyndon Baines Johnson had boarded when he attended Southwest Texas State Teachers College in the late 1920s. A decade or so later, the big white house had become BSU's campus headquarters. My parents lived in an upstairs apartment, and it was to this "home" that I was brought from the hospital.

Dad parked the Camry curbside. We got out, and my father pointed his cane toward a stand of tall oaks just behind the newer building. "Those trees," he said, "are probably *still* ringing with your cries." It seems that I had entered the world squalling and did not stop for nearly five months. My parents walked the floor day and night, never quite sure if I suffered from colic or was just at odds with life itself.

For Dad, the short walk to the BSU Center was a stroll down memory lane; for me, it was a mere curiosity. I had no recollection of the current building or of the older house. When contemplating the latter, I could only imagine the cacophony of sounds that must have filtered up to our apartment: giggles and guffaws from college kids, the hollow *thwap!* of ping-pong balls, a screen door's slam, the ratchety crank of a Coke machine, voices belting out tunes from *Singspiration* songbooks:

> Heavenly sunlight, heavenly sunlight,
> Flooding my soul with glory divine!
> Hallelujah, I am rejoicing!
> Singing His praises, Jesus is mine.

My First Home: The Baptist Student Union

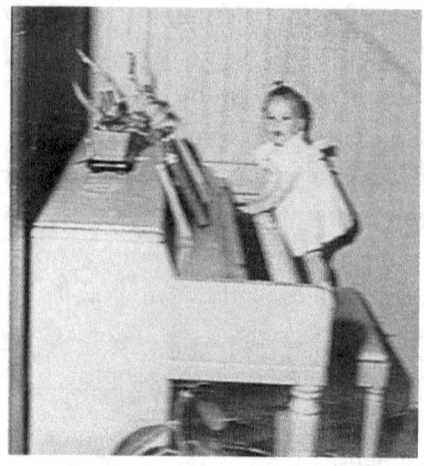

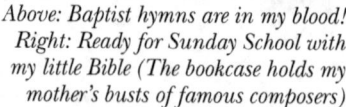

Above: Baptist hymns are in my blood!
Right: Ready for Sunday School with
my little Bible (The bookcase holds my
mother's busts of famous composers)

A new generation of students now congregated on the center's front steps, listening to Walkmans and swigging cans of Mountain Dew from computer-chipped machines. Several backpacks bore political decals from the previous year's presidential election.

"Were your students concerned about McCarthy's anti-communist witch hunt?" I asked Daddy as we picked our way through a clump of coeds. I was recalling my own college days in the rebellious Vietnam era ("Hey, hey, LBJ, how many kids did you kill today?"). "Did they protest the Rosenberg executions?"

"Not really." He shrugged, holding the front door open for me. "Most of them were from farms or small towns, and a lot of the guys were on the GI Bill. They were just grateful for the chance to get an education."

As BSU director, my father would have coordinated activities, planned weekend retreats, brought in guest speakers, and facilitated group discussions. In the 1950s, the students' roundtable topics may have touched upon the "sins" of dancing and card-playing or the dangers of frequenting honky-tonks that lined the road to Austin. Dad was by no means a fire-and-brimstone preacher (and his social and theological views would broaden greatly as he aged), but like all Southern Baptist leaders of that time, he *did* cotton to the denomination's "no drinking/

smoking/dancing" position.

Since the current BSU director was out of the office, Daddy and I did not spend a great deal of time at the center. We nodded to a few students who sprawled on the lounge's sofas, leafed through a rack of brochures, and examined a brick wall's contemporary fireplace, which my father said had been quite a spiffy feature back in 1953. We then descended to a basement-level recreation room. Noting an upright piano, I asked Dad if my mom had accompanied sing-alongs. He said that a couple of college students usually played but that Mother sometimes filled in for them.

I fingered the piano's keys while Dad studied a nearby bulletin board, neither of us speaking for a few moments. For better or worse, we often communicated with a silence that bonded us more strongly than words. We rarely talked about my birth mother—not because the subject was taboo or my father was reluctant to answer any questions. It was just that her relevance to our busy modern lives and "newer" family unit had faded into near oblivion.

But on that day in San Marcos, I could sense an almost palpable presence hovering around us.

I had never heard a negative word spoken about my mother—not by Daddy, her family, or anyone who knew her. Nor did I have any negative memories, save for those occasional spankings that *all* of us preschoolers got during the 1950s. Having never discussed Mother's apparent perfection with Daddy, I now raised the question: "In her thirty years on earth, did she tally up *no* faults whatsoever?"

"Well . . ." Dad hesitated, mulling over his answer. "Jean could get frustrated and irritated like anyone else. But I honestly can't think of any major flaws." He then described his first wife with the familiar adjectives and nouns I had always encountered: radiant, deeply spiritual (although in no way persnickety or self-righteous), compassionate, gracious, witty and fun, level-headed, a "center of calm" in the midst of chaos.

I formed a silent chord on the piano. Along with her dimples and thick brown hair, I had inherited a respectable amount of Mother's musical ability (my father bequeathed his buck teeth, weak eyes, and ingrown toenails).

"Jean," Dad continued, "was a beautiful person, both inside and out. She was always immaculate, with every hair in place. Sometimes that *did* make her a bit late when we had to go somewhere. And she kept you dressed to the nines."

"That's probably why I spent so much time *crying*," I quipped. For my entire life, I had hated to be gussied up and spent little time primping in front of mirrors. All the same, I now removed my hands from the piano, suddenly self-conscious about my torn cuticles and uneven fingernails.

"So," I summarized a moment later as we retraced our way to the stairs, "aside from sometimes getting frustrated or being late, Mother truly didn't have any faults?"

"Well," Daddy paused. "There *was* one thing."

"Yeah?"

"Jean was a *terrible* cook."

* * *

Had my family continued to reside in the original BSU Center, I might be able to claim that I was potty-trained on LBJ's toilet. But when I was six months old, the grand old house was razed, and construction began on its replacement. Had this occurred a couple of decades later, Dad would have been lambasted for overseeing the destruction of an architectural "gem" and potentially historic structure. But in 1952, few people guessed that Lyndon Johnson would one day be president.

It was late afternoon by the time Daddy and I left the campus. We were scheduled to meet some old friends for dinner, but he first drove us to one last destination: a residential street and the rental house where my family had next lived. It was in that small gray rambler (I recalled it as being pale blue) that my first true memories had gelled. In one room, I had lain on a nubby white bedspread while a doctor pricked my thigh with a smallpox vaccine. A heating grate set into the hallway floor had once checkered my bare bottom when I sat down on it after taking a bath. I recalled that in my bedroom, Mother often rocked me to sleep while singing "Goodnight Ladies," the closing song of *The Dinah Shore Show*. By day, I had stood beside her at the kitchen's screen door, knee-high to her billowy cotton skirt, and tried to mimic her whistle and finger snaps as she called to our dog.

I had named the little terrier "Pea-Winkle." I usually enjoyed our frolics but would rage whenever he clamped his teeth onto my cloth diaper and sometimes pulled it clean off. This striptease always took place in the backyard, which was where I once stepped on a cocklebur—a seemingly innocuous memory, except that to my toddler mind, the thing was as large as a tennis ball. Our yard was also the setting for cookouts with Dad's students and other family friends, some of whom had young children. One of my first toddler playmates was Howard E. Butt III, whose father was both a lay evangelist and heir to the H-E-B grocery store chain. Early on, the grown-ups had labeled us "girlfriend and boyfriend." I was quite fickle about our romance, but years later, whenever I heard the *ding!* of an H-E-B cash register, I would regret not nurturing that relationship.

As it turned out, social intercourse proved as difficult for me as teething. Although I was often content and even gregarious in the presence of others, my personality demanded solitude at frequent intervals. I seem to have been born with ultra-sensitive wiring and easily fell apart when overwhelmed by stimuli. (As an adult, I am utterly unable to multitask, and hearing a store's endless PA announcements competing with Muzak and radio commercials can push me toward neurological meltdown.)

At a young age, I routinely sought refuge from life's hoopla by retreating to some quiet corner where I entertained myself with solo play or books. My most prized possessions were fifteen red-bound volumes of the *Childcraft* encyclopedia. For over sixty years, I have refused to part with these raggedy tomes, a couple of which have stiff, crinkled pages from being dropped in bathtubs. I cut my literary teeth on the first volumes, which were full of nursery rhymes, poems, and fairy tales. Years before I could read, I had memorized each watercolor illustration on every page. I knew as well as my own name that Jack and Jill tumbled down seafoam grass speckled with dandelions, and that the Knave of Hearts bore a platter of pink-iced tarts. I could cite each piece of candy decking a magnificent "Sugar-Plum Tree" whose boughs spread across two whole pages of Volume One. Above all, I loved the gnomes who stepped from their tree-root dwellings and fairies who ring-danced across moonlit glades.

As Dad's car now idled in front of the blue-gray house, I realized anew that those nocturnal creatures had been a good fit for me. Having been born on a Sunday, I should have been "bonny, blithe, and gay," according to a popular verse. Sometimes I was. But all too often, I was a drowsy, reflective child who preferred isolation to crowds and who felt far more comfortable brooding under moonbeams than scampering in the sunlight's harsher glare.

For the next few moments, Daddy and I continued to study the rental house, occasionally in silence, sometimes voicing our thoughts. Dad reminisced about various neighbors, about the sandbox he had set up for me in the backyard, about a nearby park and pond where my mother had taken me almost every day because I loved to feed the ducks.

He recalled the time a group of migrant workers came to San Marcos and trooped door-to-door, begging for food and clothing for their families. Feeling sorry for the slovenly bunch, my mother had immediately donated some canned goods, along with several fairly nice outfits from her closet. A few days later, she and Daddy were driving just outside of town when they crossed a bridge, and Mother suddenly hollered, "Stop this car!" Daddy screeched onto the road's shoulder and, following Mother's instructions, backed up. "Those are *my* clothes!" she cried, pointing to a dry gully beneath the bridge. There, several migrant families had set up a flea market. On a commercial clothing rack, several familiar outfits hung beneath a large hand-lettered sign that read: "Cheap Dresses."

Dad chortled over the memory, and I grinned just imagining the scene. "Had Mother ever gotten her clothes back?" I asked. Daddy said no—she figured that if the farm workers were that desperate for money, she ought to let them have a go at it. What *really* ticked her off was the insinuation that she wore "cheap" dresses. Grandmother Withers, he reminded me, had sewn or given her some beautiful outfits. And Mother was the type of woman who could wear the simplest skirt or an inexpensive dress with *style.*

"That was a good thing," said Dad, "because we sure didn't have much extra money." He put the Camry in gear but kept his foot on the brake, as if reluctant to pull away from the curb. "Still," he mused, "Jean and I had everything we needed, and by the time we rented this house, it felt like we were finally moving up in the world. We bought some living-room furniture on credit and got our first television set." Pointing out two grassy ruts in a side yard, he recalled their secondhand '49 Pontiac that often sat there. It ran well, he said, but like other cars of that era had no air-conditioning.

My father then described the 1,300-mile eastward trek our family had made each summer, the memories of which now caused him to groan and massage his temples. Still, I knew that the trips were essential to Daddy, for his *only* regret during these early years had been the geographical distance between himself and his Carolina kinfolk. As we gave the rental house a final gander, I pondered the differences between my visit to the Hill Country and Dad's annual pilgrimages to his own boyhood home. As special as this day had been for me, my desire to visit San Marcos felt more like a whimsy than a necessity: had I never returned to my barely remembered birthplace, it would not have significantly altered my life. But for Daddy, the homing instinct had been far more powerful. And I knew that nothing—not his aching hip or bumper-to-bumper traffic on narrow highways, not the lack of bypasses or the endless stoplights in every city and Podunk town throughout the South, not a sweltering car or the damp cloths that Mother placed on me to prevent prickly rash—would have kept him from retracing the path to his loved ones and to the land that had held them close for almost two hundred years.

2

Carolina Moon

George and Ollie McIver

I see the moon,
The moon sees me;
God bless the moon,
And God bless me.

This is a memory:

I am sitting in a car seat—the old-fashioned kind that is little more than a vinyl pouch with leg holes and flimsy aluminum handles that hook over a seat back. Sandwiched between my parents, I have a perfect front-and-center position for watching our Pontiac's giant hood gulp mile after mile of asphalt. It is nighttime, but I am wide awake, heady with being up so late and invigorated by a wintergreen scent that rushes through the car's open windows. The trees that line both sides of the narrow highway seem close enough to touch as they whip by in furry rows. They are different from those I know in San Marcos: taller, more uniform, and so dense that they block out everything but a perpendicular slot of sky directly in front of us. It is into this opening that an enormous sugar-cookie moon slips up from the end of the road. "I see the moon!" Mother exclaims, and she begins to chant the singsong rhyme.

My memory probably comes from one of our annual trips to visit Daddy's parents in North Carolina. Perhaps we were carving our way through a Tennessee forest, climbing the spine of a Blue Ridge mountain near Asheville, or maybe on the tail end of our long journey, coasting into the woods around Chatham County. My grandparents' modest white bungalow sat on the outskirts of Siler City, a town that in the 1960s would partially influence television's *Andy Griffith Show*. In later life, Dad would fondly reminisce about "the hills of home," but that was a stretch since his neck of the Carolina Piedmont lay smack in the center of the state and was a good two hours from any Blue Ridge foothills. Still, the rolling, pine-studded landscape was pleasant enough to foster nostalgia in those who had moved away.

For nearly two centuries, my paternal ancestors had tilled the area's orange clay soil, married their neighbors, and begat generations of McIvers and Moodys, Dunlaps and Emersons, Alstons and Rives. The McIvers had descended from stern and frugal Scottish Presbyterians; my grandmother's family, the Moodys, tended to be more laid-back and boisterous, with a gift for humor and storytelling. In the late 1800s, their cash income depended upon the corn, peanut, and tobacco harvests. If a crop season had been good, then all ten Moody children could be properly shod on Sundays for the half-mile walk to Rives Chapel Baptist Church. If the harvest had been poor, half of the kids would walk to and from morning preaching, then hand over their shoes so the others could attend an afternoon service.

My grandmother, Ollie, was the proverbial Earth Mother who fussed over her siblings and nurtured any living thing that sprouted, blossomed, crept, or flew. She had learned early on to be a caretaker of all creation, to "do unto others," and to talk so easily with Jesus that He might have been picking butter beans alongside her. My grandmother's faith ran deep, but she did not parade her spiritual life with great show; she was more likely to giggle over her own foibles than to cluck disapprovingly at another's.

When Ollie Moody married George McIver in 1919, the newlyweds moved a few miles from their rural homeplaces to the town of Siler City. There, my grandfather worked in a chair factory and hand-built the small white house in which my father was born in 1925. Although he grew up during the Great Depression, Dad had a relatively secure and normal childhood. Extra cash was seldom available for frills, but there was always ample food for Dad; his older brother, Sylvester (nicknamed "Sip"); and his younger sister, Ella George. With his best friends Billy and Russell Fitts (and sometimes with their twin brothers, Earl and Pearl), my father explored woods and fished in creeks. Like many of his peers, Dad tended several animals, shot marbles, read Tom Mix books, and mimicked Charles Lindbergh in his aviator goggles. On Saturdays, he could usually finagle a quarter for a double-feature matinee at the Elder Theater, along with popcorn and a drink.

The McIvers provided a loving but disciplined home. My grandfather was a small man who rarely raised his voice in anger, but who brooked no back talk, disobedience, or hissy fit from a child. If one look from his steel-blue eyes did not squelch a rebellious attitude, there was always the woodshed. Once, when Daddy was around five, he was standing in the rumble seat of a Model T Ford as the family motored to his Aunt Beulah's wedding. Something prompted Dad to utter his first four-letter word: *Dern!* My grandfather never took his eyes off the road nor gave a word of warning. He simply reached out and, in one swift motion, backhanded his boy across the mouth. But this was also the same man who, to soothe his small daughter, would gently roll her trundle bed around the room until she fell asleep. And the same man who told my teenage father—after punishing him over some serious infraction— "Son, I want to be your pal."

Top left: The McIver Siblings: Sip, Bruce (middle), and Ella George

Top right: Dad with his oldest brother, Sip

Bottom right: A loving father with his sons

Dad had been brought up in Siler City's First Baptist Church, but as a boy, he had no intention of becoming a preacher. In fact, he had never even intended to "get saved" the night he and Russell attended a local tent revival. Throughout the sermon, the boys had been acting as nine-year-olds will: squirming, passing notes, dropping songbooks. Dad never heard a word the evangelist said. When time came for repentant sinners to approach the altar and freely accept God's gift of salvation, an older woman seated behind Daddy whacked him on the shoulder.

"Young man," she said, "don't you think you ought to go up there?" So Dad obediently walked down the grassy aisle in the direction she was pointing. Then Russell got up and followed, "to see where Bruce was going." Before they knew what hit them, both boys had gotten themselves baptized and formally added to the First Baptist Church membership roll.

It was shortly after this that Dad was playing baseball one day and slid into home base with enough force to injure his hip. The injury failed to heal, and he developed osteomyelitis. In those pre-antibiotic days, this life-threatening bone infection required my father to undergo multiple surgeries and to spend sixty-nine days at Duke Hospital in Durham. Back home, he used crutches and depended upon classmates to carry him up and down the school's staircases. And for the rest of his youth, Dad's permanently fused hip would keep him sidelined from physically strenuous activities. As a semi-cripple, my father could have pitied himself, but his likable personality and self-deprecating humor ensured his popularity with both sexes. Although frequently introspective, Dad was socially outgoing: if he could not be in the middle of the action, he at least wanted to be on the fringes. Unable to pass a football for Siler City High, he happily served as water boy; unable to shoot baskets, he settled for being a cheerleader.

When he was a junior in high school, Dad told his mother that he was thinking about becoming a doctor. She smiled and said, "That's nice, son."

One evening in 1941, Dad and Russell set out on foot to attend yet another revival in town. They really did not intend to worship or spiritually renew themselves; they were most likely going because their mamas *made* them. Joining a couple of pals in the back row, the boys settled in for some good entertainment. Throughout most of the service, they snorted and snickered at the evangelist's appearance and mannerisms. It seems that the next part of this story should be accompanied by trumpet fanfare and neon lights, but my father never elaborated on what happened toward the last part of the service. Suffice it to say that at some point during the teens' shenanigans, he quieted enough to hear a "still small voice" and underwent a genuine conversion.

Later that night he stood at his bedroom window, contemplating his experience and the overwhelming peace that now filled his soul. Looking out upon a moonlit orchard, he prayed, "Dear Lord, if this is heaven, let me die right now!"

Three nights later, my father returned from another service and told his mother that he had "surrendered" his life to preach. After expressing her joy, his mother confessed that when Dad's life had hung in the balance several years earlier, she had done some haggling with God, promising that if He would spare her boy, she would dedicate him to the ministry. My grandmother did not have a falsely pious bone in her body. Her bedside covenant had been simple and sincere, and she had wisely never spoken of it. Had she done so, my father might have felt unduly pressured toward the pulpit, or guilty had he chosen another career.

But once Dad had answered The Call, his mother *did* pressure him in one area: she made him sign up for singing lessons with Miz Brower, who had a studio uptown. In those days, many small Baptist churches expected their pastor to both preach and direct the singing, and my grandmother was simply helping her son improve his marketability. The problem was that my father had no aptitude for music. He wasn't exactly tone-deaf, but when he was once chosen to be a singing wise man in a Christmas pageant, the scene was quickly downsized to "We *Two* Kings of Orient Are."

Dad's exposure to high culture lasted exactly two weeks. Not only could Miz Brower work no magic on his voice, but "the fellas" (as he called his friends) stood beneath an open window and hooted. After the second lesson, Dad refused to go back.

Even though he couldn't carry much of a tune, First Baptist Church was still proud to ordain my father to preach the gospel. This he first did "down in the country" at Rives Chapel, delivering a halting sermonette to pews full of Moodys and Rives and Dunlaps, within a stone's throw of the burial ground where many of his forebears lay.

During his senior year of high school, Dad plotted his next steps as he prepared for the ministry. One option was quickly eliminated in December of 1941, when the Japanese bombed Pearl Harbor. Upon hearing the news, my father and some of his adrenaline-charged buddies rushed to the local army recruitment center to enlist; there, Uncle Sam took one look at Dad and sent him limping back out the door, 4-F card in hand.

Thus the early autumn days of 1942 found him safely stateside—not dodging bullets in Europe or slashing undergrowth on a Pacific island but studying Old Testament battles at Mars Hill College, a small Baptist school tucked in the Blue Ridge Mountains near Asheville.

One day during his freshman year, Dad was summoned to the administration office. An elderly man, he was told, had died a few hours earlier in a nearby "holler." The family would not arrive until the next day, and they needed a volunteer to go up to the cabin and sit with the corpse overnight. Knowing that my father was a ministerial student, one of the deans convinced him that this would be a perfect opportunity for him to "serve the Lord with gladness."

Coerced or not, Dad allowed himself to be driven to an isolated cove and dropped off within walking distance of the two-room cabin. As twilight fell, he lit a kerosene lamp and began to study at a rickety table, trying not to dwell on the corpse laid out in the next room. He also tried to ignore other sounds that seemed magnified in the gathering darkness: a hoot owl's screech, the *scritch-scritch* of pine boughs on a window, the wind keening through the rafters, and then a long gutteral groan rolling from the next room: *ArrRUGGHH.*

If that cabin had not already had a door, my father would have created one as he tore outside and down a steep ravine, moving for once like an all-star quarterback instead of a crippled preacher boy. He would never be quite sure how he made it to the main road, but he never once looked back.

Dad had inherited from the Moodys a knack for storytelling, and when he was safely back on campus, he regaled his classmates with "The Tale of the Groaning Corpse." It was the type of story that was fully appreciated by his friend Russell Fitts, who had followed Dad to Mars Hill and into the ministry, just as he had followed him down an aisle at the tent revival. Russell would eventually spend his career pastoring small churches in the Blue Ridge foothills. (For the rest of their lives,

Dad and Russell would phone each other long-distance on many a Saturday night to compare sermon notes and swap jokes.)

Dad envisioned a similar future for himself: he would earn a divinity degree at Wake Forest University, meet a nice Carolina girl, and settle close enough to Siler City so that he could attend church suppers, go fishing with his uncles, and enjoy homegrown tomato sandwiches.

The person who utterly derailed this plan was Ralph Langley, a brilliant and eloquent ministerial student who was one year ahead of Dad at Mars Hill. Upon graduation, Ralph decided to venture to Texas and complete his four-year degree at Baylor University. My father had heard of this large Baptist school "out West" but was unsure of its exact location.

"Where is Baylor?" he asked his friend.

"In Waco."

"Do what? Where's Waco?"

Ralph made the long journey to Central Texas and for the next year sent back glowing reports of intellectually stimulating professors, beautiful coeds, and a campus electrified with spiritual passion. During the summer of 1944, he returned to North Carolina and, along with my father, helped conduct a series of statewide revivals. Dad had just completed his two years at Mars Hill, and as he and his mentor sought to convert tobacco farmers and mill workers, Ralph evangelized just as fervently to turn my father into a Baylorite.

"Bruce," he urged, "you *must* come to Texas. Wonderful things are happening at Baylor, and I will expect you there for the fall term."

Ralph's persuasive skills paid off, and after weeks of resisting, Dad finally relented.

I personally have never understood it. How *could* my father leave the rumpled blue-green beauty of Carolina for a sweltering and sparsely wooded prairie land? Dad himself didn't understand it. How could he move so far away from a loving, close-knit family that had lived in the same ten-mile radius for generations? His older brother Sip didn't understand it. "Why the hell do you want to go off to Texas," he snorted, "when you can make $17 a week driving a truck for my heating-oil business?" His parents probably didn't understand it either, but to their credit, they gave their son $50, a sack of ham biscuits, and their blessing. Thus provisioned, Dad carried a cardboard suitcase onto a Trailways bus and, like the proverbial bear, went over the mountains "to see what he could see."

3

Deep In the Heart of Texas

WHAT MY FATHER SAW on the banks of Waco's Brazos River was a campus brimming with Texas friendliness, football fever, and Bible Belt fervor. Most Baylor students took their religion quite seriously: the 1940s-era yearbooks feature not only fraternities and sororities, but also the goings-on at local Baptist churches. Several group photos testify that hundreds of young people attended Sunday school at the town's two largest Baptist churches, the women having risen early in unair-conditioned dorms to wrangle with girdles, fancy hats, and shoulder pads the size of goalposts. (In 1944 and 1945, the ongoing war meant that Baylor burgeoned with far more women than men; although its medical and dental colleges had been cranking out slews of commissioned officers, those campuses were located in Houston and Dallas.)

As a junior transfer student, my father not only enrolled in a local church's Sunday school and Sunday-evening training union, but also joined the on-campus Baptist Student Union, of which he was soon elected president. Along with spiritual support and the chance to participate in community missions, the organization provided a social outlet for students. Few Baylorites would ever let a drop of whiskey pass their lips, and the school would not sanction on-campus dances until 1996, but BSU members still found ways to make merry: the yearbooks' musty pages capture all manner of talent shows, picnics, formal banquets, and candid clowning around.

Such giddy moments were a necessary release, for the word that best describes my father's classmates is *earnest*. Those students had come of age during the Depression and wartime rationing. Many had witnessed friends, sweethearts, and kinfolk march off to battle zones and not return. Some had survived combat themselves. The Greatest Generation was dead serious about life. Its members did not dillydally their way through an education, and many were just as earnest about their religious faith.

During Dad's junior year, a spiritual awakening swept across Baylor's campus, its initial sparks lit by a series of spontaneous and informal prayer meetings. Within weeks, evangelistic services were held in Waco, led by a handful of ministerial students. These services were the first of hundreds that would eventually spread throughout Texas and across the South. Dad found himself at the heart of all the action. As one of the original group of student preachers, he launched an era of his life that I would later tend to take for granted. But the experience had such a profound effect on others and so strongly shaped my father's identity that, decades later, his name would still be associated with the Youth Revival Movement.

The core evangelists of this movement were passionate in their sermons, but off duty they were good-looking, fun-loving, prank-playing young men who bonded well with other college students. During altar calls, multitudes of female coeds made sincere commitments to "follow Jesus," but many also followed the handsome preachers around as if they were movie stars.

HEAR BRUCE McIVER

Baylor University Youth Revival Leader

Speaking Sunday morning to Joint Service of Senior I and
II Departments of the Sunday School

His message will prepare our hearts for our fast-approaching Youth
Revival in Dal-Hi Stadium July 29 - Aug. 3. Please be on time: 9:30.
Your Superintendents,
MISS RUTH HELSLEY and MRS. HULEN RICH

GASTON AVENUE BAPTIST CHURCH

Baylor's administration fully endorsed the revivals, which were supervised by the Texas Baptist Student Department. And nearly all faculty members cut my father slack when his traveling schedule created academic conflicts. One of his most memorable teachers was Dr. A. J. Armstrong, an English professor both feared and revered by Baylor students. "Dr. A," as they called him, was infamous for giving "Triple Fs" and refusing papers that had been submitted early, because the student "clearly had not had time to do *quality* work."

But Dr. Armstrong was also inspirational, interspersing his lectures with maxims that would have caused eye-rolling among the hippies of my own generation, but which Baylor students eagerly copied into their textbooks:

The greatest happiness in life comes to us in the path of duty.

I had rather fail with a great ideal than succeed along the road of the commonplace.

The most that we can get of beauty, of satisfaction, of God, is the least that we should strive for.

For Dr. Armstrong, *beauty* was a virtue in itself—one that was right up there with *duty* and *godliness*. Over the years, Dr. A had acquired the world's largest collection of Robert and Elizabeth Barrett Browning papers and memorabilia, and he would eventually design a lovely library and museum to house the collection. If I make too much of this professor whom I never knew, and who taught at a college I never attended, it is partly because my maternal uncle would one day become director of the aptly named Armstrong Browning Library and Museum; it is also partly to demonstrate that in transferring to a Baptist school in Texas, my father had not landed in some cultural and intellectual wasteland.

Dad's friend Ralph Langley had already become a protégé of Dr. Armstrong, and under their dual influence, my father joined Sigma Tau Delta. Sponsored by Dr. A, the club promoted "appreciation of the fine arts" and hosted world-renowned poets, actors, and musicians.

But while concerts and poetry readings certainly broadened Dad's world, he always preferred the Grand Ole Opry to Mozart and would

Dr. Armstrong (with a bronze cast the Brownings' clasped hands). To his right is Ralph Langley, who would play important roles in Dad's life.

rather watch a football game than a Chekhov play. Still, if Dr. Armstrong never turned my father into a dilettante, he was nevertheless an inspiring teacher who challenged him to digest volumes of literature, hone his analytical skills, and appreciate Elizabeth Barrett Browning's awareness that

> Earth's crammed with heaven,
> And every common bush afire with God.

Daddy's IQ was not stratospheric, and his sermons would never be brilliantly erudite. He was not the type to discuss Shakespeare or parse Tennyson for pleasure. But he would always be a prolific reader (especially of history and biographies), and while his spiritual convictions were deeply rooted, he would become a lifelong "seeker," with a mind that was continually exploring, testing, discarding, expanding, reconsidering.

In 1945, one of my father's most pivotal reconsiderations concerned his attitude toward the Japanese. Like many Americans, he felt a bitter antipathy that was quite understandable during that time. For four years, Daddy and his Carolina buddies had been *itching* to go kill, maim, or disembowel some "dirty Japs." But then he got to Baylor and, in a seismic shift that caught him by surprise, befriended two American-born Japanese students. One of these Nisei classmates preached and prayed and traveled with him (with the revival team once "teaming up" to shield the young man from a crowbar wielder at a gas station). And on an August morning in 1945, Daddy spontaneously fell to his knees and prayed alongside his other Nisei friend as a dormitory radio crackled

My father (between two front-row women) joined "Dr. A's" Sigma Tau Delta club. Although his cultural horizons expanded, he never became as "dandified" as some fellows!

the words "atomic bomb" and "Hiroshima." The latter, he had learned, was his classmate's ancestral city and home to his extended family.

* * *

"A course in life is worth far more than a course in school." Despite the wisdom of his own words, Dr. Armstrong still demanded a great deal of coursework from his students. For example, they were required to take voluminous lecture notes, which they then typed onto onionskin paper and glued into their textbooks. Dr. A's lectures included not only unique insights and interpretations of the literature, but also eyewitness accounts of visiting poets, such as Robert Frost and Amy Lowell.

Decades later, I would use those valuable notes in my own teaching, for they are still permanently affixed inside two texts that now sit on my living room bookshelf. Daddy's name is penned inside the cover of *The Complete Poems of Robert Browning*. The other tome, *Modern American Poetry*, belonged to my mother.

4

Buckingham-On-The-Bayou

My birth mother, Mary Jean Withers, was born in 1926 and raised in Baytown, thirty miles southeast of Houston. Here, the earth was so flat that it seemed a giant hand had smacked it flush with the horizon and then pounded it in a few more feet. Filling the indentation were soggy marshes and bayous that merged into a pewter sky. The same pulverized oyster shells that paved Baytown's streets had created an ocean of thick black oil beneath the waterlogged ground, and hundreds of rigs pumped up and down, forcing it to the surface. With all of the equipment needed to pump, refine, store, and ship the petroleum, the community was surrounded by a metallic latticework that continually spit sulfur and fire into the Texas sky.

My maternal grandparents, Edward and Etta Withers, had been born over a hundred miles inland in the "Big Thicket" piney woods, to which their forebears had come by way of Kentucky, Georgia, and Virginia, with almost all branches originating in England. Grandmother was quite proud that she had descended through the Sheffield family—a line of Elizabethan courtiers, poets, and musicians. There was also an alleged connection to a Duke of Buckingham, who built his namesake house in London. In 1762, King George II acquired the house in lieu of back taxes and turned it into a full-size palace (and that, I like to say, is why Elizabeth lived there instead of *us*).

Back on this side of the pond, the Spindletop oil well "came in a gusher" in 1901, forever changing the South Texas economy. During the early twentieth century, scores of Big Thicket families flocked to the

Etta Sheffield Withers, my maternal grandmother

Gulf Coast, drawn by the lucrative new petroleum industry. My newlywed grandparents were part of this migration. In 1922, they settled in Goose Creek (later renamed "Baytown"), and Granddaddy went to work for Humble Oil (now Exxon), whose refinery sprawled beside the Houston Ship Channel.

After delivering a stillborn son, Grandmother bore two daughters in close succession: my mother in 1926, and a year later her younger sister Martha Edwina, who was nicknamed "Winkie."

My mother was a beautiful child who, as a toddler, modeled clothes for a Houston department store. Grandmother herself was an excellent seamstress and dressed her girls in hand-crocheted or hand-embroidered outfits. With her Sheffield DNA still carrying traces of English nobility and a love of life's

My mother modeled clothes for a Houston department store

"finer things," Grandmother taught my preschool-age mother to identify the works of several famous painters. As a five-year-old, Mother played "school" each day with an older neighbor girl and learned enough to totally skip first grade. Thus she was only six when she neatly printed the following in her second-grade notebook:

> The Pilgrims lived in England. The King was mean to them. They went to Holland. The Dutch were good to them. They did not want their children to speak Dutch. They went back to England and got ready to come to America in the *Mayflower*.

Along with arithmetic problems, spelling words, and pencil-colored pictures ("This is a goldenrod. The goldenrod is yellow. It blooms in the autumn."), her composition book is full of many facts that were likely dictated by the teacher:

> Tomorrow will be March 4 [1933]. This is the last day for Mr. Hoover to be President. Franklin Delano Roosevelt, our new President, will take his office tomorrow.

Three weeks earlier, Grandmother had reported every detail of her daughter's seventh birthday party to the *Goose Creek Daily Sun*:

> Mr. and Mrs. R. E. Withers entertained their daughter, Mary Jean, Saturday afternoon with a party in honour of her seventh birthday. Valentines and red paper hearts were used as the attractive decorations in the living room. Readings were given by Jim Bob Braine, James Ingram, and Edwina Withers. After several games were played, the hostess called the children into the dining room where cake and punch were served from the linen-covered table which was adorned with a large red heart centered beneath the white birthday cake. Streamers of ribbon with tiny hearts attached extended from the cake to the individual plates.

Jean and Winkie Withers

The Withers girls were not just loved, but *beloved*. Their parents were profuse with "darling," "sweetheart," and other terms of endearment. A housekeeper named Ruby pampered Mother and Winkie, even when they were big grade-schoolers: on cold winter mornings, she insisted on carrying them from their beds to the bathroom so they would not chill their feet on the hardwood floors.

Granddaddy was equally protective of his daughters. At one time, the family kept an evil rooster that constantly nipped at Mother and Winkie. One day, after they were attacked once too often, my grandfather barreled out into the backyard and wrung the bird's neck. That evening—as could only happen in Texas—he invited all the neighbors to a picnic where the main course was "Rooster Tamales."

Despite the attention showered upon them, the Withers girls were not spoiled in any detrimental way. Raised in a churchgoing Baptist home, they were taught strong moral and spiritual values. They were disciplined, punished when necessary, and sometimes denied their wishes.

Although the sisters were quite different in looks and personality, they were close and usually enjoyed doing things together. Just like my father, they often went to the picture show, where they could watch their distant cousin Jane Withers act as a "bad girl" foil for Shirley Temple.

Mother and Winkie sometimes got into trouble together. When they were old enough, Grandmother frequently sent them to a market several blocks away. After leaving the store, the sisters developed a system whereby one would carry the grocery sack for a block, then hand it off to the other. Once, when they were midway home, the girls began to squabble about whose turn it was to tote the groceries. When they couldn't come to terms, they just set the bag in the middle of the sidewalk and returned home empty-handed—for which they were duly spanked.

Another time, Mother and Winkie discovered Christmas presents hidden in the attic. When Grandmother left to run errands one morning, they unwrapped a game of checkers and identical pairs of the Chinese- style footed pajamas, for which they had begged. The girls not only played with the checkers but donned the pajamas and traipsed all over the house. Then, they rewrapped the gifts. On Christmas morning, they feigned surprise over the presents while their mother studied the new pajamas, wondering how on earth the soles had gotten so *filthy*.

My grandparents never became wealthy from the oil industry, but their comfortable Depression-proof income allowed them to give Mother and Winkie some of life's "extras." At age seven, my mother began taking both piano and ballet lessons, the latter being an acceptable dance form for more cultured Baptists. She was quite good at both but was such a naturally gifted musician that her parents soon pulled her from the barre and put her solidly on the piano bench. After a couple of years, the teacher told my grandparents, "I've taught your daughter all I know. You need to take her to Mrs. So-and-So across town." And a few years later Mrs. So-and-So said, "Mary Jean has now surpassed *me*. She needs to be studying with Ruth Burr, the finest teacher in Houston." Thus twice a week, my grandfather drove his teenage daughter an hour into Houston for her lessons.

"Do you know *why* your mother wasn't a good cook?" Aunt Winkie asked me decades later. "It was because every afternoon before supper, I was expected to help Grandmother in the kitchen. But my parents would not let *anything* interfere with Jean's piano practice. So while I was learning to cook, she was shaking the house with Chopin études and Beethoven sonatas."

Because she skipped a grade, Mother graduated from high school at age seventeen. For herself and her friends, that 1943 event was celebrated with a spate of teas and receptions. Some of these were reported to the *Goose Creek Daily Sun*, where they were fancied up by a society writer:

> The spacious home of Mr. and Mrs. R. E. Withers, 113 West Humble, was the scene of [an] Open House on Thursday, when Mesdames Withers and Young honored their daughters with a reception tea. . . . A graceful arrangement of pink and white larkspur was used in floreating [!] the reception hall. House party members wore spring formals with corsages of sweetpeas. In the dining room, the refectory table was laid with linen cutwork, and candles gleamed in crystal candelabra.

(The "reception hall" was just a small foyer, and the "refectory table" a plain old dining table. In contrast, I recently located an old copy of the *Chatham County News*, which noted that the family of Jasper Moody—my paternal great-grandfather—had surprised him with a sixtieth birthday celebration at his North Carolina farmhouse. The writer simply stated that "a long table was full of good things to eat.")

After graduating from high school, Mother attended a local junior college while her piano teacher finalized plans for her to study at The Julliard School in New York City. Around this time, Mother attended a weekend retreat with her church youth group and underwent a life-changing spiritual experience. During a period of meditation, she sensed that her destiny was to go to Baylor University, meet a ministerial student, and become a preacher's wife.

This unexpected U-turn broke my grandparents' hearts, but they knew that while their daughter was quite spiritual, she was not given to impulsive whims. They quickly came to respect her decision, offering support as she applied to Baylor and—with the lights of Manhattan a fading dream—packed a steamer trunk for the move to Waco.

5

Keepsakes

MOTHER NEVER AGAIN studied classical piano. Once at Baylor, she took organ lessons in the school's excellent Music Department, knowing that this skill would be handy for her chosen career as a minister's wife. Preparing to be a good homemaker and gracious hostess, she also signed up for a crash course in Home Economics. Some of her recipes—neatly typed on index cards—survive, including the following:

> Coffee
> 1 Tbs. per cup
> Add cream and sugar as desired

Baylor yearbooks note her membership in the Console Club (for organists) and the mission-focused Young Women's Auxiliary of Seventh and James Baptist Church. Along with Melba Brown, her roommate and new best friend, she sat on her dormitory's Executive Council.

Several years ago, Aunt Winkie sent me a long-closeted cardboard box overflowing with mementos Mother had saved from her Baylor days. These included receipts ($39 for quarterly room and board) and a handbook for the women's dormitories, with pages of rules:

- No [female] student may go to town alone or ride in a car after 6 p.m. [without permission].
- No young lady may go out with a young man without first introducing him to the dormitory director.

My mother (center) on her college dormitory council. The dark-haired girl on her right is Melba Brown, mother's best friend.

- Hose are to be worn at all times on Sundays.
- Radios may not be played after 11 p.m.
- Do not holler out of dormitory windows.

Packed into the musty box were numerous greeting cards, valentines, and telegrams (WILL SEND SANDALS TOMORROW—MOTHER) as well as memorabilia from the Baptist Student Union, which Mother had joined as soon as she arrived on campus. There, she met my father, who had also entered Baylor in 1944. The Youth Revival Movement was just beginning, and Mother not only served as pianist for some of the local services but threw herself wholeheartedly into those early days of planning, praying, and publicizing, often working shoulder to shoulder with my father.

I have little idea what transpired between my parents over the next couple of years that led them from casual dating into true love and a more serious relationship: Daddy was my main source for this information, and men tend to take far less notice of romantic details. I do know that at some point, Mother began to paste into a separate scrapbook every news clipping, flyer, or program that mentioned "Bruce McIver."

The cardboard box contained dozens of sentimental keepsakes from Mother's dates with Daddy: pressed corsages, ticket stubs, and concert / theater programs, some with handwritten notations:

> Double-dated with Treva Davis and Ralph Langley. An enjoyable evening!

If penmanship is an art form, then my mother was a virtuoso. Her handwriting was exquisite, comprised of perfectly balanced loops and flourishes. My father, on the other hand, half printed his words with a more masculine flair. Inside the cardboard box, several miniature envelopes contained cards that had accompanied flowers. On most of these, Daddy simply dashed off, "Love, Bruce." On one—commemorating a football game—he had scrawled, "Smear SMU!" But on another, my father's businesslike handwriting contrasted with an uncharacteristically mushy sentiment: "These [flowers] are dainty, darling, just like you."

On the back of each envelope, Mother had written her own descriptive notations:

> Corsage of white gardenias for Jr.-Sr. Banquet at Roosevelt Hotel. Triple-dated with Virginia Morgan and Howard Butt, and Betty Compere and Bill Cody in Howard's car. I wore a pink net and satin dress.

> Sent me beautiful pink carnations for my birthday, Feb. 11, 1946. We went to B.S.U. Council meeting and party afterwards and then Howard left his car for us and we rode around.

Bill Cody, Ralph Langley, and Howard Butt all preached alongside Dad in the youth revivals. Howard seems to have been the only one who had a car.

* * *

Jean Withers and Bruce McIver ("Campus Couples" at Baylor)

My parents' photo was featured in a "Campus Couples" section of Baylor's 1946 Yearbook, and their engagement was announced a few months later.

After graduating in the spring of 1947, my father moved a hundred miles north to Fort Worth, where he enrolled in Southwestern Baptist Theological Seminary. Although Mother stayed in Waco to complete her degrees in Bible and Speech, she followed the tradition of many young coeds and took a semester off to plan her wedding.

During this hiatus in Baytown, she chose patterns for her crystal, silver, and "Dolly Madison" china, with a pink rose centered on scalloped ivory plates. Struggling newlyweds might have had a greater need for a toaster or bath towels, but in this era, it was *de rigueur* for a bride to acquire enough place settings to entertain in style.

Mother decided that her attendants would wear champagne-pink dresses with wide-brimmed Gainsborough hats, and she was fitted for a cathedral-train wedding gown. Special music was selected (Liszt's "Liebestraum" and Grieg's "I Love Thee"), and pink-tinted pearls were purchased for the bridesmaids. Gifts arrived from friends and soon-to-be-entwined family members from Texas and North Carolina, each meticulously recorded in a keepsake book, *Milady's Wedding*.

- Silver cake server—Aunt Bertie Withers
- Silver salad fork—The E. L. Sheffield family
- Chenille bedspread—Aunt Minnie Moody
- Crystal gravy bowl—Uncle Charles and Aunt Julia McIver
- Pillows and handmade desk—Mr. and Mrs. McIver
- Clock—Russell and Mary Fitts
- Money—Howard Butt

My parents were married in Baytown in the summer of 1947, after which they journeyed to North Carolina for a honeymoon and a chance for Mother to meet Dad's relatives.

Back in Texas, they settled in Fort Worth while Dad continued studies

Mother and Daddy with my Withers grandparents

The Bride (a rare photo of my grandparents' living room)

for his Divinity degree at Southwestern Seminary and Mother worked at the telephone company. On weekends, Daddy preached at a small church in Walnut Springs, where his most memorable worship service involved a wasp, a snoozing parishioner's bald head, and a little old lady with a rolled-up Sunday school quarterly.

Once my father completed his graduate degree in 1949, a full-time BSU teaching job at Southwest Texas State brought my parents to San Marcos and the Hill Country. There, Mother was a church organist and substitute schoolteacher, but she also served as Dad's helpmeet and kept whatever "house" she could in their tiny apartment. She tried to improve her culinary skills, and Aunt Winkie later told me that Dad's criticism of her cooking was exaggerated. Personally, I think that my father just longed for his own mama's country-style, fresh-from-the-garden meals; since my parents were on a tight budget, Daddy quickly tired of hamburger goulash and franks and beans. He grew so sick of tuna casseroles that in later life he would mutter a bad word if he discovered one on the dinner table.

At any rate, Mother kept testing recipes in the kitchen and sometimes passed them on to her friend Melba (Brown) Shelton:

> Dearest Melba,
>
> Well, here I am again. It just dawned on me that I forgot to enclose the recipe in your last letter. Guess I'm just an absent minded school teacher. [Here follows the recipe for Lemon-Pear Jello Salad.] . . .
> Sound just like a cook, don't I?
> I haven't had any shoes on all day because of a sore foot. You'd think I was a country girl from Arkansas [Melba's home state]. . . . Mother and Winkie said hello.
>
> Love, Jean

She and Melba had stayed close after their graduations and weddings, where each served as bridesmaid for the other. Half a century later, Melba gave me several letters that Mother had written to her, including the one above. Another letter gently spoofed Aunt Winkie, who had just graduated from Baylor with a degree in Education:

> Last week, Bruce and I drove to Waco and moved Winkie out of the dorm. She and all the "little girls" around were crying and drinking Cokes when we got there. Then when we went downstairs to see Mrs. Staples [the dorm mother], there she sat crying. They all had a wailing good time.

When I first read these letters, I was surprised to discover Mother's sense of humor and wondered if it could have influenced my own. But since preschoolers don't usually detect subtle wit or irony, it seemed more likely that my tongue-in-cheek worldview came from decades of being around Daddy.

One trait that Mother *did* pass to me was at least some of her musical ability. While genes certainly played a role, so did an environment where, even in the womb, I would have been surrounded by piano, organ, and choral music.

When I was born in 1952, my mother considered naming me "Melody" but settled on "Kathlynn," with an accent on the first syllable and no middle name. My nickname quickly became "Kathie"—and I thus joined the legions of Kathys and Pattys and Lindas born in the 1950s. (I switched to "Kate" as an adult but will always be "Kathie" to family and longtime friends.)

In my blue satin-covered *Baby's Milestones* book, Mother listed a slew of gifts. Many were from students and colleagues, but once again, others reflected my parents' interwoven families and lifelong friends:

- Dress—Aunt Minnie Moody
- Bonnet and sacque—the Lee Moody family
- Bottle warmer and rattle—Bertie Withers
- Blanket—Aunt Ida (Sheffield) and Uncle Jerry
- Diaper shirts—Ella (McIver) and Bill Payne
- Cradle-gym crib toy—Uncle Charles and Aunt Julia McIver
- Silver cup—Melba Shelton
- Pink diapers—Russell and Mary Fitts
- Dress and $10—Howard Butts

She transcribed the formula recipe for my bottles and dated every sniffle, babble, and new-cut tooth. Doctor visits and inoculations were recorded, as well as first Christmas gifts.

She noted that at twenty months, I enjoyed all pets, the game Ring Around the Rosie, and my *Childcraft* books, with their beautifully illustrated poems and fairy tales.

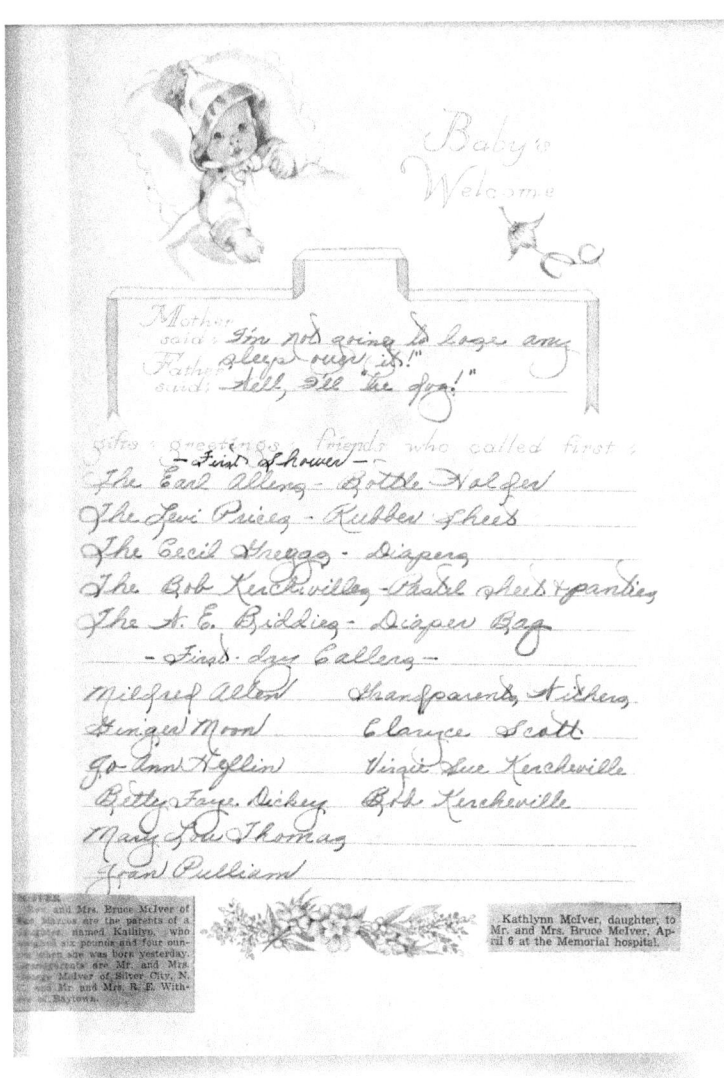

Mother's beautiful handwriting in my "Baby's Milestones" book

6

Recording Machine

DADDY: *(clears his throat) Hello, folks, and a very Merry Christmas from all of us McIvers way out here in Texas. Now Mother and Dad, what we're going to do this year is a bit different. We borrowed this recording machine from the church and have set it up in our living room . . . and we just want you to come into our home for a while and see how we live. I've written to Reverend Lynch, and he is going to bring you his machine and play this tape for you. Maybe later we'll take this contraption into the kitchen and let you hear us eat a meal. (A rustling sound in the background, like book pages being turned. Then whining.) Right now, we're in the living room, where Kathie is sitting in her mother's lap, wanting her to read the book. So we'll let her take over for a moment.*

(crackly sound of microphone being moved)

DADDY: *Kathie, can you say "Merry Christmas"?*

(silence)

MOTHER: *Hmm? Can you wish everyone in North Carolina a "Merry Christmas"?*

(silence, then nervous chuckling)

DADDY: *Can you say, "Hi, Mommie Mac"?*

(silence)

DADDY: *"Hi, Daddy Mac"?*

(silence)

DADDY: *Kathie, look here. Who's this in your book?*

ME: (unintelligible)

MOTHER: *Yes, that's Mother Goose.*

DADDY: *And what's this over here?*

ME: *Bear!*

MOTHER: *And what does the bear say?*

ME: *Woo-woo-woo!*

DADDY: *No, not "woo-woo."*

MOTHER: *Yes, that's the old Indian. But what does the old bear say?*

DADDY: *Hmmm?*

(silence)

ME: Grrrrr!

MOTHER: *Oh my, what a ferocious bear you are!*

* * *

On a spring day in 1973, my father's secretary was cleaning out the closet in his office and discovered an old reel-to-reel tape that had lain dormant for two decades. She located a tape deck, positioned the reels, and pressed PLAY. She later told us that she got chills when she realized what she was listening to.

When Daddy heard the recording, he recalled that it had been made in our San Marcos living room as a Christmas greeting for my North Carolina grandparents, whom we called "Mommie and Daddy Mac." The date was November 1953, and I was twenty months old. At some point, the reels had made their way back into Dad's possession, and then been stored in a closet and completely forgotten. The recording was a treasure, not only because it captured forty-five minutes of our family's everyday life but because amateur audiotapes were extremely rare in the early 1950s. None of my peers had ever had their earliest words preserved in this fashion.

Dad immediately asked his choir director to transfer the reel's contents onto a cassette and to make extra copies. When I came home to Dallas during a college break, my father and Lawanna excitedly called me into the kitchen, where a "modern" shoebox-sized recorder sat on the breakfast table. A moment later Daddy depressed a lever, and voices filled the room—as clear as if the speakers had been an elbow's length away.

DADDY: *Looka here, Kathie, what's this a picture of?*
ME: *Cow!*
MOTHER: *And what does the cow say?*
ME: *MOOOOOO!*
(my *parents laugh*)
DADDY: *Can you tell Daddy Mac what the cow gives?*
ME: *Grass!*
DADDY: *No, the cow doesn't give grass.*
MOTHER: *Yes, the cow eats grass.*
ME: *Milk!*
MOTHER: *That's right, and she gives us milk to drink.*
DADDY: *Can you tell Uncle Sip and Aunt Ella what you spilled at the supper table tonight?*
ME: *(in a guilty tone) Spill milk.*
DADDY: *Yes, you spilled your milk. You spilled it twice.*
ME: *Coke?*
DADDY: *Yes, you spilled your Coke too.*
ME: *Cow (unintelligible)*
MOTHER: *Do the cows spill Coke? No, just Kathie. . . . Would you like to go to North Carolina next summer and see the big old cows up there?*

Sitting in our Dallas kitchen in 1973, I was listening to my mother's voice for the first time in seventeen years.

Did I remember it?

Well, not consciously: if I had heard it in a crowded room, I would not have exclaimed, "That's my *mother!*" And yet it sounded almost mystically familiar, as if it were part of my blood, my fiber, my very being. It was a pleasant voice, with a lyrical alto tone and a soft Texas drawl. I was struck by how similar it was to my own, with nearly identical intonations and phrasings.

The cassette tape was full of other revelations. As it spooled around, I was surprised by how many of my personality traits and adult tastes were already apparent at twenty months (e.g., my love of music, passion for naps, and even lifelong addiction to soft drinks and Diet Coke). I was verbally precocious, and it was obvious that my parents were using the tape to showcase my skills. With their prompting, I counted, recited favorite foods, made animal sounds, and identified pictures in what I am certain were my *Childcraft* books. And while my folks were undoubtedly putting their best foot forward for the recording, their true parenting styles could not be faked. As an adult, I had sometimes wondered if I had idealized Mother's gentle, nurturing nature. To a great extent, I did. But the tape confirmed that she *was* tender, patient, and a born teacher. She was also able to interpret my garbled words, instinctively understand my needs, and come to my defense when necessary. Daddy, on the other hand, was a sometimes bumbling and occasionally frustrated father, but one who was oh-so-proud of his firstborn.

These family dynamics were quite apparent throughout other portions of the tape:

MOTHER: *Can you tell the folks what Mommy brought you home from the store this morning?*

ME: *Mama bring pony.*

DADDY: *Yes, Mother brought her a pony. [probably a stick horse]*

MOTHER: *And what does Kathie do on that pony?*

ME: *Kathie ride pony.*

DADDY: *She rides the pony. And what do you say when you get on the pony?*

ME: *Hang on.*

(laughter)

DADDY: *Say, "Hang on the pony!"*

ME: *Hang on. Hang on . . . Mama Mac.*

DADDY: *Hang on, Mommie Mac! Can you say, "Hi, Mommie Mac"?*

ME: *Hi, Daddy.*

DADDY: *No, not "Hi, Daddy." Say, "Hi, Mommie Mac!"*

ME: *Hi, Daddy Mac!*

DADDY: *(laughs) Well, what is this a picture of?*

ME: *Find the moon?*

MOTHER: *Find the moon?*

DADDY: *Find the moon, Mother.*

MOTHER: *All right . . . (with her Texas accent, the words come out as an unhurried "All rahhht.")*

ME: *(more demanding) Find the MOON!*

MOTHER: *Well, I believe it's in the other volume. You want to . . .*

DADDY: *Yeah, why don't you go get the other book.*

(The sound of small feet running across a hardwood floor, fading at first, then growing louder before stopping. A few seconds of page-rustling.)

ME: *NO!*

MOTHER: *No what, darling? . . . You don't want me to turn the pages? Well, you turn them. You're a big girl. (the sound of crunching paper)*

MOTHER: *(sighing) Oh, my . . .*

ME: *Kathie turn page!*

MOTHER: *(somewhat wearily) Yes, Kathie's turning the pages . . . Oh, look! There's the moon in your book! (a distressed whine from me)*

MOTHER: *Yes, that old moon just fell all to pieces! [I know exactly where that picture is—in Childcraft Volume Two. In the illustration, a griffin-like creature "hatches" from the moon, breaking it open like an eggshell.]*

DADDY: *Look here, Kathie, what's this?*

ME: *(ignoring him) Find "Free Blind Mice"?*

MOTHER: *Find "Three Blind Mice"? All right . . . (rustling pages) I bet the McIvers and Moodys in North Carolina would like to see your book and all of these pretty pictures.*

* * *

DADDY: *Okay, folks, we're getting ready to have lunch, and we've taken the recording machine into the kitchen so that you can hear us eat. Mother's getting our food ready, but Kathie's sitting in her high chair and already eating . . . let's see—Kathie, what do you have here in your dish? (silence, except for my feet banging on the footrest, and Mother opening drawers in the background)*

DADDY: *Hmmm? Can you tell Sip what you're eating?*

ME: *Sip eat?*

DADDY: *Yes, Sip eats. But what do you have here?*

ME: *Jeeze!*

DADDY: *Jesus?*

MOTHER: *Can you say, "Jesus loves me"?*

ME: *Jeeze love me.*

MOTHER: *(singing) Jesus loves the little children, all the children of the world . . . .*

ME: *Daddy sing too!*

MOTHER: *She wants Daddy-Boy to sing, too.*

DADDY: *(joining in, somewhat shakily) Red and yellow, black and white, they are precious in His sight. Jesus loves the . . .*

ME: *Tick-TOCK! Tick-TOCK!*

MOTHER: *(singing) This is what the clock says, "Tick-tock! Tick-tock!"*

DADDY: *This is what we do around here every day—we have to sing for our supper.*

ME: *Kathie play piano.*

DADDY: *Kathie plays the piano?*

MOTHER: *Where do you play the piano, darling? (silence)*

DADDY: *Hmm?*

MOTHER: *Say, "I play the piano in Sunday school!" . . . Uh-oh, there goes the phone. You and Daddy-Boy go ahead, and I'll answer it. (leaves the room)*

DADDY: *What's in your cup, Kathie? What are you drinking?*

(silence, then a loud clatter)

DADDY: *(in a frustrated tone) Great day in the morning, you dropped your spoon! . . . Watch out, there! You almost spilled your milk. . . . Here's your spoon. Can you say, "Thank you, Daddy"?*

(silence)

DADDY: *"Thank you, Daddy"?*

(silence)

DADDY: *(muttering)* *"Thank you, Daddy."*

MOTHER: *(coming back into the kitchen, she murmurs something to Daddy, then speaks in an amused tone)* Well, as usual, some girl wants Daddy-Boy on the phone!

(the sound of an oven door opening and closing)

MOTHER: *Kathie, you'll have to tell the McIvers and the Moodys and the Paynes [my Aunt Ella's married name] that Mommy and Daddy are having Mexican food for lunch: enchiladas, tacos, hot tamales . . . And you haven't learned to eat those foods yet. Ooo, they're hot! They're hot with fire . . . and they're hot with seasoning. They're too hot for Kathie, but she has a good lunch of her own.*

(sounds of foot banging and babble, then another louder clatter)

MOTHER: *Kathie, you dropped your spoon. (silence)*

MOTHER: *(in a playful tone)* *You dropped your spoon, little girl. . . . Kathie, who came to see you today?*

ME: *Lee-Mo.*

MOTHER: *Lydia Margaret? That's a mouthful, isn't it?*

ME: *Lee-Mo!*

MOTHER: *Yes. And what did you play with Lydia Margaret? (silence)*

MOTHER: *Did you ride the pony?*

ME: *Lee-MO!*

MOTHER: *Um-hmm. And they read the book together!*

DADDY: *(coming back in the kitchen and muttering)* *Oh, great . . .*

MOTHER: *What's the matter?*

DADDY: *That phone call . . . hey, what happened to the food?*

MOTHER: *Uh, it wasn't hot enough, so I put it back in the oven.*

DADDY: *Well, it was one of my students . . .*

(I began wailing, interrupting him.)

DADDY: *(irritated)* *What on earth's wrong with you, Kathie?*

MOTHER: *What's the matter, sweetheart?*

ME: *BED!*

MOTHER: *Have you finished all the lunch you're going to eat? Would you like one of those little animal crackers to finish up on?*

DADDY: *You don't want to go to bed. It's too early for you to go to bed.*

ME: *BED!*

MOTHER: *Well, I imagine she is sleepy. She was up late last night and got up early this morning.*

DADDY: *Let me tell you this before you put her to bed. I think the folks would enjoy this story. (Daddy talks for a minute, but I cry even harder, and you really can't hear him over the noise) . . . Anyway, this student had said something in class this morning that she thought might have offended me, and she just wanted to apologize. It didn't even register with me.*

(Mother chuckles. I stop crying but still whimper.)

DADDY: *Man, you catch it from all sides when you're in this line of work.*

MOTHER: *Oh dear, Kathie. I can't seem to get your apron untied. It's in a knot, and this plastic doesn't work very well when it gets in a knot.*

DADDY: *Kathie, are you going to leave Daddy and go to bed?*

ME: *Leave Daddy, go bed.*

MOTHER: *Can you tell everyone where you go when you sleep?*

(silence)

MOTHER: *Hmm? Tell them, "I go to Sleepytown!"*

ME: *Sleep Town!*

MOTHER: *And what do you do when you go to Sleepytown?*

(silence)

MOTHER: *Hmm? Can you say, "Play with the fairies in Sleepytown"?*

(silence)

MOTHER: *And what do you play with those fairies?*

ME: *Ring-a-rosy!*

(my parents laugh)

MOTHER: *(sings) Ring around the rosy/A pocketful of posies . . .*

ME: *See-saw . . .*

MOTHER: *Say, "See-saw, Margery Daw . . ."*

ME: *Pat-a-Cake.*

DADDY: *Goodness gracious! You play all of that when you sleep?*

MOTHER: *Say, "Yes, sir!"*

ME: *Duck.*

MOTHER: *You see a little duck out in the yard? That's not your duck—you dragged that home from a neighbor's yard. [It was probably a pull toy.]*

ME: *That . . . Bill's . . . duck? [I struggle mightily with this difficult phrase, but manage to pronounce every consonant.]*

MOTHER: *I believe that is Bill's duck.*

DADDY: *Yes, Bill's the little next-door neighbor.*

MOTHER: *Well, look here—tell the McIvers and Moodys and the Paynes, "Night-night."*

ME: *Night-night.*

MOTHER: *Say, "I'm going to Sleepytown!"*

ME: *Sleep Town!*

DADDY: *There goes the phone again. I don't think we're gonna eat this meal . . .*

7

Social Register

From the *San Marcos Daily Record*:

A birthday party, using the Easter theme, was given on April 8 on the lawn at the home of Mr. and Mrs. Earl Allen [family friends], Bluebonnet Drive, honoring Little Miss Kathlynn McIver on her second birthday.

As the guests arrived, each little girl was given a yellow ribbon bracelet with tiny chickens attached, and the boys received green chickens attached to a lapel pin.

The birthday table was covered with a yellow dotted Swiss cloth with eyelet embroidery, and featured a yellow cake covered with green coconut. A miniature nest was perched on top of the cake. Other decorations included Easter-bunny candles, eggs, and chicks.

After outdoor games were played, cake and sherbet were served to Kathlynn and her little friends. They included Moyra McLaurin, Lydia Margaret Quarrels, Kaye and Norman Alexander, Pat Ivey, Michael and David Elliott, and Howard Butt III.

8

Little House On The Big Plains

SHORTLY AFTER MY SECOND BIRTHDAY, we McIvers moved 400 miles northwest to Lubbock, where Daddy had been hired as BSU Director for Texas Tech University. There, we rented a small white house that was close to the campus. It was also near the home of Buddy Holly, a gangly teenager who would soon rock 'n' roll himself to fame.

Our family's relocation to Lubbock carried me into an environment that was sometimes harsh and occasionally dangerous. As the saying goes, "There's nothing to stop the wind between Canada and Texas except a barbed wire fence"—and the Panhandle seemed to catch the full blast of that wind. Even on the calmest days, tumbleweed bounced across highways, and powdery black dirt sifted through open windows. During more turbulent seasons, giant dust storms could deposit a thick layer of silt inside houses that *had* been battened down. Swarms of locusts could descend like a biblical plague to leave windows blackened and cracked. Tornadoes spun across the high plains to flatten anything taller than a prairie-dog mound, and winter blizzards could sculpt five-foot-long icicles and (as one photo proves) hang them from the eaves of our house.

I was oblivious to these dangers, for I was still too young to pay much attention to any geography beyond my own backyard. I recall not only that yard, but nearly every inch of the house itself, whose floor plan and furnishings I can still visualize.

The focal point of our living room was an upright piano, where Mother gave weekly lessons to several students. As fascinating to me as the ivory keys were two objects on top of the piano: a music-box ballerina who pirouetted beneath a glass dome, and a metronome whose slim rod could be weighted to swing in slow arcs or to *clip-clop* along like the Lone Ranger's horse. The rest of the living room was filled with furniture that my parents had bought "on credit" a few years earlier. Although low budget, the suite's gracefulness reflected my mother's personality. The sofa and chairs were supported by French Provincial legs that curtsied floorward, their wood honey-colored in the glow of a gas space heater. Atop our coffee table a copper fondue set posed on its own ladylike feet. Tea roses scrolled across the double globes of a pale-green lamp, and end tables showcased dainty knickknacks: a tiny gold pitcher, a porcelain magnolia, one of my baby booties that, instead of being bronzed, had been eternally "pinked." Even the ladder-back chairs crafted by my Carolina grandfather seemed feminine with their curved slats and delicately spooled legs.

Behind the living room was what should have been a dining area, but since Mother had no table worthy of her Dolly Madison china and no hutch in which to display her Melrose crystal, we used this space as a den. Daddy's contour recliner was angled into one corner, my mother's more sedate chair in the other; in between, I sat in a little rocker and watched such TV fare as *Romper Room, Howdy Doody,* and a local program that featured singing cowboys and cowgirls (the term "Country Western" was not yet in vogue, so we just called it "Cowboy Music"). Rounding out our sitting-room furniture were a four-drawer desk and two small bookcases. I could easily open the cases' glass-fronted doors to fetch a *Childcraft* volume or to study the plaster busts of famous composers (awarded to Mother by her piano teachers) arranged in a semicircle on a middle shelf.

We took our meals in a cramped kitchen where, until I was older, I sat at my own toddler table with a Howdy Doody spoon and Hopalong Cassidy cup. It was in this kitchen that my mother and I fed salmon bones to our cat Smokey—a replacement for Pea-Winkle who, because we had no fenced yard, had been given to San Marcos friends.

One day, I was in my bedroom playing "house" with Smokey, when I put him somewhere . . . and then completely forgot what I did with him. Later that afternoon, my mother was making salmon croquettes for supper. She called Smokey to come get his bones, but he didn't come. I recall both of us hunting all over the house, and Mother asking, "Sweetheart, think hard: *what* did you do with the cat?" That evening, she opened a dresser drawer to get my pajamas and out jumped Smokey. I had apparently shut him up in what I thought would be a nice soft "bed" and then forgot all about him. Smokey's days with us were numbered, for he ran away the next morning and never came back.

My other "kitchen memory" is of drinking purified water from a bulky glass dispenser that stood beside the back door. When I later asked Aunt Winkie about this, she explained that Lubbock's tap water tended to yellow children's teeth. In retrospect, I probably should have just drunk from the faucet. Not only were childhood antibiotics *already* staining my teeth, but future studies would reveal that Lubbock's water contained high levels of lithium—a mineral that would one day be used to treat manic depression. Apparently, it contributed to the citizens' happy, laid-back dispositions and kept the city's suicide rate exceptionally low.

* * *

When I was two, the top of my head would not yet touch the doorknobs in our house. Since my parents had told me that I would be a "big girl" when I turned three, I took their word literally, assuming that on the morning of my third birthday I would automatically shoot up a couple of inches and be as tall as the doorknobs. I don't remember being disillusioned when this didn't happen. What I do recall is the party that was held in our makeshift dining room. Mother and I spent all of that morning moving furniture out of the room so that we could set up a borrowed folding table to seat the half dozen preschoolers who had been invited. We also dragged my red rocking horse and a few other toys into the room, and I was reminded to "share" with my friends. My mother then took down my pin curls and fitted me into a frilly blue party dress. All I remember about the party itself were the refreshments. For days, I had begged for a cake in my favorite color: blue. Mother must have instructed the bakery well, for they concocted the most beautiful treat I had ever seen: a round white cake with powder-blue icing, topped by a blue-and-white ballerina. Even today, I can close my eyes and taste its unique sweetness that I have never since found duplicated by any kitchen or bakery.

My mother had a different memory of that party. According to what she told Daddy, instead of playing London Bridge and farmer in the dell, I huddled in a far corner, hogging my new doll and refusing to interact with the other children.

Just as I had expected to grow a couple of inches on my third birthday, my parents had probably hoped that I would become less reclusive. Throughout my preschool years, they did all they could to help me become a citizen of the world, arranging playdates or taking me to events where other kids would be present. Their efforts occasionally paid off. But as a child who needed little outside stimulation, I preferred to spend time in my bedroom, a toy-filled sanctuary where I could entertain myself for hours on end.

In one corner of the room stood my crib, upon which I was almost neurotically fixated. The baby bed was gray, but that dull color was redeemed by a headboard scene of kittens playing blindman's bluff. The bed's very best feature was a row of chunky spinning balls—alternately pink and blue—set into that same headboard. When I was around three, I became obsessed with the cribs in other homes and nurseries. Did the infant's bed have ornamental playthings along the rails or headboard? What colors and shapes were they? Did they spin? And, above all, were they *pretty*? I remember one particular time when I accompanied my parents to visit a couple who had a baby. Before they could finish greeting us at the front door, I tugged at our hostess's skirt and interrupted: "Does your baby have balls?"

"I beg your *pardon?*"

"Does your baby have BALLS?"

I don't recall any shock waves created by my question—probably because I had already dashed down a hallway to see for myself. This kind of snooping took place in quite a few houses, and at times, I was disheartened to find a plain wooden crib, with no decor whatsoever. Whenever I saw a baby bed without any eye-pleasing balls, beads, or discs, I concluded that the parents must not love their child very much.

Although there was a double bed in my own room, I refused to give up my crib until I was nearly four years old. When I was three, Aunt Winkie came from Colorado to visit us, bringing six-month-old Cousin Leslie. The infant needed a place to sleep, and my parents bribed, reasoned, and pleaded with me to let her use my baby bed. I would not be moved. We ended up borrowing a portable crib for my cousin.

I was equally possessive about two blankets that had survived my infancy: one with pastel alphabet blocks, the other with yellow moons and stars against a blue background. One evening a young couple visited our home, bringing their newborn son. They placed the tiny baby on my double bed, squarely in the middle of a blanket that my mother had provided.

MY blanket.

The one with alphabet blocks.

The grown-ups moved to the living room, and while they chatted, I stood glaring at this usurper who was snoozing away on MY blanket. In one swift motion, I reclaimed my rightful possession by grabbing a flannel corner with both hands and jerking as hard as I could.

Tha-whump!

That baby went flying off the bed and landed headfirst on the hardwood floor. I don't know who squalled louder: the frightened newborn . . . or *me*, when I got the spanking of my life.

Despite this incident, I could be quite maternal with my own dolls, who slept in a miniature bed that Daddy Mac had made for me back in North Carolina. My grandfather had also constructed an enormous shelving unit to hold the rest of my books and playthings. A lower hinged bin held wooden blocks, stringing beads, and several infant and crib toys that I had held onto for sentimental reasons. Spilling off the pink shelves were stuffed animals, tea sets, jump ropes, and a pair of brightly painted maracas that Daddy had brought me from Glorieta, the Baptist conference center in New Mexico. I had a toy telephone that went *brrriinngg!* when you dialed, and a half dozen puzzles (including one of a frog, whose green foot was eaten by my mother's Hoover vacuum cleaner). I owned a small toy stove with Lilliputian pots and pans as well as doll-care items galore: my favorite was a miniature sterilizer whose wire rack held glass nursing bottles. Unhampered by any child safety standards, I loved assembling the detachable collars and rubber nipples; the nipples could easily be stuck up one's nose, and my parents had to perform more than one emergency extraction on me.

The remaining space in my bedroom was filled by a red wooden rocking horse, a small table and chairs, and a record player that spun canary-colored discs of children's songs as well as popular tunes of the day: "The Yellow Rose of Texas," "Zip-a-Dee-Doo-Dah," "The Syncopated Clock." I once asked my mother what *syncopated* meant, and she was somehow able to explain this complex musical term so that I understood.

Without prodding, I would have been content to spend whole days in my bedroom, absorbed in records and dolls and storybooks. (I was setting a precedent here: for the rest of my childhood, frustrated adults would nag me to "Get your head out of that book! Go outside and *play!*") My parents lured me into fresh air by providing a tricycle, wading pool, and sandbox (how I still recall the pungent, loamy scent of that black Panhandle dirt!). I also enjoyed the homemade swing attached to our backyard's single large tree. Unable to pump myself, I waited until Mother came outside to hang laundry and then pestered her to "Come push me!"

One day I was standing beside her as she pegged fresh-washed sheets onto a clothesline. Hearing a distant roar, we both looked high overhead to see a white line etching across the blue sky. Mother told me that it was made by a new type of airplane called a "jet." I deduced that as the jet flew, its tail scraped the underside of heaven, leaving a long white scratch. I knew where heaven was and soon concocted another theory about the celestial world: when the people who lived up there were happy, they danced so merrily that they cracked a hole in heaven's floor. God then dumped out a bucket of water and—*voilà!*—we got rain.

I knew that Jesus had long hair and loved me, and that God was an old man with a beard. Beyond this, my theology was pretty muddled. My parents had told me that "Jesus is our Savior." I had no earthly idea what a "savior" was, but I was quite familiar with Life Savers candy. So as I knelt in my crib each night, I mentally lifted my bedtime prayers to a gigantic peppermint Life-Saver-in-the-Sky. The Lord got even more mixed up for me when I accompanied my parents to BSU fellowships, where everyone sang, "Lonng-ing, longing for Jeee-sus . . ." The way they drew out the word *long* made me picture a little weenie dog I had once seen at someone's house.

If I envisioned the Holy Trinity as God-Candy-Weenie-Dog, it was not because my parents neglected my religious and moral instruction. I learned one of my first hard lessons when my mother and I went to visit a lady who had a daughter my own age. While playing in the girl's bedroom, I saw a toy broom that I coveted for myself. It never occurred to me to be sneaky, for I saw nothing wrong with simply taking what I wanted. How I ever got such a large object into our car without attracting attention, I will never know. But Mother spotted the broom right after we pulled into our driveway. She firmly explained the meaning of stealing and told me why it was wrong. We then drove back to my friend's house, and I returned the toy.

In the *Milestones* book, Mother wrote under "Reactions to Discipline" that I was "extremely sensitive and deeply impressed when scolded."

Sometimes I was "deeply impressed" on my backside, for the '50s was a decade when parents did *not* spare the rod . . . or the hairbrush, yardstick, or hickory switch. If my mother had to spank me, it was just plain old hand-to-posterior. I was more afraid of Daddy, whose hand was larger and whose voice louder. My father had inherited from Daddy Mac an aversion to noise, commotion, arguments, tears, sassing, and disobedience. Like his own father, he could usually tame an unruly child with a warning look. On some days, especially if his back was "splitting in two," there might be no warning before his swift temper erupted. Daddy's bark was generally worse than his bite, but I still feared the bark: a loud reprimand could send me into tearful self-pity. In a *Milestones* entry, my mother wrote that after being scolded, I once prayed, "Dear Lord, please help Daddy-Boy be nice to me."

Despite his low tolerance for some of parenthood's frustrations, my father had a genuine love for children and a tender heart that often made him a pushover. My favorite illustration of this comes from a day in 1955 when Davy Crockett fever was sweeping the nation. Like most every kid in America who was transfixed by a TV series about the frontiersman, I owned a coonskin cap and clamored for any product that bore the frontiersman's logo. I had asked my parents to buy me a record of the popular "Ballad of Davy Crockett," so one Saturday morning Daddy and I drove downtown and made the purchase at a music store. My father then escorted me back to our angle-parked Pontiac, boosted me onto the passenger seat, and handed me the paper sack containing a child-sized record.

"Honey, I have to run in to the hardware store," Daddy said, this being an era when it was perfectly acceptable to leave a child alone in a car. "You sit tight, and I'll be right back."

I did sit tight—right on top of the paper sack. There was a splintering *crrr-rack!*, and a moment later I extracted from the bag two halves of the yellow disc. When Daddy returned to the car, he grumbled and probably did some low-key scolding. But he trudged back to the music store and soon emerged with another flat parcel.

"Here," he said, handing me the package. "Now I need to step into the dime store a minute. You stay right here . . . and DON'T break this record!"

I recall that in that instant I felt profoundly loved by a father who had given me the grace of a second chance.

"Davy, Daaavy Crockett," I sang, caressing the record's edges. I gently held the disc up to the sun, its rims supported by my palms. Still singing, I flipped the record back and forth, then marched it toward my door . . . and a slot where the window had been lowered.

"King of the wild frontier!"

Ker-PLOP.

The disc slipped into the groove and disappeared down the door frame.

I honestly don't remember my father's reaction when he returned, but I know that he went back to the music store a third time. We were both giggling as we drove home with yet another copy of the hit song (and perhaps in some West Texas junkyard there reposes the hulk of a '49 Pontiac with "The Ballad of Davy Crockett" still buried deep inside its door).

One ritual that I particularly enjoyed sharing with Daddy-Boy was our Saturday-morning excursions to a neighborhood candy store. We would set off on foot, holding hands and singing our way down the cracked sidewalk. I always stopped to point out the place at the end of our block where I had once tumbled off my tricycle into a bed of Texas-sized fire ants. We then continued a few more blocks to the mom-and-pop store with its creaky screen door. Our return trip usually found Daddy-Boy limping and my face sticky from Tootsie Rolls, but we still held hands and sang in high spirits:

> Hot diggity, dog ziggity,
> Boom! What you do to me—
> When you're holding me tight!

9

As Tall As Doorknobs

Grandmother Withers made my dress

By THE TIME I WAS THREE YEARS and seven months old, I stood at three feet and eight inches—almost doorknob height. Not only had I grown physically, but my geographical horizons were rapidly expanding to include new places and experiences. Our family went on excursions to the Palo Duro Canyon, Prairie Dog Town, and the county fair. I saw *Bambi* and *Lady and the Tramp* at the movie theater and visited a farm with my Sunday school class. At the municipal airport, I could almost reach through a chain-link fence and touch the beautiful triple-tailed

Constellation that had just brought Aunt Winkie and Leslie for a visit.

A few of my new experiences were unpleasant, such as the week I spent in a Catholic hospital being treated for pneumonia. Some schoolchildren learned to fear nuns because they bore stinging rulers for small hands. I learned to fear them because they bore stinging hypodermic needles for my small bottom. An even worse experience occurred when our family went to the Ringling Brothers Circus. We sat in the front row, which was great fun . . . until a clown lit a firecracker practically under my nose. The resulting *BANG!* almost ruptured my eardrums and blew to smithereens any trust I had placed in clowns. Wailing hysterically, I clung to Daddy's neck as my parents rushed me out of the arena. For the rest of my life, I would never go back to another circus and would be freak-out phobic about explosions (even *balloons*) in enclosed spaces.

Given my circus trauma, no one could really fault me for being afraid of loud pops and bangs. And Dr. Spock would have found some of my other childhood fears entirely normal. What kid *hasn't* cried out during the night until her parents flip on a light to reassure her that the "witch" in the closet is really just a bathrobe hanging on the door? Or that the rumbling "thunder" she heard was simply Daddy-Boy adjusting his contour chair in the living room?

But overall, I was much more of a scaredy-cat than my peers. At the local carnival, I cried into my mother's lap while we swerved about on a relatively tame bumper car ride. When we visited the coast, I panicked if Galveston beach waters lapped at my ankles. For a while, I was even afraid of cameras, howling if anyone took my picture. I also tended to be clingier than most preschoolers and was overly demanding of my parents' attention. In a section of my *Milestones* book labeled "Dislikes," Mother wrote: "The idea of having a little brother or sister!"

The first word I learned to spell was *j-e-a-l-o-u-s*. Many a time, my mother would glance pointedly at me and recite these letters to women friends who had brought small children to our house. And I knew exactly what she meant.

Just when it seemed that I would be an apron-clinger for life, I began to show signs of maturing. Shortly before turning four, I graduated to

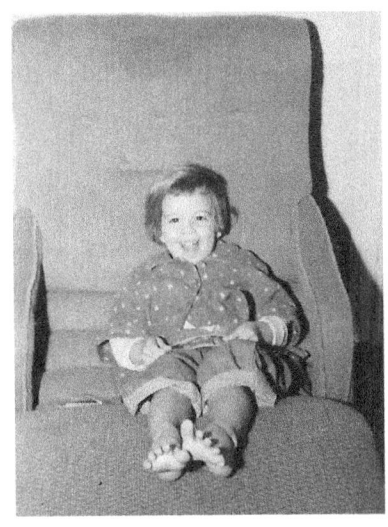

a big bed and quit wearing nighttime diapers. Occasionally, I found it quite clever to call my mother "Jean," as if we were equals. I consciously imitated her women friends when they sat in our living room and crossed their silken legs with such poise. And while I *hated* to be dressed up for church or special events—and threw seismic tantrums in department-store fitting rooms—I did enjoy parading around the house in my mother's hats and high heels, pretending to be a lady.

I was especially fond of one of Mother's handbags that was entirely covered with small colored beads. When the two of us ran errands, I sat next to her in the car and played with the purse, fingering the plastic beads and squeezing the bag so that it rippled in waves of color. Many a night I would lie in my big bed and lull myself to sleep by thinking of that pocketbook. In my fantasy, I was no longer a child playing with the purse, but instead "the Mother" who kept it nearby while I steered a car full of my own youngsters, gently tapping the brake pedal with my high-heeled foot.

I had mostly overcome my hatred of cameras, and photos from this time show that I was happily modeling other "womanly" actions of the 1950s. Using miniature appliances, I cooked meals or ironed clothes. In one picture, I tottered in cast-off stilettos while pushing a doll buggy; in another, I cradled a baby doll in the crook of an arm and—with my legs gracefully crossed—bottle-fed her as competently as any good mother.

At long last, it seemed that I was growing up.

10

April Showers

ONE MORNING AROUND the time of my fourth birthday, I was sitting Indian style on my bedroom floor, listening to a favorite yellow record as it circled the turntable:

> Drip, drip, drop, little April shower,
> Beating a tune as you fall all around;
> Drip, drip, drop, little April shower,
> What can compare with your beautiful sound?

The song was from the movie *Bambi,* and the tune evoked forest scenes where baby animals gamboled among primrose and buttercups. The music was upbeat, but I had always been intrigued by a section where the cheerful melody dipped into a more ominous mode, suggesting something akin to a cloud sliding across the sun. Of course, I knew nothing about harmonics or the concept of major and minor keys. I only knew that for a few seconds the tune floated on a dark undercurrent that was both mysterious and elusive . . . and then, just as I was about to identify the strange tug it gave my heart, the melody sprang back into sunlight.

On that morning I was playing the *Bambi* record over and over, each time hoping to capture those slippery chords and slot them into something I could name and understand. During the third or fourth playing, I realized that another far-off sound had joined the singer and instruments. It rose faintly at first, like a distant flute sustaining a high

C. Then the sound grew closer . . . and louder . . . until it was no longer music but an ear-stabbing wail that penetrated my bedroom walls.

I ran down the hall and joined my mother on the front porch, just in time to see the back side of a large red fire truck disappear onto a boulevard at the end of our block. Before its siren died away, another began to crescendo in the distance. Neighbors stepped onto their own porches, and we all watched as four . . . five . . . then *six* fire engines blared down our street and careened onto a thoroughfare bordering Texas Tech's campus.

It did not take long for radios, telephones, and over-the-fence chatter to spread the word: the Lubbock Coliseum was on fire.

I was familiar with the coliseum, for it was close to my father's university office, and it was the site where I had been terrorized by the clown's firecracker. But my most recent memory of the building was a pleasant one, stemming from our family's visit—just days earlier—to a furniture exhibition. I had shown little interest in futuristic dishwashers and modular sofas; instead, I had been captivated by a display of children's furniture, a blue-enamel doll crib in particular that I deemed one of the prettiest objects I had ever laid eyes on. I had spent so long twirling the pink disks set into its headboard that my parents had to physically drag me away.

It was this doll bed that worried me when, later on the day of the fire, my folks and I piled into our car and drove a few blocks to view the damaged coliseum. Although the fire caused no injury or fatality, it had been a bad one. I was stunned speechless at the sight of a gargantuan black hole that flames had chewed through the dome. Up until then, the only Really Bad Things in my world had been along the lines of booster shots, spankings, misplaced toys, or nightmares in which the ugly witch cooked Hansel and Gretel for dinner. But *this*—this badly hurt building—opened a whole new realm of pain for me. (I would not learn the word *tragedy* until much later, but on the day of the fire, I sensed that it involved the collapse of something familiar and dependable. And I also developed a new awareness that Really Bad Things could happen in the larger world beyond my house and yard.) The hole in the coliseum's dome matched the one in my heart as our Pontiac slowly circled the arena. I felt deep sorrow for the injured building, and I grieved for the doll bed that I feared was still inside, perhaps melted into a pile of pink-and-blue ash. "Good Lord," my father would say years later. "You worried us sick over that doll bed. You asked about it for *days.*"

Eventually, I forgot about the crib. I went back to the security of my small white house—to playing with my own doll furniture, reading fairy tales, and sitting on my bedroom floor with a stack of yellow records. My playthings were all familiar and unchanged except for one: the *Bambi* record was now almost too painful to listen to, for its ominous chords had become inseparable from sirens, black holes, and charred doll beds.

For the rest of my life, "Little April Shower" would remain one of the saddest songs I had ever heard.

II
August 1956

11

Eight Scenes

Etched in my mind are eight memories from the summer of 1956, each as distinct and self-contained as a Kodachrome slide projected with an audible "click" onto a movie screen:

Our Lubbock living room is full of wooden crates and cardboard boxes. A gray-uniformed man with a floppy cap squats by the coffee table and gives me a toy truck. It is made of orange metal, with the letters B-E-K-

I-N-S stamped on its side. The moving man shows me how to wind up the truck, and I watch it roll across the floor.

(Click)

We have just moved to Dallas, and I am at my new pediatrician's office, where a witch of a nurse is about to give me a polio shot. It is the first injection I have ever gotten in my arm. Then the nurse says, "All done!" and I scream—not with pain, but with rage and betrayal. The old hag gave me the shot when I wasn't looking. She didn't give me a chance to cry.

(Click)

My parents and I, along with another couple, stand outside a redbrick hospital. Tall pine trees sway nearby, and the landscape seems greener and cooler than in Texas. We have come to visit a three-year-old boy but cannot go inside his ward because he has polio. My father boosts me up so that I can peer over some hedges and see the boy through a window. He lies on his back in an enormous crib, his head toward the window. His only clothing is a pair of pale-blue rubber pants that cover a diaper. The boy cranes his head far back so that he can see me, and the two of us stare at each other.

(Click)

I am playing in the living room of our new Dallas duplex. Kneeling on the hardwood floor, I wind up the toy moving van and watch it whir across the room. I am wearing a sunsuit and am clammy with heat. Central air-conditioning is still in the future, as are the window units we will eventually install. The duplex's only heat relief comes from electric floor fans and a water-cooled contraption that spins an attic fan.

I send the moving van on several trips under the coffee table, then wind it once again—this time, so tightly that it freezes up. I pound on the truck and pinch my finger trying to budge the metal key. When I set to whining, Mother comes from the kitchen and sits beside me, the skirt of her tan-striped housedress fanning across the floor. "Sweetheart," she says, examining the truck, "I think you may have broken it." She fiddles with the windup mechanism, but my patience lasts about one millisecond. In full meltdown mode, I yank the van from my mother's hands, whereupon she hauls off and slaps my bare leg.

Now I begin to cry earnest tears. I bury my face in Mother's cool skirt, wailing from physical pain, bruised feelings, fury over the broken truck, and frustration with the whole sweltering, summer-sticky world.

(Click)

I am at the Galveston seashore, wearing a swimsuit imprinted with violets. Little wavelets lap my ankles, and I am frightened. Mother and Aunt Winkie stand on either side of me. They lift my hands high and gently hoist me a few inches, encouraging me to "jump the waves!" I shriek in terror.

(Click)

I wake up on a Sunday morning back in Dallas. Daddy tells me that we are not going to church because Mommy has a bad headache.

I am surprised.

My mother is never sick, and we always go to church.

(Click)

It is that same Sunday night. Daddy's secretary, Betty Faye, has taken me on an afternoon outing just to get me away from the house. We have now returned and stand on the front porch of our two-story duplex. Betty Faye leans down and says, "Now, we must be quiet when we go inside because your mommy is very sick." We walk through the front door. Mother is lying on our green sofa, violently ill while one woman holds an enamel basin and another holds her head. Betty Faye leads me upstairs to my bedroom, but I keep looking back through the stair railings. I have never in my short life seen anyone so sick.

(Click)

Daddy and I walk through the back door of our duplex. We have just picked up boxes of fried chicken from Youngblood's Fried Chicken out on Northwest Highway. It smells so good, and I am starving. I scurry through the kitchen and into a small dining area . . . where I suddenly stop short. The adjacent living room is full of people. Grandmother Withers sits on the sofa, tears streaming down her rouged cheeks while she stares at me. No one has ever looked at me in such an odd way, and I have never before seen an adult weep.

I ask Daddy why Grandmother is crying.

My father kneels down beside a bookcase and faces me, taking my hands in his own. He says that Grandmother is sad because Mother was so sick that she couldn't get well, and she has gone to heaven to live with Jesus. Oh.

I am eye level with the Famous Composers lining the bookcase's top shelf. I wonder how my mother got up to heaven. Did she climb a staircase or maybe ride an escalator like the one at Volk Department Store? Then I imagine Mommy and God—a bearded old man—sitting at a little tea-party table atop a white cloud. I wonder what they are having for their supper. Hamburgers? Hot tamales? Tuna casserole?

We are having fried chicken . . . if Daddy will just hush up talking and fix me a plate.

12

The Cookout

I WISH THAT I COULD REMEMBER the last full day I spent with my mother.

I cannot.

In later years, I would learn the complete story of her illness and death from Daddy's recollections, family anecdotes, and written records—including hundreds of letters, cards, and telegrams. But for me, one of the most poignant mementos was a simple shopping list penciled on an index card. I would not discover it until the twenty-first century, when I unearthed a taped-up carton in our Dallas garage. It held Baylor yearbooks, some of Dad's old papers, and a Betty Crocker recipe box.

The latter was not heavily filled. Inside the red-checked cardboard box, a few tabbed dividers separated two dozen index cards, each with a typed or handwritten recipe: Tuna Cutlets, Asparagus Hollandaise, Strawberry Shortcake. Tucked behind these lay a ten-cent coupon for Birds Eye frozen peas. And at the very front, just before the first

Shopping list

manila divider, stood a separate index card with Mother's unmistakable handwriting:

The recipe box had traveled from Lubbock to Dallas, where our family moved in June of 1956. Daddy had been promoted by the Baptist General Convention of Texas to oversee BSU activities on campuses throughout the state. We rented one side of a two-story orange-brick duplex on Marquita Street, near Skillman Street and the Live Oak district.

Shortly after our arrival, I was indeed taken to my new pediatrician for a polio shot—a fact noted in my *Milestones* book. Parents still hailed the fairly new Salk vaccine as a miracle, for they had long feared that their child might swim in a public pool one day and be encased in an iron lung the next. (Daddy later confirmed that during our annual summer trip to North Carolina, we had stopped at a sanitarium in Warm Springs, Georgia. The little boy in blue pants was the son of missionary friends. Stricken with polio, he was not in an iron lung, but his legs had been paralyzed.) Years later, I learned that Mother had asked my pediatrician if she, too, could be vaccinated but was told that because of a nationwide shortage, the serum was reserved for children and pregnant women.

And yes, Mother and I *were* at the coast in August. The two of us had traveled to Baytown to see my grandparents and Aunt Winkie, who was visiting from Colorado. A year earlier, Grandmother Withers had suffered a stroke that paralyzed her entire left side. She could walk with a cane but gone were her days of sewing, cooking, and being an active society matron. My grandfather, having retired from Humble Oil, took over all caregiving and domestic duties. Mother and Winkie tried to visit Baytown whenever they could and were especially happy when they could reunite with each other. During this August trip, one of their excursions was to Galveston Island where, according to Winkie, we spent a fun-filled day at the beach.

* * *

On Saturday evening, August 11—only days after our return from the coast—my parents attended a backyard cookout. For years, I had believed that they hosted the event at our *own* duplex. Indeed, Mother's shopping list seemed to support this theory: ground beef, onions, potato chips.

It was not until very recently that I learned differently.

In July, our family had united with Wilshire Baptist Church, a small but rapidly growing congregation pastored by Dad's close friend Ralph Langley. My parents joined a young adult Sunday school class, whose members included Dot and Asa Newsom. At ninety-three, Dot still had an ironclad memory. "That cookout was held at *another* couple's home," she told me when I revisited Dallas in 2018. "It was a social for our Sunday school class."

In retrospect, Dot's news made more sense than my aunt's version, for my parents would not have been sufficiently settled to entertain guests. Not only had they had little time to form new friendships in Dallas, but they were still unpacking boxes and hanging curtains in our duplex. (Mother's shopping list? It must have been a mere coincidence, although I cannot explain why she needed a "crate").

As for myself, I have no memory of that Saturday evening. I might have spent the time at another home, or perhaps a babysitter had kept me at the duplex. But it is unlikely that children would have attended the cookout. Whatever the case, I can only imagine the scene as adults mingled in someone's backyard. While burgers grilled, the women likely traded child-rearing and household tips while their husbands chatted about their jobs or sports. The men possibly admired my father's "new" secondhand Studebaker, for which the Pontiac had been traded. "It had a plush interior," Daddy would later reminisce, "and a sorry engine."

Whether they discussed them or not, the guests would have been aware of recent world and national events, such as the tragic sinking of the *Andrea Doria*. Most would have known that the GI Bill had just expired, ending an era of free college education for veterans; that Adlai Stevenson would be running against "Ike" in November; and that a group of Southern senators had effectively blocked President Eisenhower's Civil Rights Bill ("Death for Civil Rights" proclaimed a *Time* magazine headline, as if the movement had been permanently defeated). The previous week's cover of *Sports Illustrated* featured Louise Suggs, who had just won the LPGA All American Golf Open. In other

Wilshire Baptist Church. 1956

Pastor Ralph Langley in Wilshire's baptistry

news, the National Association for Better Radio and Television had recently blacklisted the children's TV program *Hopalong Cassidy* for its "typical Western crime element."

Mother and her friends, still enamored over Grace Kelly's fairy-tale wedding to Prince Rainier of Monaco, had perhaps recently seen the movie *High Society*, in which she starred.

During the summer of '56, teenagers were flocking to theaters to watch less sophisticated fare, such as *Earth vs. the Flying Saucers*. Some parents undoubtedly shook their heads over their kids' lack of taste, but most were far more concerned about the invasion of Elvis Presley into their properly ordered world. The controversial rock 'n' roll singer currently dominated the radio; his "wild" music assaulted sedate, suburban lily-white Americans, and his live concerts were sending young girls into mass hysteria. On this very August weekend, Elvis was performing in Miami. "I am *not* a lady-killer," he protested to an interviewer. The statement would do nothing to reassure parents and Baptist preachers that "Elvis the Pelvis," with his frenetic rhythms and suggestive hip thrusts, was not dragging their teenagers straight down to hell.

My mother and her women friends probably listened to their car radios whenever they drove to the grocery store, but chances are that they avoided stations that played Elvis's "Shake, Rattle and Roll" or "Hound Dog." Instead, the women might have enjoyed Vic Damone's "On the Street Where You Live" (from the current Broadway hit *My Fair Lady*), as well as Doris Day's popular new song "Que Sera, Sera (Whatever Will Be, Will Be)."

* * *

I don't know how late the cookout lasted, but we McIvers were surely well prepared for churchgoing the next morning. Back at the duplex, shoes would have been polished, dresses and ties and shirts ironed, my hair washed and pin-curled. Mother would have studied her Sunday school lesson. In Lubbock, she had taught a class of young women, and I inherited a small binder full of her lesson notes. On the topic of

"Juvenile Delinquency," she had enumerated "Causes" and then listed the following "Cures":

1. Parental *care* and attention
2. Church—youth programs
3. Home—provide security, family activities
4. *Careful* provision of "things" (rather than material overabundance)
5. Guidance clinics for parental development
6. Material aid—cleaning up slums, etc.

Although she did not teach at Wilshire, my mother was a conscientious student and would have read over the next week's lesson. She might also have practiced some music, for she had already joined the choir and was serving as a substitute organist. A notepad lay beside our desktop telephone on that Saturday night, and for whatever reason, Mother had written the names and phone numbers for the choir director and several members.

At some point during the evening, I would have been put to bed, either by a babysitter or my parents. Once darkness fell, I can envision myself slipping out of bed to kneel at a nearby window and study the Dallas skyline a few miles distant. My second-floor perch gave me a good view of two especially interesting structures. The tallest was the thirty-six-story Republic National Bank Building, whose spire could be seen across 120 miles of prairie. At night, a row of tiny red lights skittered up to the spire's tip, held for a moment, then vanished; the pattern was repeated with blue lights; finally, the spire flaunted both colors at the same time . . . and the entire sequence began anew. While I never tired of watching this neon animation, I was also captivated by Pegasus—the revolving red horse atop the Magnolia Building (and a well-known logo for the Magnolia Oil Company).

At a later hour, I might have been wakened by orchestral music drifting upstairs from the living-room television—the melancholy theme of *The Honeymooners,* which I heard most every Saturday night. Having returned home, my parents perhaps ended their long day by laughing at the shenanigans of Jackie Gleason and Art Carney.

Finally—after a stray dish was carried to the kitchen, a newspaper refolded, a last lamp clicked off—I can picture Mother and Daddy climbing the stairs, tired but content, looking forward to the next chapter of their lives in a new neighborhood, new church, and vibrant new city.

Later, as the attic fan went *thumpety-thump* above a tiny landing dividing the two bedrooms, my parents and I drifted to slept, never dreaming that this would be one of our last nights together as an intact family of three.

13

Psalm 116

THE VIRUS UNLEASHED inside my mother's body during the wee hours of August 12 did not come on gently, but struck like a tsunami. She woke to crashing waves of nausea and a severe headache. After my early-morning surprise that we would not be going to church, I remember nothing else until that same evening when Daddy's secretary returned me to the duplex after an outing, and I saw Mother sick on the couch.

Her symptoms were so intense that several women had arrived earlier in the day to help with caregiving, and someone had decided to get me out of the house. Daddy would later save a telephone notepad, whose pages hint of the unfolding drama inside our duplex. Next to Mother's blue-inked list of choir members, another person's handwriting—feminine but different—suddenly intrudes with penciled notations: Dr. Asa Newsom and Dr. W. E. Carswell. Both physicians were Wilshire members, and it would have been logical to summon either one to make a house call or write prescriptions for what was still thought to be a run-of-the-mill, although acute, virus.

The medications didn't work, and on Monday morning Mother was taken to Methodist Hospital. I don't know for sure if I was home at that time, but I have a dreamlike image of a boxy ambulance backed into our driveway. ("Was it mint green?" I once asked Daddy. He confirmed that it was.)

After that, my mind went blank, deleting all memory of the next couple of weeks.

On Tuesday morning, my father went to the hospital, hoping that a night of IV fluids and stronger medications had helped Mother to turn the corner. But there had been no improvement. In addition, her neck was now stiff and her speech slurred. As Daddy visited with her, she asked about me and was told that I was being kept by some friends. She then wondered aloud, "Do you think I might have polio?"

At that point, a nurse asked my father to step outside while she gave Mother a bed bath. Daddy went downstairs to the soda fountain, where he ordered a cup of coffee. My father did not go around toting an ostentatious Bible, but he sometimes carried a small Psalms/New Testament inside his coat pocket. Sitting at the counter, he pulled it out and began idly flipping through its pages, seeking some guidance or consolation. His eyes had just fallen on a verse in Psalm 116—

Precious in the sight of the LORD is the death of His saints. (verse 15)

—when a Code Blue pierced through the hospital's PA system. Moments later, a nurse rushed up to the counter and summoned Dad back upstairs.

He was unable to enter the semi-private room, for it was crowded with doctors and technicians and machines. According to the nurse, my mother had suddenly stopped breathing in the middle of her bed bath. For the next several hours, Dad stood in the hallway while the staff tried to resuscitate his wife. They performed a tracheotomy, hooked her up to some kind of primitive respirator, and finally stabilized her vital signs. These frantic interventions managed to keep her alive—but barely, and she was in a deep coma. The doctors did not know why every system in Mother's body had crashed, but they suspected a polio-type virus. It was thus decided to transfer her across town to Parkland Hospital, which had state-of-the-art isolation facilities.

Back at our duplex, other notations appeared on the phone pad: contact information for distant relatives, a phone number for the "Drs. Bureau" (a human-staffed answering service), and messages: "Bob Dunn called from San Marcos." The same female scribe had underlined or drawn boxes around some of the information, the pencil's deep, repetitive impressions betraying her anxiety. During this time, Dad's boss at the Student Department was mailing mimeographed progress reports/prayer requests to Baptist leaders throughout the state. In turn, telegrams began arriving at the hospital and at our duplex:

BE ASSURED OF OUR PRAYERS AND DEEP CONCERN
FOR JEAN. WE ARE HAVING SPECIAL PRAYER AT NOON
TODAY AND AGAIN TONIGHT AT OUR PICNIC.
                    BSU, TEXAS WESTERN COLLEGE

* * *

BRUCE OUR PRAYERS ARE WITH YOU AND KATHIE IN
THIS CRITICAL TIME.
                    FIRST BAPTIST CHURCH, LUBBOCK

* * *

PRAYING FOR YOU AND JEAN AT THIS HOUR. TRUST IT IS
GOD'S WILL FOR HER TO RECOVER.
                    RUSSELL AND MARY FITTS, SILER CITY, NC

Although Mother remained unconscious, family members were guardedly optimistic until Friday, when her temperature soared to nearly 107 degrees. Doctors performed an exploratory craniotomy, and the head physician then advised my father to go home and rest, saying that he would call him later.

Leaving the hospital, Daddy shared an elevator with a physician who had been involved in Mother's case, and who was now chatting with a colleague about an upcoming hunting trip. A few minutes later, Daddy was walking through the parking lot when he saw this same physician opening a car's trunk.

"Excuse me, sir." Daddy approached the young doctor, who hoisted a hunting rifle from the trunk.

"Yeah?" The fellow brought the scope up to his eye, squinted, and squeezed the empty gun's trigger.

"You operated on my wife this afternoon . . . Jean McIver."

"Uh-huh." The doctor stared straight ahead. *Aim. Squint. Click.*

"Could . . . well, could you tell me what you found?"

"Total effusion of the cerebral cortex."

"And what does that mean?"

"The brain is gone."

Aim. Squint. Click.

The doctor never put the rifle down, never once made eye contact with my father.

"Thank you," said Daddy. And he slowly walked off to his own car.

Later that afternoon, the attending physician phoned our duplex and broke the news with more empathy: "Bruce," he said, "I'm so sorry to tell you this, but Jean's brain has been irreversibly damaged. The person you once knew as your wife no longer exists."

✼ ✼ ✼

Once the outcome was deemed hopeless, our duplex began to fill with kinfolk. My Grandparents Withers made the all-day drive from Baytown. Aunt Winkie and Leslie flew in from Colorado (leaving Uncle Roger back in Boulder, where he was teaching and working on a doctorate in English Literature). My North Carolina grandparents were on standby. Daddy later told me that the deathwatch took place at our house rather than at the hospital, mainly because Mother was in strict isolation, and *no* one was allowed to see her.

As an adult, I once asked my father where *I* had been during that critical weekend. He honestly could not recall, because those days had been so topsy-turvy. Both of us assumed that I must have been staying at someone else's house. I was astonished when Aunt Winkie told me many decades later, "No, you were at the duplex the whole time. When I got to Dallas, I asked Bruce what I could do to help. He said, 'Please take Kathie upstairs and try to keep her out of all this commotion. Just do your best to entertain her and keep her routine as normal as possible.'" (Grandmother Withers was unable to climb stairs and could do little to help; she and Granddaddy apparently spent the nights at someone else's house.)

Upon hearing Winkie's version, I was shocked, envisioning myself held prisoner in a hot, cramped bedroom: a double bed, massive toy chest, bureau, and reassembled crib for Leslie would have left almost no room to move. I can also imagine how annoyed I must have been when a toddling cousin messed with *my* toys or drooled on *my* old blankets. But Winkie recalled that Leslie and I played very nicely together. My aunt was a born storyteller who likely kept us girls entertained with books, songs, and rhymes:

> This old man, he played one,
> He played knick-knack on my thumb

And on second thought, I doubt that the bedroom door was shut— not during stifling August days in Texas. Against the imagined clack of puzzle pieces and clink of doll dishes, I can almost hear the steady *whop-whop* of the hallway's attic fan. Today, I think of it as a loving heartbeat—a white-noise buffer to protect me from "all the commotion" going on downstairs.

Throughout the weekend, the living room steadily filled with people. The telephone must have rung continually, and each doorbell chime signaled another visitor, casserole, or Western Union telegram. Surely I noticed the heightened activity, for there is no way I would have been kept upstairs around the clock. As I now picture myself racing out the back porch's screen door or tearing through the living room en route to the kitchen, I want to reach back through half a century and shake those small shoulders. "Stop, child!" I want to shout. "Pay *attention*! Don't you realize what is *happening* here?" But even if I had slowed down, I would not have fully understood the strange conditions or adult worries surrounding me. Like most preschoolers, my world was peopled with fairies, Santa Claus, and the Easter Bunny; despite my encounter with the damaged Lubbock Coliseum, I had little understanding of critical illness and none at all of death. Chances were that on that weekend, I was far more focused on finagling a grape Popsicle or pouting because I couldn't watch TV cartoons in a living room commandeered by somber grown-ups. And I was probably jealous that baby Leslie got to sip milk from her pretty pink sippy cup while I had to use a plain old aluminum tumbler.

*   *   *

On Sunday, August 19, for the second week in a row, we did not go to church.

At Wilshire, prayers would have been lifted—more for my father and other family members than for Mother herself. All hope for recovery was now gone; if by some miracle her body survived the catastrophic illness, she would have spent her remaining days in a permanent vegetative state.

This day, like those immediately following, is a gaping chasm in my memory. When I try to imagine it now, I think of my Aunt Winkie and wonder, "How did she *bear* it?" Years later, she told me that the rote motions of childcare kept her busy and distracted. Still, her heartache must have been a powerful undertone as she examined a stubbed toe, rescued a diaper pin from Leslie's mouth, or chanted mechanical rhymes:

> O Jonathan Bing, O Bingathon John,
> Forgets where he's going and thinks he has gone.
> He wears his false teeth on the top of his head,
> And always stands up when he's sleeping in bed.

Some of these poems likely came from my *Childcraft* books, which I would have hauled out at bedtime. I can envision myself in a summer gown, leaning against my aunt as she sat on my double bed and read my favorite selection from Volume One:

> Have you ever heard of the Sugar-Plum Tree?
> 'Tis a marvel of great renown!
> It blooms on the shore of the Lollypop sea,
> In the garden of Shut-Eye Town.

As she recited, my aunt might have silently reminisced about her own childhood days with her sister, recalling their games and pranks, laughter and tears, special occasions and shared memories. And her ear was almost certainly tilted toward our downstairs telephone, waiting for the inevitable call.

Later, after darkness fell, did she collapse into a numbing, dreamless sleep? Step into the bathroom to release pent-up emotions? Or perhaps slip downstairs to savor a few child-free moments with other adults?

And I wonder if I might have crept out of bed and knelt at a window, as I did most nights, to study the Dallas skyline. I can almost feel those venetian blinds balanced across my shoulders as I gazed at now-familiar landmarks: a revolving Pegasus, his forepaws uplifted, poised to vault into the Texas sky . . . and the Republic Building's spire, where the lights chased each other—*red . . . blue . . . red and blue*—in a steady, dependable pattern.

Captivated by this razzle-dazzle, I would have had no clue that beyond those skyscrapers, the expressway lights unwound like a strand of pink-tinted pearls, leading to the hospital where even now my mother was gradually letting go her hold on life.

✳ ✳ ✳

On Monday morning, August 20, the telephone scribe recorded a message from one "Dr. Cushing" at Parkland:

> BLOOD PRESSURE ↓
> SLOWLY, STEADILY SINKING

Telegrams continued to be delivered, including one to my father's secretary:

> BRUCE ADVISES ONLY MATTER OF TIME.
> PLEASE NOTIFY WHEN ARRANGEMENTS COMPLETE.

✳ ✳ ✳

The hospital's final call came shortly after 4 p.m.

Like an earthquake's fissures, additional information began to radiate at odd angles across the telephone pad:

WEILAND-MERRITT FUNERAL HOME_ROSS AVENUE
DALLAS MORNING NEWS—FRONT DESK 4-5577
COUNTY HEALTH DEPARTMENT 6-3435
CALL AMERICAN RED CROSS

Flight arrangements were noted for my North Carolina grandparents, and food flooded our kitchen:

HAM AND VEGETABLES—CHOIR
ASPARAGUS_MRS. ESTES
CHICKEN—MRS. ASA NEWSOM JR.
CHOCOLATE CAKE_LADIES ACROSS THE STREEt

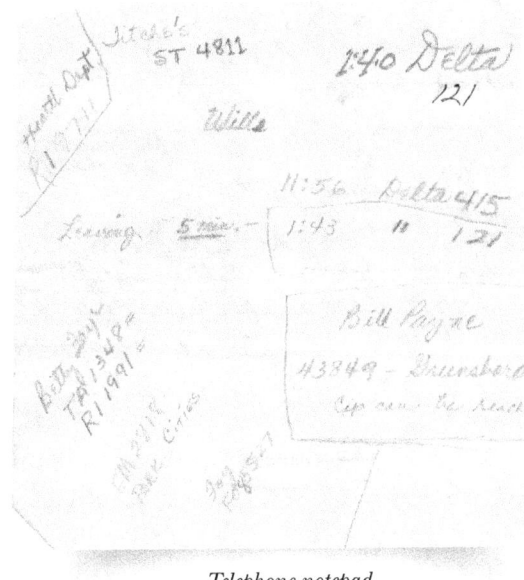

Telephone notepad

Western Union now brought messages of sympathy:

BRUCE—YOUR GREAT LOSS IS HEAVEN'S GAIN QUOTE
PRECIOUS IN THE SIGHT OF THE LORD IS THE DEATH OF
HIS SAINTS QUOTE.

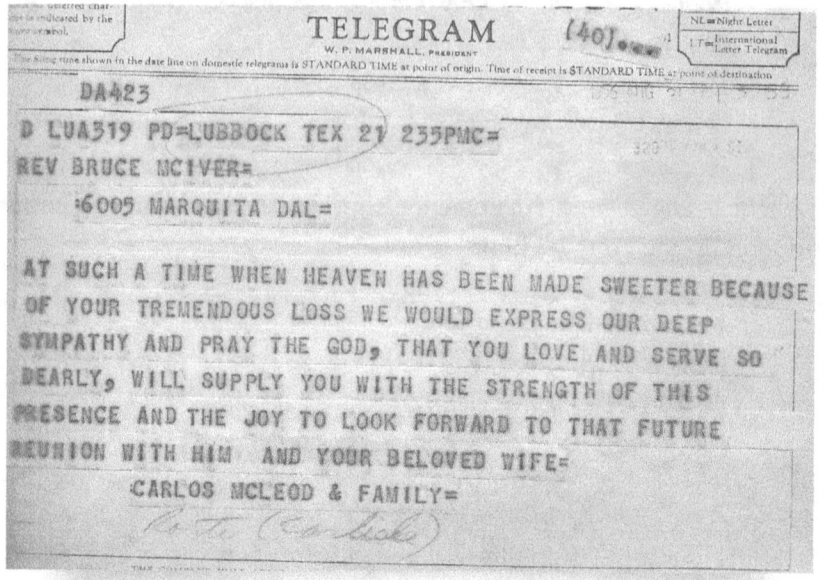

TELEGRAM

W. P. MARSHALL, PRESIDENT

DA423

D LUA319 PD=LUBBOCK TEX 27 235PMC=

REV BRUCE MCIVER=

6005 MARQUITA DAL=

AT SUCH A TIME WHEN HEAVEN HAS BEEN MADE SWEETER BECAUSE
OF YOUR TREMENDOUS LOSS WE WOULD EXPRESS OUR DEEP
SYMPATHY AND PRAY THE GOD, THAT YOU LOVE AND SERVE SO
DEARLY, WILL SUPPLY YOU WITH THE STRENGTH OF THIS
PRESENCE AND THE JOY TO LOOK FORWARD TO THAT FUTURE
REUNION WITH HIM AND YOUR BELOVED WIFE=
         CARLOS MCLEOD & FAMILY=

MAY GOD COMFORT YOU AND YOUR LITTLE ONE IN THIS
TIME OF SORROW.

CONDITIONS HERE WILL PREVENT OUR PRESENCE
AT THE SERVICE, BUT OUR PRAYERS FOLLOW YOU
CONTINUALLY TOWARDS THAT BRIGHT DAY WHICH HAS
JUST DAWNED FOR JEAN.

The funeral was held on Wednesday at Wilshire Baptist Church,
officiated by Ralph Langley and Rev. A. L. Jordan, the Withers' pastor in
Baytown. No transcript of the service exists, but according to a Memorial
Book (signed by all who had paid their respects), two pieces of special
music were included: the hymn "Blessed Redeemer," sung by JoAnn
Seelig, a concert artist and voice teacher at Southwestern Seminary;
and a choral anthem:

> My God and I go in the fields together.
> We walk and talk as good friends should and do.
> We clasp our hands, our voices ring with laughter.
> My God and I walk through the meadow's hue.

Mother was buried in the Woodlands section of Restland Cemetery. A flat headstone was added a few weeks later, inscribed:

Mary Jean McIver
1926–1956
PSALM 116

III
Wayfarers

14

Aftershocks

"Make them go away!" I shrieked, swatting my father's pajama top. "This one's crawling up your arm, and that one's eating your nose!"

It was the middle of the night, and I had woken up sick. Daddy had barely snapped on my Little Bo Peep lamp and sat down beside me when the first snake detached itself from his pajama-sleeve cuff. Like the cuff's maroon piping, the creature was thin as a licorice whip but still quite menacing. It was also zippity-quick and had a remarkable ability to reproduce. I now watched in horror as the writhing cuff stitch morphed into another two red worms. One darted diagonally up the gray pajama top; the other coiled around a button and then split into three more baby snakes.

"They're going under your collar!" I screamed, still flailing at Daddy's chest. He tried to restrain and comfort me, but I knew that those snakes were as real as the daisies embroidered on my nightgown.

They were, in fact, more real than almost anything else I had experienced in the previous days. Little more than a week had passed since my mother's funeral and burial service—neither of which I attended. Instead, Leslie and I had stayed with a lady who, according to Aunt Winkie, kept us happy with a basketful of toys.

In fact, I had not even been told of the death on that Wednesday of the funeral. And I was equally unaware that on that same evening, Daddy was grappling with a dilemma. Within a few days, he was slated to preach the closing message for Youth Week at Glorieta, a Baptist conference center in New Mexico. Ironically, his preassigned topic was

"Is My Faith Adequate?" (*How can I* not *go?* he asked himself.) After much deliberation, he decided to keep the commitment, reasoning that kinfolk were still on hand to tend me and that he would only be gone for a couple of days. His mother was supportive but adamant about one thing: "Bruce," Mommie Mac said, "you *must* tell that child about her mother before you fly off to New Mexico."

Late that afternoon, Daddy decided to drive to Youngblood's Fried Chicken. Our kitchen overflowed with food, so he probably just wanted to get away for a while and saw this as an opportunity to be alone with me. We got in the Studebaker and headed over to Northwest Highway, a former farm-to-market road that until very recently had marked the limits of northeast Dallas. Years later, this greatly widened thoroughfare would be an inner loop of a city whose suburbs fanned out for fifty miles. But in 1956, it was still just a two-lane road edged by a few new housing developments and great swaths of windswept prairie. Dad would later recall that he pulled onto the shoulder of the highway, shut off the ignition, and tried to explain to me where my mother had gone. And I reportedly responded, "I'm hungry. When are we gonna get the chicken?"

My own chronological memory unfolds like this:

> *I see Mother sick on the couch. A mint-green ambulance possibly sits in our driveway. My father and I carry the take-out food into our duplex, and after Daddy explains why Grandmother is crying, I wonder if Mommy climbed stairs or rode an escalator up to heaven. I imagine her eating hamburgers with God on a puffy white cloud.*

The next thing I knew, snakes were crawling all over Daddy's pajamas.

And then it was morning. A middle-aged woman from our church sat on our living room's sofa, cuddling me in her lap while Daddy hovered nearby. Above the sofa, dark-green cafe curtains and venetian blinds were closed against sunbeams that hurt my eyes. Daylight had not banished the snakes, but after our long night together, they seemed about as worn out as I was. Instead of darting, they now slugged across the front of the lady's blouse. I no longer had the energy to scream.

Resigned, all I could do was weakly swipe at her collar and moan, "Mrs. Brannon, they're all *o-ver* your neck."

The three of us were the only ones in the duplex on this late-August morning. All of our visiting relatives had left, and Daddy—now returned from New Mexico—was adjusting to his first days as a single parent. I would not learn until much later that my future was being discussed over phone lines strung from Colorado to Texas to North Carolina. Grandmother Withers was physically unable to care for me, but my paternal grandparents had offered to take me in, as had Aunt Winkie and my father's sister, Ella. And one of my great-aunts wrote to Dad: "I would be happy to raise Kathie, and would love her as if she were my own."

Daddy would consider none of these offers. "She's already lost a mother," he explained. "She doesn't need to lose *another* parent." All the same, he was going need a great deal of help—something he realized with new urgency after nursing me through a snake-filled night. At daybreak, he had phoned Myrtle Brannon, a Wilshire member and mother of four who had already assisted our family in many ways. The first thing Myrtle did after she arrived was reassure Dad that I had not gone stark raving mad: I was simply running a high fever, which had triggered hallucinations. But the fever itself caused a new worry.

Mother's autopsy report had been released two days after her burial, listing "polio encephalitis" as the cause of death. Family members suspected that during our trip to the Gulf Coast, she might have been infected by a mosquito bite. Whatever its origin, the polio virus bypassed her spine and went straight to the brain.

Everyone who visited the funeral home or attended the memorial service was advised to get a gamma globulin shot to boost their immunity. Aunt Winkie disinfected every surface in our duplex. All sheets and towels were hot-washed in bleach, and Mother's clothing was removed from the premises. During a day or two of bureaucratic confusion and overreaction, the Dallas County Health Department even posted a QUARANTINED sign on our front door.

My polio vaccine was declared sufficient to protect me, but so much mystery and fear had surrounded Mother's illness that when my own fever soared, Daddy was certain a second nightmare was about to begin.

Blessedly, his concerns were not prolonged . . . because within a few hours, I was splotched from head to toe with German measles.

*   *   *

Within a few days, my father had to resume his job at what we called "the Baptist Building" in downtown Dallas. Following a friend's recommendation, he hired a housekeeper to tend me on weekdays. Annie Kaye Howard was a young single woman whose coffee-toned beauty would later remind me of the actress Phylicia Rashad. She was good-natured and fun to be with, and she cared for me with a balance of firmness and affection. Annie Kay was quite competent with childcare and household chores, but she did not do a great deal of homestyle cooking: I mainly subsisted on dry cereal, soups, sandwiches, and canned fruit cocktail. When Daddy came home at suppertime, he fixed something from his own limited repertoire: poached eggs, beef potpies, or fish sticks (the latter two being frozen entrees that only needed heating in the oven).

In the evenings, my father supervised bath time, read me a couple of stories, helped me say my prayers, and tucked me into bed. Then he would go downstairs to sort through the day's mail:

> Bruce—Words cannot express the agony of my soul when I read in the *Baptist Standard* of Jean's passing.

*   *   *

> Word has just come to us that polio has claimed your wife. All of us who have children live in fear of this disease.

*   *   *

> Bob Dunn just relayed to us the shocking news of Jean's passing. Realizing that there is little we can say to a Christian heart that is broken, we can only pledge our prayers.

*   *   *

You are fortunate to have had such a lovely, charming wife with whom to company through the years. She was a light of inspiration certainly beyond compare.

Several letters mentioned Mother's memorial service, and others referred to my father's closing message at Glorieta:

Words cannot express the gratitude I have for the blessings which were mine at Jean's "Commencement Service." The presence of the Holy Spirit was so real, and heaven seemed so close! . . . I tried to put this into words for our Sunday school class Sunday morning [in Lubbock]. So many of the girls were close to Jean. We had special prayer for her Monday night (we know now that she was already with the Lord), and sixteen girls raised their hearts in such earnest prayer, I have never felt such a marvelous Presence!

* * *

Ellen told me about the service last Wednesday—that it was more like a revival than a funeral. . . . She told me that Mrs. Withers had "seemed to see Christ standing next to Ralph as he preached."

* * *

Some of our [church's] young people have just returned from New Mexico where they heard you give a very courageous testimony concerning your faith in such a crisis.

* * *

I heard that you delivered a marvelous message at Glorieta, and the young people and their leaders were greatly blessed. Friends report that you are a constant source of inspiration to them.

* * *

Bruce, God used you in a wonderful way at Glorieta to bless all of our lives! Your testimony will bear much fruit in the years to come.

* * *

Betty Faye told us that Kathie had the measles. Know that you must have been worried sick for a while.

Daddy realized that it would be an impossible task to personally respond to the hundreds of people who had sent letters, cards, telegrams, flowers, and other gestures of sympathy. He thus typed his own thank-you letter and mailed mimeographed copies to everyone. In addition to expressing gratitude, he voiced his spiritual convictions:

> I fully believe that if we could know what Jean is experiencing today, we would covet her joy. . . .
> In light of the above, I cannot find it in my heart to be overwhelmed with grief. In saying this, I do not minimize my personal feelings, nor am I oblivious to the rough days of adjustment ahead. . . . As I have been prone to despair these last days, I can almost hear Jean say in a subtle tone, "What did you preach last Sunday?" For nine years, we sought to proclaim the Christian truth together. I shall now live by it as never before.

As an adult, I would reread that letter and wonder if my father might have repressed his grief. In retrospect, I do not think so. For despite his strong and sincere spiritual beliefs, I am sure that he gave way to tears in private and often felt crushed by loneliness.

And what about me?

Upon losing my mother, I—who had been so heartbroken over the Lubbock Coliseum—Felt. Absolutely. Nothing. I—who could worry the most trivial notion into the ground—rarely asked about her. I shed not one tear of grief and have no memory of missing her.

The adults around me saw all of this and were relieved. "The child seems to be adjusting well," they told each other. "So let's don't upset her by talking about her mother."

Their intentions were good, and they had my best interest at heart. This was just the way things were done in the 1950s: every effort was made to shield bereaved children from the pain of loss. They were not rushed into "trauma therapy" and were not encouraged to memorialize or remember the deceased family member.

Adults have fairly standard rituals to help them grieve: the funeral-home visitation/wake and viewing, the funeral itself, a burial or ash scattering, the receiving of cards and flowers and memorial gifts. I participated in no such rites and would not have fully comprehended them *had* I done so.

As an adult, I would look back and wonder: Was there ever some anvil-dropping moment when it hit me that Mommy was *never* coming back?

Probably not, since I didn't yet understand the meaning of *never*.

But how did I feel when almost every trace of her was removed from the duplex? After closets and drawers were emptied, shoe racks stripped bare, and not a single hairbrush, earbob, or tube of lipstick left behind?

Did I miss that pretty beaded purse?

If so, I cannot recall.

15

Earth Angels

Dear Brother Bruce—May God continue to bless and comfort you during these difficult days. . . . Kathie, I know that you will make Jesus and your mother proud as they watch you from heaven's window.

ONE MORNING AFTER I had recovered from the measles, I was squatting on the sidewalk in front of our duplex. A passing cloud had left big rain splats on the concrete. They smelled hot and leached a tangy scent from the nearby grass. The air almost visibly sizzled as the wet patches vanished before my eyes. Our yard was small and virtually treeless, but I had still found ways to entertain myself. If I was not watching rain patches evaporate, then I might sample the honeysuckle nectar from a porch-side bush or maybe snag a doodlebug inching out of the grass.

I was getting ready to do the latter when something farther down the sidewalk caught my eye. A dozen steps later, I stood over a pink-and-white object lying on the concrete. I picked it up. It was a small baby rattle, shaped like a cherub sleeping on a cloud. It was made of unusually sturdy plastic and had no handle. Instead, a pink ribbon had been threaded through a hook above the cherub's head, suggesting that the rattle was designed to be tied to a child's stroller. Fingering the ribbon's loose ends, I wondered where the toy had come from. No babies lived on our block. Cousin Leslie had gone back to Colorado, but it probably wasn't hers because (1) my aunt didn't bring a stroller, and (2) I was such a connoisseur of infant products that I would have spied and coveted that little angel from the get-go. It was the most perfect toy ever.

Deciding that this was a clear case of Finders Keepers, I carried my new treasure back to the duplex and up to my bedroom. The crib was still set up, probably because no one had had the time or energy to take it down. I hoisted myself over the side rail and tumbled into the baby bed. Then I called to Annie Kay, who was downstairs ironing Daddy's shirts and watching *As the World Turns.* When she came to my room, I asked her to tie the rattle onto a crib railing. She obliged and then headed back to her ironing and soap operas. Meanwhile, I unfolded an old baby blanket—the one with crescent moons and stars. Even though it was the middle of the day, I lay down, tucked the blanket around me, and swayed gently from side to side. I imagined that I was an infant, rocking myself back to a warm, womb-like world where pain never entered and problems fled. In this fashion, I floated to sleep under the pink-and-white watch of the baby angel.

* * *

The crib eventually came down (and at some point, the angel rattle vanished from my life, never to be seen again). But I did not let go of my longing to be babied. And like grown-ups who sometimes drown their sorrows in liquor, I hit the bottle hard.

One day I was snooping around a garage-side storage room and stumbled upon some of my old nursery items, including a bulky sterilizer filled with a dozen glass nursing bottles. Their nipples were inverted, secured with black screw-on collars and protective disks. I removed one of the dusty bottles and carried it back to the house. In the kitchen, I asked Annie Kay to fill it with Kool-Aid, which—after a good scrubbing—she did. I then went to the living room and sat in front of the TV, happily sucking away while the Three Stooges bonked each other around.

Not long after this, a lady in our church kept me for an afternoon. Like everyone else, she felt sorry for me. So when we went to a drugstore, the lady told me that I could pick out whatever I wanted and she would buy it. (I was not a stupid child: I was quickly learning that hangdog eyes and a forlorn expression worked like magic on adults.) Instead of heading for the toy or candy aisle, I beelined to the infant products. The Evenflo company had recently begun to make *plastic* nursing bottles in pastel colors; even better, the ugly black collars and discs now came in pink, blue, and yellow! I could not decide between the pink or blue bottle, so the lady bought them both for me.

They became favorite possessions. I lugged the bottles most everywhere I went, and grown-ups humored me by filling them with Kool-Aid or Dr Pepper. The bottles didn't do much for my buck teeth or nutrition, but they did soothe my soul.

* * *

Meanwhile, Daddy found solace in more conventional ways, such as poring over the mail that still arrived:

Bruce, Jean's death still seems an impossibility. I told Jesse that I thought going to the funeral would help me realize that she was gone—but I can't. So many of the girls who were in her Sunday school class have said the same thing to me.

* * *

I don't know when anything has crushed me as this has. Jean was one of the loveliest persons I have ever known. Not many weeks ago, Mabel [the writer's wife] commented to me how sweet and fine your wife was.

* * *

We may not be able to trace God, but we can trust Him. We see part of the picture. He sees all of it.

* * *

Thank you for your Contribution to the last service at Glorieta. Our whole year's BSU program is going to be more spiritual because of that one service.

* * *

To think that Jean will always remain young and beautiful, and her Christian witness an inspiration—a benediction. Her life will be untouched by so many of life's sorrows and disappointments.

* * *

Brother Bruce, it is likely you will not remember me since you only saw me one time when you held a revival for us [in New Braunfels, Texas]. But I want you to know how sorry I am to hear about the passing of your dear little wife. She came with you several times to the services. Since she was a Christian lady, you are sure you will see her again. . . . Here is a scripture that I just cannot get my mind away from: Psalm 116:15—"Precious in the sight of the LORD is the death of His saints."

* * *

Dear Bruce . . . I recently read about Kathie's comment that she was glad her mother died, because she will now have "lots of mommies." Man, isn't that just the Lord—to repay ten to one—"good measure, pressed down, shaken together, and running over"?

I don't know who put into my head the notion of "lots of mommies." But years later, I would reread this particular letter with mixed feelings. While I appreciated the writer's attempt to find a silver lining, part of me wanted to press *him* down and shake *him* up for so glibly equating the loss of a parent to some tent-revival cheer.

All the same, in the autumn of 1956, Daddy and I did need the help of any "earthly mothers" we could get. Annie Kay met our most urgent need, and other friends from church or the Baptist Building frequently followed the biblical admonition to care for widow(er)s and orphans.

One of Dad's biggest problems was that he didn't always keep banker's hours. His job often required evening activities or weekend travel to college campuses across Texas. In addition, he sometimes accepted preaching engagements in distant cities and towns. In Baptist circles, he was still widely known from his youth revival days; now, folks hungered all the more to hear inspiring messages from this young widower who had just trod the Valley of the Shadow. Decades later, feeling guilty about being away so much of the time, my father would explain that the preaching opportunities were not optional: not only had our family lost income from my mother's organ playing and piano teaching, but Dad now had to pay for a housekeeper. He *needed* the fees or gratuities from those extra jobs.

Whenever Daddy was away for a weekend, it was most often Forrest and Myrtle Brannon who opened their home to me—so often, in fact, that I would practically become a member of their family during the next few years. They lived only a couple of miles from us and just blocks from our church, where Forrest served as a deacon. The Brannons went about the Lord's work with good humor and an easy grace. They had an older son in college, a teenage daughter, and two preschool boys. Myrtle was the type of person who stepped into our lives with no fanfare and little discussion. "Hey," she told Dad with a cheerful shrug, "I've already got four kids. What's one more?"

Myrtle not only provided bed and board, but she often ferried me around town. Even if Annie Kay *had* known how to drive, Daddy had no second car to leave with her. So if I needed new shoes, it was Myrtle who took me shopping for Buster Brown shoes. For other apparel, we usually went to Volk Department Store, where my fitting-room tantrums set tongues to clucking.

Shortly after my bout with the measles, Myrtle chauffeured me to a beauty shop. On a recent Saturday evening, Daddy had tried to primp me up for Sunday-morning church. My light-brown hair had always been fairly short and naturally straight, but Mother sometimes gave me Toni home permanents, and on Saturday nights she always sent me to bed in pin curls.

Following the advice of some Wilshire women, Daddy decided that he would take the "tried and true" and *improve* on it. The first thing he did was dispense with bobby pins and purchase a new product called

Spoolies—rubbery pink rollers that secured the hair when a spool-end was inverted and snapped down. In itself, this change might have been workable. But my father had also heard that applying a bit of lanolin to the hair would give it more body. Sadly, Daddy interpreted "a bit" to mean "half the bottle." When the rollers were removed on Sunday morning, my hair was a sopping, greasy mess.

And so I ended up in a styling salon, having my already short locks cut down to nearly nothing. I would wear this pixie style for the next three years: it was currently fashionable for young girls and was easy to care for, requiring only an occasional trim and some bangs-shaping. But I didn't particularly like it. I might have been taken to a beauty shop, but with my buckteeth, plain-Jane features, and boyish haircut, I did not feel at all beautiful.

16

...And One Ugly Witch

On a crisp autumn day, I sat on a paper-covered table in my pediatrician's examination room, a stark cubicle devoid of any cheery pictures or kid-friendly decor. Packed into the space were Annie Kay, Mrs. Brannon, and Dr. Doris Spegal. This was not the first time we had thus congregated. My bout of measles was only a prelude to what would become a two-year string of illnesses: mumps, chicken pox, stomach viruses, strep throat, tonsillitis, ear infections.

The latter had brought us here on this day.

My pediatrician was a middle-aged woman with salt-and-pepper hair and a nasal voice that scared me. She was nice enough, but it was hard to warm up to someone who held such power. Every time I went to her office, it was a toss-up whether she might send me home with a painless prescription . . . or order my butt to be stung by what felt like a hundred yellow jackets.

Dr. Spegal had finished her examination and now helped me back into my dress (really sick kids sometimes wore their pajamas to the doctor's office, but *dresses* were still the norm for girls). She then placed a firm hand on my thigh, peered over the top of her bifocals, and asked if I would mind taking some penicillin.

"A pill or a shot?" I asked. Four years old, and I already knew the p-word.

"A shot."

Yes, I minded *very* much. But I also knew there were three grown-ups in the room who were *not* going to give me a choice in the matter.

Dr. Spegal stepped out to issue the order. Normally, she would have moved on to see another patient or write chart notes; instead, she reentered the room, perhaps to offer extra support to me and my caretakers. She told Mrs. Brannon that I might have to be hospitalized *unless* I was brought back to the office daily for four additional injections.

I sat on the table, legs dangling and heart thumping. My stomach plunged as another child's torturous shrieks penetrated the walls between cubicles.

While we waited, the three women discussed my diet, sleep patterns, discipline problems. I was vaguely aware that surrounding me were some of the "lots of mommies" who were concerned about my well-being. Only in retrospect would I more fully appreciate their efforts to keep me from becoming a runny-nosed, malnourished, ill-mannered vagabond.

"Someone needs to help her with toothbrushing," Dr. Spegal was telling Annie Kay. "And she should be eating more fresh fruit. You can keep apples and tangerines in the refrigerator so that she can easily get them . . ."

Without warning, the cubicle door swung open, and in strode the same barrel-chested old hag who had given me my polio shot a few months earlier. In her hand was an unforgivably long hypodermic needle, its tip spearing a damp wad of cotton.

Suddenly self-conscious in the crowded room, I decided that I wasn't keen for this many people to witness my ordeal.

"Mrs. Brannon," I said, "I want you to leave." Myrtle stepped out into the hallway. Following orders, I lay face down on the crinkly paper and lowered my drawers. Off in the corner, Annie Kay grimaced and covered her eyes.

Even though I didn't struggle, the nurse pinned me down with a sumo-wrestler arm and hiked my dress. Then, before I could blink, she stuck the living fire out of my bare bottom. (For the rest of my life, I would be severely phobic about butt shots: "Give it to me in my arm, my leg, my eyeball, my big toe!" I would plead. "But stay the hell *away* from my backside!")

I screamed like a banshee when the hypodermic went in but shed no tears. Afterward, I sat up and grudgingly accepted a cellophane-wrapped lollipop (hardly a fair trade, in my opinion). I told the nurse that I hated her and called her an "ugly witch" to her face. Then, I posed a question that encompassed every injustice of life: "Why," I groused, "do they have to make the needles so *sharp*?"

17

Wayfarers

"WHY DO YOU HAVE to go away again?" I whimpered from the passenger seat as Daddy backed our Studebaker from driveway. It was just after daybreak on a chilly Saturday, and both of us were still groggy. My father's suitcase and hanging clothes were stashed in the back of the car, along with a smaller bag that I would carry to the Brannons.

Daddy said that he wished we *could* stay home together, but this trip was part of his job. He paused to adjust the heater, then put the car in gear and steered us down Marquita Street. The few trees on our block were bare, and a broody overcast sky reflected my own mood. It was not that I really minded staying with the Brannons, because I usually had a good time once I was settled in at their house. But it was the leave-taking that hurt. I rarely wept, but the thought of parting with Daddy put a knot in my throat. Cradled in my arms was a favorite baby doll, swaddled in one of my old receiving blankets. As we turned north onto Skillman Street, I moved her closer to the heating vent so that she would feel safe and warm.

My father and I cruised by residential side streets in silence. True, we were still half-asleep, but silence was also how we responded to the cloud of melancholy that had become a third presence in our lives. The two of us could not see or touch it, but it loomed everywhere; if you pressed too close against it, your heart would sink into your stomach. So Daddy and I tiptoed around this murky cloud, either in silence or by talking about everything in the world *except* the cause of our sadness.

In hindsight, I realize that Daddy must have missed everything about the helpmate who, after nine years, had become as familiar as a second skin. Not only was he confronted daily with a vacant chair, a half-empty bed, and an oppressive silence, but he now had no one with whom to smile over private jokes, discuss world events, laugh at *The Honeymooners,* or share the details of a trip the minute he walked through the front door.

I, too, felt bruised but could not link this sadness to my mother; once she vanished, all conscious desire for her was severed as completely as an amputation. Instead of longing for her, I had almost immediately begun to select possible "substitute" mothers who might be willing to marry Daddy. Some of these prospects I found at church, others on television shows and even in commercials. Almost any woman who was young and pretty was fair game (middle-aged matrons, such as Myrtle, were out of the running, no matter how nice they might be).

I had reacted to Mother's death by skidding backward toward the good old days of babyhood. But, conversely, I had also grown quite protective of Daddy and did what I could to fill my mother's high heels with my small feet. I was already an expert at locating missing cuff links and reminding Daddy to smooth down his stubborn cowlick. Whenever his back hurt, I fetched the heating pad. If he seemed sad, I tried to lift his spirits. Sometimes, I simply climbed into the contour chair and snuggled with him. At other times, I might sing *The Mickey Mouse Club* song or demonstrate how to slide down a staircase on your butt.

"Do you have a headache?" I now asked my father, who was rubbing his temple. Without Mother's example and encouragement, I had stopped calling him "Daddy-Boy."

"Just a bit," he said. "But you don't need to worry about me."

We had stopped at a traffic light on Mockingbird Lane, which despite its quaint name was a major thoroughfare. Several blocks to the left sat the enormous Dr Pepper bottling plant and national headquarters. On our right, a small shopping strip was anchored by the Wilshire Theater; when our church was formed in 1951, services were held in the movie theater until its own facilities could be built nearby. It was from this movie house that the church had taken its name.

"Did you remember your toothbrush and razor?" I nagged Daddy.

"They're in my suitcase. Do you have your bottle?"

"Uh-huh." My pink plastic nursing bottle was in the overnight bag. I wouldn't publicly display it at the Brannons', but I still wanted it close by.

I wished that the traffic light would stay red forever. We were only a couple of blocks from the Brannons' street, and I wanted to hang onto these last precious seconds with Daddy.

"Can't I go with you?" I pleaded.

"Not this time, honey," my father said. "But I have to preach in Abilene in a couple of weeks, and maybe I can take you with me then."

The light turned green. I swallowed hard, rewrapped the doll in my blanket, and pulled her close.

* * *

"Here I come to save the day!"
That means that Mighty Mouse
Is on the way!

Sprawled on the Brannons' den floor, I alternately scribbled in a coloring book and watched cartoon characters *ca-room* across a console television screen. I was flanked by four-year-old Ricky and three-year-old Tommy, whom everyone called "Bo." The boys had their own coloring books, and we shared a cookie tin full of Crayolas.

Ricky (who would grow up to own an art gallery) was fusty about aesthetics and got upset if a crayon broke or lost its paper wrapper. He was a pudgy, sweet-natured child with dreamy brown eyes. His high-pitched voice and closely buzzed haircut made me think of Curly from the Three Stooges. Ricky's greatest ambition was to be a trapeze artist.

Although Bo was smaller, he was All-Hyperactive-Boy: wiry, tough, primed for a fight, continually conjuring mischief. He was not really cruel nor did he have pent-up anger (there was *nothing* "pent up" about this kid who careened happily through his days with steam almost visibly shooting from both ears). He was simply a rambunctious male who loved for me to come over because it gave him the chance to annoy fresh prey: a *girl*—and one close to his own size. On this morning, Bo greeted me in his usual fashion. Moments after Daddy kissed me goodbye and left through the back door, the youngest Brannon snarled and pounced, seizing me with a bruising grip. My doll popped like a cork from my protective arms. Bo then cannonballed his head into my stomach and propelled me backward through the spacious den and attached kitchen, then out to a hallway. There he shoved me into a coat closet and slammed the door, bodily blocking my exit while I screamed and pounded from within.

I was not particularly afraid, but the mistreatment angered me. Mrs. Brannon soon came to my rescue, scolding Bo and gently chiding, "Oh, Kathie, you know he's only teasing you!" I was fast developing a reputation as a whiner and a drama queen.

But like most young children, I was resilient. Thirty minutes later, I had downed a pancake breakfast and settled in with the boys for a marathon of cartoon-watching. With a laid-back, 1950s version of multitasking, we watched Bugs Bunny outsmart Elmer Fudd while scribbling in our coloring books. The three of us would spend the next few years swapping broken Periwinkles for stubs of Burnt Umbers, our progress measured by how well we had learned to "stay in the lines."

In 1956, none of us were very good at this. And on this morning, our coloring grew even sloppier as we elbowed, kicked, grabbed, and jerked. Bo was the main offender, being genetically wired to imitate every cartoon bully that crossed the TV screen. With a cry of "Geronimo!" he suddenly dove onto the cookie tin and scattered our crayons. He arm-wrestled Ricky and pounded drumbeats on my back. Unaccustomed to roughhousing, I would never learn to fight back. My reaction to stress was to curl up like a doodlebug and bleat an irritable "*Stop* it!"

"Bo!" Mrs. Brannon warned. She stood at a nearby sink—set into a bar that divided the kitchen from the den—and kept a half-watchful eye on us. But like most mothers in the '50s, she did not seriously intervene in our playtime unless we were on the verge of drawing blood.

Bo stopped his antics, but only because he was now distracted by the Lone Ranger crying, "Hi yo, Silver, awaaay!" Taking advantage of the reprieve, I crossed the room and hefted a Sears & Roebuck catalog from under an end table. I lugged it back to the TV area and began to turn great slabs of pages until I came to the Baby Furniture section. For the next half hour, while the boys bickered and Tonto thundered across TV Land, I retreated into a world of high chairs, cribs, and playpens.

I was trying to decide which bassinet I liked best when a pair of hands suddenly dug into my ribs, followed by tickling fingers. "Kitty-Kitty-Kitty!" chirped sixteen-year-old Rosemary, who had just come into the den.

"Quit!" I hollered, swatting her hands away. Although I was warming up to Rosemary—whom everyone called "Sis"—I did not like to be tickled, and I *hated* the nickname "Kitty."

"You got your nose buried in that book again?" she asked, mussing my hair. Picking up the cue, Ricky and Bo began to chant:

Baby Kathie! Baby Kathie!
Looking at the ba-by fur-ni-ture!

"Gimme it!" I hollered as Bo tried to pry the book away from me.

"Sis!" called Mrs. Brannon. "You all leave her alone!"

I thought about sneaking off to Forrest Jr.'s bedroom, which was where I slept since he was away at college. It was quiet and dark back there, and I might be able to find some solitude with my nursing bottle. Whenever I went to the Brannons', I kept it hidden in my suitcase, having learned that its presence not only invited merciless teasing but put the bottle itself at risk of being thrown, squashed, set afire, or given to the dog to chew on.

Before I could slip away, the boys had turned their attention back to the TV. In the background, Rosemary excitedly commiserated with her mother over high-school gossip and the latest Hollywood scandal. Left to myself, I resumed my nursery-furniture daydreams while all manner of commotion swirled around me. That was just how things were at the Brannon house: noisy and busy and always in motion. Radios blared. Doors slammed. Teenagers came and went. Mr. Brannon worked for a Chevrolet dealership. When he was home, he sat in his vinyl chair in the den, drinking coffee and smoking cigarettes. He was a jovial man who smiled a lot, but he didn't have many chances to get a word in edgewise.

* * *

Across town, my father was sitting in a Love Field boarding lounge and possibly penning one of the sporadic journal entries he had begun to keep in a large blue ledger:

DAD'S JOURNAL
....
November 17, 1956

Today I am headed to Shreveport [Louisiana]. Tomorrow I preach at Queensland Baptist Church—the pastor will meet me at the airport.

I just finished reading a chapter in one of Weatherhead's books on death. His feelings are similar to mine—that death for the believer is a beautiful experience! The only sorrow is that which comes to the loved ones left behind in their loneliness. Yet God in His goodness can even supply this need. I shall be eternally grateful to Him for the peace He has given me!

* * *

In the Brannons' den, *The Lone Ranger* gave way to *Sky King*. The latter program featured a modern-day cowboy who righted wrongs by flying his own plane throughout the West. His sidekick was Penny, an attractive girl with long blond hair. It didn't matter to me that Penny was Sky King's teenage niece: I saw her as his adult girlfriend. Shoot-'em-up Westerns normally bored me, but on this morning I was agog as Sky King managed a tricky canyon-rim landing, killed a rattlesnake, and fought some bad guys. I wished that Daddy were Sky King so that he could marry Penny . . . and she would then be my mother.

By the time Sky King flew off into the sunset, we kids had been so inundated with commercials for Sugar Smacks and Bosco chocolate syrup that we ran over to the kitchen and begged for a midmorning snack. Myrtle agreed to fix us some ice cream if we promised to go outside later, where we could play in the sandbox or ride trikes in the driveway. The three of us trooped back to the television and flopped to the floor. After a few minutes, Myrtle brought us small unbreakable bowls, each with a mound of vanilla ice cream. I copied the boys when they began to stir their scoops into a soft mush, our spoons clacking against melamine.

"I'm making a milkshake," Ricky announced.

"I'm making dog food," said Bo. "What are you making, Kathie?"

"Baby food."

DAD'S JOURNAL
....

Next week will be Thanksgiving. A year ago, our family gaily commemorated this occasion. Today, Jean is with her Lord. And yet Kathie and I have so much for which to be thankful. The world is filled with people with greater needs than ours.

Today, I am thankful for memories. The beautiful ones, the ones that linger even as the afterglow of a sunset. What a blessing to feast on these!

I remember Jean! Lovely, attractive, radiant, positive. She lived life to the fullest and pitied the person who could not. Strange—all my memories of her are beautiful. Even those petty quarrels, those little tiffs (and we had them) are cherished. I suppose it's because they always led to a beautiful reconciliation. This is the course of true love.

* * *

Only you can make this world seem right,
Only you can make the darkness bright

Later that afternoon, the Brannon boys and I crowded into Sis's bedroom. I stood at one end of a long dresser, watching cross-eyed as a 45 rpm record wobbled around a turntable. Nearby, Sis swayed romantically with her eyes closed, crooning along with The Platters:

Only you can make this change in me,
For it's true, you are my destiny

Behind me, Bo was using the double bed as a trampoline, mussing its chenille spread. I played the perfume atomizers lined up on the dresser's other end. Ricky had opened an adjacent closet and was inspecting a row of crinoline petticoats and prom dresses. Sis went to Woodrow Wilson High, whose pennants and pom-poms decorated the bedroom walls. Stuck in the dresser's mirror frame were mums and corsages, some of which matched her pastel gowns.

Baptists were really not supposed to dance, because it could lead to all sorts of licentious behavior; in fact, some of the stricter ones wouldn't even listen to rock 'n' roll music. (President Eisenhower himself would soon form a congressional committee to study "The Effects of Rock-and-Roll on Juvenile Delinquency.") But the Brannons were not hard-shell Baptists and didn't mind if Rosemary played the latest radio hits or went to school dances.

> When you hold my hand,
> I understand the magic that you do.

"That's Sis singing on the record," Ricky told me, pointing to the phonograph.

"Is that you, Sis?" I asked, interrupting her lip-synching.

"Sure is," she said. "And I come in again . . . right here at the very end":

> You're my dream come true,
> My one and only you!

That final high falsetto note convinced me that it *was* Sis singing on the record.

Before The Platters could fade out, Bo hollered, "Play 'Hound Dog!'" His sister removed one disc and dropped another onto the turntable. Seconds later, with gyrating hips and penny loafers swiveling, she launched into the tune that we had been hearing around here for weeks:

You ain't nothin' but a hound dog,
Cryin' all the time!

Decades later, I would scan a compilation of Billboard's Top 40 Hits and be surprised to discover that Elvis Presley's "Hound Dog" had peaked on the charts on August 18, 1956, two days before my mother died. But even more astonishing was that Perry Como's "Hot Diggity (Dog Ziggity Boom)"—the song Daddy and I had sung back in Lubbock —had peaked the previous March.

Those two hits were made only five months apart . . . but in my mind, they might as well have belonged to different centuries.

18

Condolences

DURING THE DAYS and weeks after Mother's death, scores of cards, letters, and telegrams had flooded both our mailbox and Daddy's desk at the Baptist Building. Still reeling from the shock of losing a spouse and overwhelmed by new responsibilities, it is likely that my father had not had the time or energy to fully digest this avalanche of condolences. Perhaps on quieter evenings, he found an hour or two of solitude in which to reread older messages and peruse more recent cards and letters that continued to trickle in.

The envelopes had been sent from places far and near, but most bore Texas postmarks. Expressions of sympathy came from friends and former classmates, the BSU leaders of dozens of colleges, and the staff and members of churches where Dad had preached revival services. Most began with "Dear Bruce," but a few included my name as well. Many writers shared memories of Mother, while others offered spiritual advice or observations. But whether the condolences were awkward or eloquently expressed, each was heartfelt and helped Daddy to bear his burden of pain.

> Every time I have tried to express the loss I have felt over
> Jean's Homegoing, I just haven't had the words. *You* know
> I loved her in a special way. . . . Each time I drive out on
> Seminary Hill I recall the fun Jean and I had several years ago
> as we were together when you were away preaching. . . . Kathie
> is a darling, and please, *please* bring her to Fort Worth any

time. We have some fine beef in the freezer, and we'll plan on a good steak for you when you bring our sweet girl over to play with Jane Anne.

* * *

Jean always had every hair in place. . . . Her voice was unique, her handwriting unforgettable, her person immaculate.

* * *

Bruce, you are one of the most stable, spiritual, sincere, and practical Christian young men I have ever met. The test of a man's faith can only be met when he faces adversity. If he can remain calm, strong, poised, and humble without being possessed by cynicism, bitterness, and doubt, God can use him unspeakably in the years that lie ahead.

* * *

I have not had opportunity to write you until now, for my fourteen-year-old son is in the hospital with polio. . . . Looking back one day, it will be clear why these things happen. God doesn't make "cosmic pets" of us just because we are His children. He permits us to suffer all the experiences common to man.

* * *

May God continue to comfort and bless you, my precious boy. I feel you are becoming the fulfillment of the prayer you once asked me to pray that you might be the man Dwight Moody said: "The world has yet to see what a life fully consecrated to the Lord can be."

* * *

You will be glad to know that Mr. and Mrs. Howard Hampton have given two books, *All the Women of the Bible* and *Streams in the Desert*, to our church library in memory of Jean.

* * *

Lives like Jean's are a formidable argument for why there
must be a heaven.

* * *

We believe that many students shall have cause to remember
Jean's influence for years to come. Thus we are placing a copy
of *Leaves of Gold* in the Baptist Student Center of Sam Houston
State Teachers College in her memory.

* * *

I'm not sure how soon you will be resuming preaching
engagements, but if you could supply us on Oct. 14, I know our
people would love to have you [in McKinney, Texas].

* * *

Enclosed is a check from many of your friends here in Lubbock,
to express in a small way the esteem which our people [at First
Baptist Church] have for you and yours.

* * *

The fine work you and your wife helped organized in San
Marcos [BSU] is a most fitting tribute to her and will continue
to influence the lives of many young people.

* * *

Ruth and I will be glad to keep Kathy any time you have BSU
work near Austin. I'm sure you will be at the University of
Texas sometime this fall. While you are there, why not just
make our home your headquarters?

* * *

When you are in Lubbock next month, Wylene and I would
love to have you and Kathie stay with us. We have an extra

bedroom, and our girls would enjoy having Kathie with them again.

*   *   *

I am so glad that you are coming to our BSU State Convention. You will mean a lot to our Kentucky students, and I know the Lord will use you in a special way.

*   *   *

We would really like to have you as our featured speaker for the BSU Christmas Banquet on December 20. [from Texas Western College, El Paso]

*   *   *

Bruce, this Christmas will be unlike any you have ever known, but I am convinced that with your faith, there will be joy in your loneliness, comfort in your sadness, strength in your weakness. . . . May He richly bless you and cause His face to shine upon you and yours.

19

Christmas In Blue . . . With A Touch Of Pink

OUR DUPLEX'S BEST FEATURE was its staircase, which I rarely approached in any normal fashion. Several times a day, I would scramble up its steps on all fours, like a monkey scaling a palm tree; for the descent, I often sat at the top and then slid all the way down, my rear end bouncing on each hardwood riser.

But on Christmas morning of 1956, I neither bounded nor slid downstairs to see what Santa had left beneath our tree. Instead, my footfalls were slow and tentative as I stepped onto the first riser . . . then the second. It was still dark outside, and a halo of lamplight rose from the living room below. On the fourth or fifth step down, I knelt beside the banister and peered through its rails. It was from this very spot that I had last glimpsed my mother as she lay sick on the couch. Now, four months later, the sofa had been moved against another wall to make room for our Christmas tree.

A week or so earlier, Daddy and I had driven to a grocery store where holiday trees filled a roped-off section of the parking lot. Most were a natural green, but in keeping with some current fad, a few had been spray-painted white, pink, or baby blue. While Daddy examined spruces and Fraser firs that looked the way God had made them in his native North Carolina, I raced over to the newfangled pastels and quickly selected my favorite. No amount of persuasion could change my mind, and we carried home a scrappy pine that some paint sprayer had transformed into a powder-blue vision sprung straight from a fairy tale.

The tree embarrassed Daddy, even after we had camouflaged it with lights, ornaments, and tinsel.

He thought it was tacky.

I thought it was beautiful.

And it had grown even more appealing as, day by day, colorfully wrapped presents accumulated beneath its boughs, most sent by relatives or friends. Our family had always opened such gifts on Christmas Eve (saving "Santa Claus" for the following morning), and Daddy opted to keep this tradition. My father and I had received many invitations to Christmas Eve gatherings, but he preferred that the two of us spend this special time together. For all I know, we might have supped on frozen fish sticks and Fritos, although we would have received quite a few homemade sweets from church members and other local friends.

My other memories of that evening are equally vague. I do know that after we opened our gifts, I set milk and cookies on the piano bench for Santa. When I worried that Saint Nick might not be able to enter our chimney-less duplex, Daddy promised to leave the front door unlocked for him.

I now rose from my kneeling position and descended two more steps. Through the stair railings, the blue tree's upper branches appeared, topped by a gold star that tilted precariously from its perch. Another step down and Daddy came into view, reclining in his contour chair over in a far corner of the living room. His bathrobe as rumpled as his hair, he sipped a cup of coffee while carols floated from a nearby radio.

> Yea, Lord, we greet Thee,
> Born this happy morning!

Daddy called out a cheerful "hey, hey!" when he spotted me and asked what I was doing up so early.

I grinned but averted my eyes with uncharacteristic shyness. I recall feeling acutely self-conscious—not just because Santa had supposedly come, but because I was aware that this Christmas was profoundly different from those that had preceded it. I knew that Daddy was equally aware of this difference, but as usual, neither of us spoke of it.

Then my father asked if I wanted to come on down and see what Santa had brought. Still hesitant, I descended another step . . . then another. I was wearing a footed sleeper, and its plastic soles crackled against the bare risers.

The tree's lowest branches were now visible and . . .

Oh!

There were *things* beneath them! Wooden things and metal things. Plastic things and colored things and girl things.

I quickened my pace down the final steps and jumped over the floor's inset heating grate (which, I had learned, could melt your pajamaed feet if you lingered too long). Two short strides took me to the tree, where I squatted to examine my presents. Santa had brought Tinkertoys, a stuffed monkey, and a makeup kit that contained a miniature compact and mirror, along with pretend lipstick, rouge, and nail polish. He had also left a boxed set of aluminum saucepans, a coffeepot, and a whistling teakettle for my toy stove.

But this cluster of playthings was dwarfed by the item I had most wanted: a Tiny Tears baby doll who drank water from a bottle and cried it back out of her wide, lash-rimmed eyes. I picked up the box and through the cellophane window admired the doll's rose-print shirt, triangular diaper secured with a tiny gold pin, white booties, and pink nursing bottle. She also came with a bubble-blowing pipe and a wee packet of Kleenex.

Daddy walked over and helped me unbox the doll, uttering a few *dang nabbits!* while he fumbled his way through cellophane and wire ties. Tiny Tears finally popped free, and I pulled her into my arms, intoxicated by her fresh vinyl scent. Right away, I wanted to fill her bottle with water, and Daddy said he would help me as soon as we had eaten some breakfast.

I asked if, instead of water, we could put chocolate milk in the bottle. Daddy didn't think this was a very good idea.

Later, my father and I snuggled side by side in the contour chair, both of us still in our pajamas. Windows were pinking up behind their venetian blinds as Daddy sipped a second cup of coffee and I played with Tiny Tears. On the little brown radio behind us, a choir sang a chorus from what I would later learn was Handel's *Messiah*:

> O thou that tellest good tidings to Zion,
> Arise, shine, for thy light is come

Twenty minutes earlier Daddy had dragged me away from toys long enough to eat some cereal. It wasn't the fanciest holiday breakfast, but we both knew that our evening meal would more than compensate. For years, my family had driven to Baytown on Christmas Day. After an eight- or nine-hour trip on two-lane roads, we would often arrive at my grandparents' house well after dark, tired and ravenously hungry. Granddaddy Withers had always been an excellent cook, and nothing was more welcoming to our travel-weary family than the aroma of his turkey and dressing and giblet gravy.

Keeping this Christmas Day tradition, Daddy and I would shortly begin the long journey to Baytown, where Santa would have left still *more* toys. We would soon need to ready ourselves; for now, though, Daddy dallied over his coffee as we enjoyed a few extra minutes by our modest fireside. Our hearth was only a boxy gas heater, but behind its grate, blue-tipped flames flickered prettily and spread sufficient warmth throughout the room.

After breakfast, I had gone upstairs to get my old moon-and-stars baby blanket, which I wrapped around Tiny Tears (later in the day, I would get carsick on this blanket, and it would end up in a roadside trash barrel somewhere in Central Texas). With some difficulty I had also filled her bottle with tap water from the bathroom sink. Now, sitting tandem with Daddy, I angled the bottle into the doll's mouth. Some of the liquid did leak out of her eyes, but a good amount dribbled onto the chair's arm, making my father say *honey, dadgummit!* and slosh coffee on his bathrobe. But he really wasn't all that mad, and he didn't even bother to blot the spills. Instead, he looked across the room at our tree and commented that the star was all lopsided.

I surveyed my gifts piled around the tree skirt and asked Daddy if Santa had brought *him* anything.

"Yes," he said, "an electric razor."

I studied his stubbly face and suggested that he *use* it.

He mumbled an *um-hum* but made no move to get up. While he finished his coffee and I fed my doll, we listened to a lady on the radio sing about a Shepherd who fed His flock and gathered the lambs in His arms. Then the song ended.

Daddy set his cup back in its saucer and said, "Kiddo, we need to hit the road." With his free hand, he reached down and pulled a lever that raised the chair to a more upright position. We both stood. Daddy took his dishes to the kitchen, and I trailed behind with my doll's bottle, wondering if I could get her to cry some Dr Pepper tears.

20

Snapshots: 1957

DAD'S JOURNAL
·····························
January 1, 1957

1956 is now history.

As I look back over the year's joys and sorrows, I am grateful for so many things: Friends. Health. Peace of mind. My work and calling. Anything else would have to be regarded as luxury.

God has been good!

I face the coming year without my beloved Jean—yet I do not face it alone. The Lord has been very near. And in a very real sense, Jean has continued to be with me. I have felt her presence in a strange fashion. This is proof to me— whether or not to anyone else—that one never dies.

* * *

THE BRANNONS USUALLY KEPT ME whenever Daddy had schedule conflicts, but other families also came to the rescue.

Sometimes I stayed at Pastor Ralph Langley's house, where I enjoyed playing with four-year-old Leanne. Ralph and his wife, Grace, were very kind to me. At the supper table, they did not force me to eat foods I disliked. Instead, they tried gentle persuasion, convincing me that carrots would make my hair as red as Leanne's. I told them that I didn't *want* red hair.

Another surrogate was Mary Louise Valentine, who had been one of my mother's Baylor friends and whose husband, Foy, had worked alongside Daddy in the Youth Revival Movement. The Valentines attended another Dallas church and lived farther across town, but I occasionally spent a day at their house. Carol was their one-year-old daughter, but I felt no jealousy toward the baby—probably because her mother gave me lots of undivided attention.

Mrs. Valentine was young and pretty, with long butterscotch hair. She sat on the floor with me when I colored and taught me the word *turquoise*. She read storybooks and acted out the tale of "Crooked Mouth," a personified wind who was unable to blow out a candle. When Carol took her nap, Mrs. Valentine let me sit in the baby's high chair and eat banana popsicles.

DAD'S JOURNAL
....
February 25, 1957

It has now been six months since Jean went to be with the Lord. She continues to be a source of inspiration for me. How positive she was! How glowing with faith, yet realistic. She was thorough, dependable, and completely honest. She was open to truth, and deplored being orthodox just for the sake of orthodoxy. If I could only know the depths she knew! She was a far better Christian than I am. But with the Lord's help, I'll set my sails toward deeper experiences.

* * *

Whenever I was not sick, I usually went to church two or three times a week, either with Daddy, the Brannons, or other Wilshire members who might be tending me.

Wilshire sat near the intersection of Mockingbird Lane and Abrams Road, and consisted of a small orange-brick sanctuary attached to a stubby educational wing. The facilities occupied one corner of a rectangular field where members hoped to one day construct a much larger sanctuary and additional buildings. For now, a swing set and jungle gym jutted from the field like lone oil derricks on a prairie. In

Wilshire's very crowded Preschool Department, shortly before our family joined the church. My future playmates– Ricky and Bo–are in the back with their hands raised. Teacher Nina Knox is holding a crying child.

coming years, the church would use this grassy expanse each October for a Western-style "roundup," with singing cowboys and the best mesquite-fired barbecue you ever put in your mouth.

I was normally at Sunday school on Sunday mornings and Training Union on those evenings. Wednesday nights I went to Sunbeams, a mission-focused children's class where we sang,

> Jesus wants me for a sunbeam,
> To shine for Him each day!

Since I was still a bit young to attend worship services, I spent that time in Mrs. Nina Knox's preschool nursery. There, I worked puzzles, colored pictures, and dropped blocks into a shape sorter. "*Nee*-na," as we called her, was a kind-hearted older woman whose silver hair was usually pinwheeled into a flat bun atop her head. Nina reminded us to share and told David Sinclair that it made Jesus sad when he filched other kids' animal crackers at snack time.

Whenever Nina saw me in the church hallway, she knelt to hug me and coo, "Jesus loves sweet Kathie." She said that to all us kids. We were "sweet Martha," "sweet David," and "sweet Bo"—even though I knew for a fact that David Sinclair and Bo Brannon were *not* sweet.

DAD'S JOURNAL
....

I find in these days a tendency to be anxious about the future. The grief, for the most part, is gone. Of course, one could easily work himself into a morbid state if he allowed his mind to dwell in that area. He could become a neurotic, and many do. Lord, save me from this! Help me to be positive, faithful, and optimistic.

* * *

My father and I were in the car one day when I began to rhythmically gulp and bug out my eyes. It was a nervous tic that I had recently developed.

"What on earth are you doing?" asked Daddy, glancing over to my passenger-side seat.

I couldn't answer, because it felt like a big frog was stuck in my throat, and I had to swallow hard to clear it out.

"Honey, please stop that!"

I continued to gulp and pop out my eyes.

"Kathie, if you don't quit this nonsense, I'm taking you to Dr. Spegal."

That scared me, and I stopped.

DAD'S JOURNAL
....

Last night I dreamed of Jean. She was so real, and so pretty! We were going to church together. I think I never felt more proud of her than when we would walk down a church aisle together.

Jean was always dressed to perfection, yet never

gaudy. She spent much time making her own clothes, yet she was not obsessed with them. She felt that a Christian should look his best, but she was conservative in her expenditures.

*   *   *

At the Brannons', I had fallen into some bad table manners. Instead of bringing the fork *up* to my mouth, I found it easier to lower my mouth to the plate and use the fork like a shovel. That way, I reasoned, I didn't have to waste all my energy *lifting* a utensil.

To be sure, there was nothing even remotely formal about the Brannons' home. They ate their meals at a plain dinette that sat against a den wall, using sturdy dinnerware and mismatched cups. Elbows were often on the table; milk was spilled; and the dog, Blackie, prowled around our feet, waiting to snatch dropped tidbits.

But as casual as the Brannons were, my pig-at-a-trough posture crossed a line. When Myrtle's corrections had little effect, she would turn to her daughter: "Rosemary, show Kathie how she looks when she eats like that." Sis would lower her head to her plate's rim and scoop mashed potatoes directly onto her tongue. We always laughed. The younger boys imitated her, which made Myrtle groan.

I laughed too and felt no shame over being the butt of a joke. At this stage of my life, very few people had the power to hurt my feelings. Daddy was an exception, for I sobbed with grief whenever he raised his voice or spanked me.

And I had really taken to one of the older girls in *The Mickey Mouse Club* on TV: it would have broken my heart if I were ever scolded by Darlene.

DAD'S JOURNAL
....

My gratitude for friends and friendships continues to grow. Yesterday I was in Texarkana and visited with Al Stringfellow and James Coggins. Genuine people these are. I think one is wealthy indeed if he has such friends.

And the Brannons! What a blessing they have been to

my life, and to Kathie. They have "stood by" us in a way I shall never forget.

* * *

At the duplex, Annie Kaye and I got along pretty well. She laundered my clothes, helped me dress, shampooed my hair, and concocted simple meals. Daddy had given her permission to spank me when I was naughty, and sometimes she did. But we usually had a good time, with mutual affection and lots of teasing. Instead of a uniform, Annie Kaye wore housedresses or slacks with casual blouses. Five days a week, she rode buses from far south Dallas to the end of our block. I never bothered to ask about *her* house or family.

One day, the two of us sat on our sofa watching *Queen for a Day*—a TV program where woebegone housewives took turns weeping because their husband had died, their child had an incurable disease, or a washing machine had conked out just before their house burned to the ground. The lady for whom the audience clapped loudest would be given a new washing machine, a Florida vacation, and maybe a year's supply of some product.

"Annie Kaye," I asked, "can we be on *Queen for a Day*?" Onscreen, the rich harmonies of "Pomp and Circumstance" swelled as a teary-eyed winner was crowned and presented with a heap of roses.

Annie Kaye said no, we couldn't go on TV.

I asked if she and Daddy could maybe get married, and she said no.

Reaching over, I lifted my caretaker's hand and compared its cinnamon tone to my paler flesh.

"Annie Kaye, are you a nigger?" It was a word I had learned from Bo Brannon.

She told me that this was a not a nice thing to say, but that yes, she was a Negro and had darker skin than mine.

Once or twice a week, Annie Kaye and I caught the southbound Skillman Street bus for a trip to the grocery store. I enjoyed the short ride and loved to pull the overhead cord that went *ding!* when we wanted to get off. I was oblivious to the blatant glares of White passengers: a half century later, Annie Kaye described how they tsk-tsked upon seeing a Caucasian child with an out-of-uniform maid (surely she was not the child's *mother!*) who clearly didn't "know her place." And I would never be able to recall exactly *where* we sat on those buses.

Our journey was a short one, just a mile or so down Skillman to a small strip of shops near La Vista Drive and Dr. Spegal's office. At the A&P grocery store, automatic doors ushered us into frosty air that smelled of ripe melons and earthy green stalks. Annie Kaye and I didn't worry about dairy products, because the milkman delivered those to the duplex. Instead, we headed for ready-to-serve foods: canned goods, snacks and cereals, fruit, and—of course—frozen fish sticks and beef potpies. After checkout, I always stopped at the gumball machine and begged Annie Kaye for a penny. I dropped it into a slot and cranked the lever. If a black gumball tumbled into my hand, I threw a fit because I had wanted a red or green one.

DAD'S JOURNAL
....

Jean was a woman who lived between heaven and earth as few people do.

I think this is something akin to what our Lord experienced. He was the most perfectly balanced man who ever lived. He bridged the gap between this world and the next.

Jean had this balance—far more than I have experienced. I think she must have been one of God's choicest in this realm. Her life lives on!

* * *

In contrast to the scores of photographs from my earliest years, very few were taken of me between 1957 and 1960. As an adult, I would look at those "Before" and "After" snapshots and be stunned by the difference. Before losing my mother, I could certainly have sulky moments when I didn't want to smile for a camera; but overall, those earlier photos reveal a relatively happy child.

In the pictures taken after 1956, my smile has vanished, and I look like I've been dragged through a hurricane. Daddy had a camera during

*Pouting at my 5th birthday party (I was probably jealous of my
cousin Leslie, being held by Granddaddy Withers)*

these later years, but I suppose that with all he had to worry about, photography was not high on his list of priorities.

For better or worse, someone did bring a camera to my fifth birthday party in April of 1957 and preserved the special event. In every one of those photos, my mopey expression suggested that I was either in the foulest of moods . . . or very depressed.

Even without the pictures, I would have vivid memories of the party. Grandmother and Granddaddy Withers had driven up from Baytown, and Aunt Winkie was also there, with Leslie in tow. Along with Annie Kay and Myrtle Brannon, my aunt helped to plan a Disney-themed party held in our duplex. Back then, a "theme" party consisted of little more than the Seven Dwarfs marching across disposable tablecloths, napkins, plates, and cups. A dozen of my church friends showed up, and I was embarrassed when they sang "Happy Birthday." I pouted because I didn't want to blow out candles on the bakery cake or distribute ice-cream cups to the other children. I balked at playing Pin the Tail on the Donkey and worried that the balloons might pop and scare me.

I opened presents, but years later would remember only one of them (an Uncle Wiggily game). Nor would I recall what party favors were given to my guests. In my *Milestones* book, those entry spaces remained blank.

DAD'S JOURNAL
....

In some ways, Jean is as near as ever, perhaps even nearer! This makes the next life real. I am convinced we are already experiencing everlasting life *now*. Death is just a transition.

* * *

Although I rarely thought about my mother, one day I got a notion to call her up. I took my red toy telephone out to the front porch. Squatting on my haunches, I put a finger into the rotary dial and gave it a few spins. Then I told an operator that I wanted to speak to my mother in heaven.

The sky on this day was like crisp blue linen, and while I waited for the connection, I watched white clouds tower high into that other mysterious and unseen world.

I waited . . . and waited . . . until I finally realized that no one was going to come to the phone.

Not my real mother.

Not an imaginary mother.

Not even the operator.

I put the receiver back in its cradle, feeling nothing beyond a shrugged-off "Oh, well . . ."

21

Aloft

"Everyone in Dallas frets and fusses over her so much," Mommie Mac told my father. "What that child needs is to put on her panties and run around in our garden all summer."

Since I normally *did* keep my drawers on, what my grandmother probably meant was that I should strip down to them and flit half-naked through her cucumber vines and beanstalks, squishing red Carolina clay through my toes.

Happily for me, Daddy took her advice. Each summer for the next few years, I was buckled into a Delta Airlines DC-6 and schlepped eastward for a few weeks. And back then, we really did "schlep" from Texas to North Carolina. It took most of a day to puddle-jump from Dallas to Shreveport to Jackson to Atlanta to Charlotte to Greensboro. When his schedule permitted, Daddy accompanied me on some of these flights; during other summers he might send me ahead and then come out later to retrieve me. Whether I traveled solo or had my father next to me, I relished the adventure of a plane trip.

On Trip Day, I would don a freshly ironed dress, frilly socks, and patent-leather shoes for air travel was still a hat and gloves affair reserved for a much smaller segment of the population. Either Daddy or Mrs. Brannon would drive me out to Love Field, our city's only airport. After my guardian had taken care of business at the ticket counter, we would cross an enormous lobby, my Sunday shoes clicking pleasantly on the marble floor. I might pause to run a couple of laps around the statue of a Texas Ranger or wheedle a candy-counter treat out of an adult. At the boarding gate, a piece of paper with my name and phone number would be pinned to my dress in case Delta Airlines misplaced me somewhere along the way.

Getting on the plane itself required no procession through metal detectors, security checks, or jetways: my caretaker and I simply strolled out to the tarmac and clanged up the aircraft's steps. My guardian would accompany me all the way to my seat, securely strap me in, and chatter off a string of final instructions and reassurances:

> Now, you be sure to mind the stewardess and hold her hand when you change planes in Atlanta. . . . Look, why don't we put these Life Savers in your purse? Your hands are already sticky. . . . No, your doll won't fit inside the airsick bag. Are you *sure* you don't have to go to the bathroom? . . . Aunt Ella and Uncle Bill will meet you in Greensboro. . . . Here, give me a big hug!

To an outsider, sending a half-orphaned kid 1,500 miles away might have seemed traumatic, but it was nothing of the sort. Since Daddy had accompanied me on my first plane trip—to Abilene, I believe, where he was preaching—I now fancied myself a pro at going aloft. And I knew what pleasures awaited me at my grandparents' house in Siler City. As far as I was concerned, I was simply being transported from love to love, and in between, my care had been entrusted to my very own fairy godmother: a jaunty-capped stewardess who was already pinning a set of junior wings onto my dress and promising to sit with me during takeoff.

In the meantime, I savored each hum and thrum of preflight activity. Nose pressed between window curtains, I tried to spot my suitcase on the baggage trolley, envisioned the contents of box lunches being stacked in the galley, and watched a man pump fuel into the plane's wing. Once all the doors were shut, I thrilled to the climactic moment when the four great propellers began to spin, faster and faster, until their blades dissolved into roaring silver coronas.

Despite being squeamish about any carnival ride wilder than the merry-go-round, I had absolutely no fear of flying. Takeoff did not bother me in the least—not even when my stomach dropped into my ankle socks as the plane rose and sank, scrabbling for altitude.

On most trips, I passed the time with crayons, Little Golden books, or my Tiny Tears. I was normally an excellent mother to my dolls, but one day back in Dallas, I had gone completely off the deep end. First, I took a red ink pen and scribbled all over the Tiny Tears I had gotten for Christmas. Then, I wrenched off her arms and legs. Finally, I punched in her eyes so that they rattled around inside her hollow head.

At some point, I received a replacement doll for the one I had killed.

En route to North Carolina, I always took good care of Tiny Tears II and her successors, changing their clothes at least three times before we crossed the Mississippi River. At the same time, I had not outgrown my own need to be babied. During my earliest years of air travel, I brought on board a plastic nursing bottle, which I asked the stewardess to fill with Coca-Cola. Sucking contentedly, I would prop my forehead against the window and watch the only in-flight video available: patchwork farmlands and Thumbelina towns flowing beneath the rounded wing, or milky clouds towering toward heaven.

Each time our DC-6 prepared for one of its pit stops, the stewardess distributed Chiclets gum, which we chewed to "unplug" our ears during descent. Flaps lowered, the plane's wing would slide through gauzy clouds . . . dip toward furrowed fields . . . arc around barns and steeples, then straighten over highways and float low over water towers . . . over pine tops and fences . . . over runway numbers still glistening after a summer shower. This process was repeated all day long until the landscape deepened into dark greens and rich coppers . . . and I was gently set down in the lap of my kinfolk.

22

Nothing Could Be Finer

ON THE OUTSKIRTS of Siler City, my grandparents' bungalow rested in a shallow swale, surrounded by two acres of meadow, cornfields, a vegetable garden, and neatly mowed lawn. The house itself was white, with a tin roof. Abelia bushes fronted an L-shaped porch, partially hiding a row of chunky redbrick pillars from which wooden posts rose to support the overhanging eaves. I would spend many an hour swaying in a porch swing while my boy cousins stomped around the bushes' flowers, clapping bumblebees into mason jars. Sometimes they even shook the jars to make the bees angry.

I preferred tamer amusements, such as rising early to watch the morning glories open. On a typical day, I slipped out of bed with the first crowing of a neighborhood rooster and ventured barefoot down a gravel driveway that ran alongside the house. A wrought iron fence separated the driveway from a ditch (it had replaced a picket fence that my grandmother knocked down the one and only time she attempted to drive a car). Near the main road, the fence bordered a garden brimming with zinnias, daylilies, gladioli, larkspurs, and black-eyed Susans. And, just as in the song "Carolina in the Morning," morning glories really *did* twine—in this case, around the black metal railings.

With daybreak a mere crimson line on the horizon, the flowers still sagged like bits of crumpled blue tissue. But I was patient, having slowed my rhythms to the pace of this rural world. Whenever I stayed with my grandparents, my life was mostly free of clocks, calendars, and bed-hopping from house to house. Instead, the days meandered like a wide river with no particular destination.

As I stood in my nightgown waiting for the sunrise, I took stock of surroundings that were unlike any I knew in Dallas. Because my grandparents' house sat in a declivity, I often felt as if I were in the middle of a wide bowl. If I stood in the yard and twirled around, I could create a dizzying blur of cornstalks, pastures, gardens, and barns—all sloping up to the bowl's rim, where the whole cyclorama was ringed with distant pines.

Neighboring homes were separated by meadows or fields. Diagonally across the road, Mrs. Dark's enormous white house topped a wooded embankment, its central gable rising above treetops. Mommie Mac and I sometimes visited this widow, who was even more ancient than my grandmother. Since Mommie Mac almost never left home empty-handed, she would carry a "mess of greens" or a sackful of fresh okra for Bertha, Mrs. Dark's caregiver, to cook up on the kitchen's vintage iron stove. Bertha might then pour glasses of fresh lemonade and join us on the wraparound porch while we chatted. Or we might socialize in the front parlor, whose decor had not changed since Grover Cleveland was president. When I later learned the word *Victorian*, I would imagine this parlor with its sturdy wicker furniture and portraits of Dark ancestors jutting from the walls.

I sometimes played with Mrs. Dark's granddaughter Carolyn, whose house was back on *this* side of the road, one pasture removed from my grandparents'. Carolyn was a few years older than me and tended to be strong-willed and bossy. The tables were turned when I played with Rhonda Dowd, a grade-school girl who lived diagonally in the other direction. Rhonda went to a Holiness church and was so sweet and submissive that she let me boss *her* around.

Next door to Rhonda's house stood her Aunt Mozelle Dowd's brick ranch, flanked by hydrangeas. One time, Mommie Mac swallowed a fly when we were standing beside those spongy blue flowers. She had opened her mouth to say something to Mozelle . . . and the next thing we knew, a fly just buzzed right in. Before she could clamp her jaw shut, it had disappeared down her stomach.

The street curved at Mozelle's place, hiding other houses from view. Still, they were within easy strolling distance, and Mommie Mac and I would often "walk up the road apiece" to visit Mr. and Mrs. Fitts, whose son, Russell, had been Daddy's boyhood friend.

Back in my line of sight, the home of Mr. and Mrs. Brooks occupied a small knoll on the other side of my grandparents' property. There, a willow tree's tendrils brushed a side yard that sloped down to meet Daddy Mac's pasture.

My visual sweep having come full circle, I felt almost woozy from tracking the neighborhood's dips and rises. A half century later, I would drive past the same area and be shocked at how puny these undulations seemed and how quickly they zipped by. But as a child who was both knee-high to a sunflower and conditioned to the flat Texas prairies, I probably magnified every ripple of the Carolina landscape.

Although some of my perceptions were inflated, the sun that finally crested on summer mornings truly *was* enormous. From my post beside the limp flowers, I would watch it scroll above the tree line, a giant disc the color of sweet-potato pie. Its rays fanned across the Darks' tobacco field . . . burned through a layer of ground mist . . . then jumped a ditch and crossed the road.

The rooster let loose another raucous fanfare while a red cardinal swooped toward Mommie Mac's backyard birdbath. A couple of cars hummed down the blacktop road. Far behind Daddy Mac's cornfield and some distant woods, a sawmill buzzed and whined, censing the air with hickory and balsam. Over in town, the Boling Chair Factory blasted a loud whistle—two shorts and one long—alerting employees that it was time to get ready for work.

The whole world was astir, and the morning glories now joined in. In a magic act rivaling any Cinderella tale, they began to quiver as if tugged by an invisible force. Then, before I could say *bibbidi-bobbidi-boo*, their petals unfurled into China-blue gowns, and they lifted their faces to greet the day.

* * *

Although no two days in Siler City were exactly alike, I could count on several dependable routines. Chances were that as soon as the sun rose, my grandmother would call to me from the porch—not overly concerned that I was standing gowned and barefoot near the road, but worried that I had gone outside without eating a good breakfast.

Moments later, I sat in a kitchen chair while Daddy Mac wiped grit from my feet and Mommie Mac brought me a plate of sausage, eggs, and buttery toast.

Another long whistle traveled through the open kitchen window. Were Daddy Mac not retired from the chair factory, he would be punching its time clock. Instead, my grandfather would soon be working in the garden, mowing the yard, or building a table or bookshelf down in his carpentry workshop. An industrious soul, Daddy Mac moved at an easy pace but rarely spent his hours in idleness.

After breakfast, Mommie Mac always took a box of Quaker Oats from a cabinet and handed it to me, signaling a favorite morning ritual. Moments later, I would be out in the backyard, tossing a handful of cereal into a low concrete pool the size of a sandbox. Beneath a wire grid, goldfish darted through jade-colored water, greedily snapping up the flakes.

"Don't give them too much, Snookie!" Mommie Mac called from an outside porch, using her pet name for me. She tapped an aluminum pie pan against the porch railing to loosen stale biscuits and leftover corn bread. These she flung into the yard for the birds. Then, having nourished fish and fowl, the two of us went back into the house.

For the next hour or so, I shadowed my grandmother as she continued her morning tasks, delighted when she allowed me to dust a low table or polish a mirror. Mommie Mac did not force me to do chores: I simply took pleasure in being close to her and dreaming of the day when I would have my own tidy dwelling with rocking chairs, braided rugs, a ticking mantle clock, and corner hutches.

I especially enjoyed dishwashing, for which I stood on a step stool next to my grandmother, up to my elbows in fragrant suds. It was great fun to play house with adult-sized teacups and spoons—so much fun that I sometimes took clean dishes from the cabinet and rewashed them.

After completing a few indoor chores, Mommie Mac usually gathered paper sacks and colanders and headed back outside. I trailed her like a gosling as we crossed the backyard and started down a grassy lane, well-worn from years of comings and goings. To the right lay a summer-lush garden full of every vegetable that could be found on a Southern dining table. I was a child who believed that most food came from a Chef Boyardee can, and back in Dallas my closest encounter with fresh produce often involved sticking plastic ears into Mr. Potato Head. Now, under my grandmother's tender tutelage, I learned which pole beans were ready for picking and which tomatoes needed more time to ripen. For a while, I went about the serious task of filling my sack with butter beans; at other times, Mommie Mac simply "let me be" to run wild in this green new world. Squatting close to the ground, I examined pods, husks, melons, roots, bulbs. I ran my hand across fuzzy squash and sticky okra, fingered the bumps along a cucumber still cool with morning dew. I picked ladybugs from a beanstalk while a bird warbled nearby:

> Bob-o-white!
> Bob-o-white!
> Are your eggs ripe,
> Bob-o-white?

Mommie Mac had taught me the rhyme, and it inspired me to compose what was probably my first original poem:

Daddy Mac!
Daddy Mac!
Do your ducks quack,
Daddy Mac?

In truth, my grandfather had no ducks, and he no longer kept chickens, hogs, or a goat. But sometimes he and I would walk over and visit Mr. Brooks's cows, which were pastured on my grandparents' land. "*SOOOO-WEEE* cow!" Daddy Mac always called in a loud falsetto as we approached a wooden fence. A couple of Guernseys would bellow a response and amble toward us, rustling through undergrowth. I had no fear of these sloe-eyed creatures. Standing on a bottom fence rail, I would reach over to stroke their knobby foreheads while they gummed the corncobs we offered.

While I usually stayed close to Mommie Mac's side, I treasured the time spent with my grandfather. Sometimes Daddy Mac allowed me to pass a supervised hour or two in his workshop, a tar-paper-sided building at the back of the property, partially hidden in tangled vines. There, I braved splintery floors and stray wasps to pound nails into wood, creating primitive sailboats or airplanes. Even if I didn't construct anything recognizable, I had fun rummaging through bins of nuts, bolts, screws, shims, and nails: real-life Tinkertoys that made wonderful designs when hammered into a block of wood.

* * *

My Aunt Ella, Uncle Bill, and three cousins lived an hour away in Greensboro and drove down to Siler City almost every weekend. When I was five, Billy would have been three and Steve a two-year-old. Aunt Ella had been unable to attend my mother's funeral in 1956: at the time, she was pregnant with a baby girl, whom she named "Susan Jean." (Mother's best friend Melba—now married and living in Waco—had also been pregnant that summer. Even if travel had not been forbidden, her doctor would not let her attend a memorial for someone who had succumbed to a mysterious virus. When Melba's daughter was born, she too was named "Jean.") In the summer of 1957, Aunt Ella's baby was six months old. Unlike my relationship with Cousin Leslie, I harbored no ill will toward Susan. We were far enough apart in age that she didn't pester me, nor did she steal much attention. So I was perfectly willing for this little cousin to sleep in a guest-room crib and to suckle from her pink nursing bottle . . . so long as I could still drink Pepsi-Cola from *mine*.

Billy and Steve were high-octane playmates, but I managed to tolerate short stretches of their company. On hot afternoons, we were often taken to the nearby city swimming pool; on other days, we simply cavorted with a water hose out by the gravel driveway. The gravel itself fascinated me, for it was sometimes flecked with silver mica or veined with pink quartz. The only rocks I encountered back in Dallas were chunks of concrete—certainly nothing that could be imaginatively transformed into gemstones or crystals.

My cousins and I occasionally spent time with our Uncle Sip, my father's older brother. Sip was a large man, and he never entered any room quietly; instead, he stomped, thudded, and slammed around like a bull in a china closet—nor was this done with good cheer. When he was with family, Sip's normal expression was a frown, and his greeting little more than a grumble.

Ironically, my uncle—who owned a tombstone company—was an excellent businessman who had a good rapport with his customers, and he could be quite generous with his time and money. But among family, he was considered a "weird bird." Like a Southern-style Archie Bunker, Sip was extremely moody, gruff, and glum, and he could carry boulder-sized chips on his shoulder. With his penchant for armchair psychoanalysis, my father would later surmise that since his brother didn't get much attention during Dad's critical childhood illness, Sip became emotionally "stuck" at around twelve years old. Indeed, he was so fond of the Ringling Brothers Circus that when it came to North Carolina, he followed it to every city in the state, rarely missing a performance.

He and Aunt Margaret had no children, so whenever my cousins and I visited Siler City, we became Sip's "playmates." Although our uncle was not the type to toss balls or read storybooks, he did enjoy piling us into his car and whisking us off to interesting places. We cousins could do

Uncle Sip

completely unannounced vanishing acts from Mommie Mac's house.
Realizing that things had grown too quiet, a grown-up would suddenly
ask, "Where are the kids?" Another would reply, "Oh, they've gone off
somewhere with Sip." Then everyone would shrug and go about their
business.

The three of us almost always enjoyed our hours with Sip. He might
drive us out to a country store, where he would hand each of us a paper
bag and instruct us to fill it with all the candy we wanted. Or we might
end up at an all-night diner, barefoot and in our pajamas, gorging on
ice-cream sundaes. Few of Sip's other destinations would have received
parenting organizations' seals of approval. He might, for example, take
us a few miles out of town to the Devil's Tramping Ground, a large,
mysterious circle where no grass would grow; it was said that Satan
and his minions danced there on moonlit nights. Or if my uncle had
heard about a bad wreck on a nearby highway, he would carry us to the
junkyard so we could gape at the mangled car. Once, he suggested that
we ride out in the countryside and shoot firecrackers at cows. I don't
know whether he and the boys followed through with that scheme;
since I was scared of loud noises, I didn't tag along.

23

My People

UNLIKE BILLY AND Steve and Uncle Sip, who thrived on feats of derring-do, I was content to conjure more sedate amusements at my grandparents' house. I could always pick flowers, daydream in a tree swing, or carry letters to the roadside mailbox, raising a red metal flag to signal the postman. Back inside, a jar full of variegated buttons could entertain me for hours, as could a piece of string laced through empty bobbins or spools. Sometimes I took all the clean dishes from the kitchen cabinets and rewashed them just for fun. I enjoyed standing next to my grandmother while she sewed a frock for Tiny Tears on her treadle machine. And what fun it was to watch her get into or out of her corset! Half-reclining on her bed, Mommie Mac would roll around like an upended turtle as she panted, tugged, and wrangled with the rubbery contraption.

One of my favorite activities was to explore a corner hutch in the front parlor. Its open upper shelves displayed a few prized knickknacks. Midway down the hutch was a single drawer crammed with a jumble of loose photos, snapshot booklets, news clippings, greeting cards, and letters.

I would sift through these items, reaching first for the small, spiral-bound booklets that contained baby photos of my cousins and myself—each a testament to how greatly we were loved by our grandparents. Deeper in the drawer lay a cardboard fan attached to a wooden stick: a promotional gift from the Siler City Monument Company so that during funerals, the mourners could cool themselves in unair-conditioned

Blue-Pajama Girl

churches. On the front was a photo of a little girl around my own age; like me, she had light brown hair and razor-sharp bangs across her forehead. She wore blue flannel pajamas and knelt beside a bed, her hands folded in prayer and her eyes raised heavenward with a holy expression. Through the years, I would have a love-hate relationship with the Blue-Pajama Girl. Sometimes I tried to mimic her prim perfection. At other times, I imagined how good it might feel to shove her into some rosebushes.

In this same hutch drawer I once discovered a long envelope from which I extracted a newspaper clipping. I recognized my mother's photograph but could not yet decipher the heading: "Dallas Reports First Polio Fatality of 1956."

"Kathie, honey, why don't we put this away for now?" Mommie Mac had slipped into the room and now touched my shoulder. "I'm afraid it might upset you." Her voice sounded quivery. I folded the article and returned it to its envelope because I didn't want my grandmother to be sad.

* * *

Back in Dallas, I had stayed in many homes where I was surrounded by loving caretakers and almost always had a good time. Still, I was quite aware that these were not my *real* families.

This sense of rootlessness vanished when I explored a lower cabinet in Mommie Mac's hutch. Rummaging through that dark recess, I discovered scrapbooks that held sepia-toned photographs of kinfolk, both living and long dead. Those pictures, I knew, were somehow connected to the Family Records section of my grandmother's worn bedside Bible. Long before I could translate her spidery handwriting or recognize the faded names and dates, I knew that these McIvers and Moodys and Dunlaps and Rives were uniquely "*my* people."

Some family members had died decades earlier, and the hutch's scrapbooks preserved their obituaries: yellowed strips of newsprint that eventually became as familiar to me as any photograph. It would be a few more years before I could read the flowery prose that made Dallas obituaries seem as sterile as legal documents. In modern-day Dallas, people just "died" or "passed away." But in turn-of-the-century Chatham County, North Carolina, the local writers had tuned their harps and invoked muses to memorialize the deceased:

> As dawn drew nigh on Thursday morn, the spirit of little Mary Louise Gilmore took its flight to realms of perfect glory. . . . Tonight, she sleeps 'neath a profusion of floral tributes.

Another clipping rhapsodized:

> When "The Roll Was Called Up Yonder" last Sunday, brother Jordan McIver was there to answer.

Yet another scribe concocted this badly strained image:

> Mrs. Dunlap had not passed on life's highway the stone that marks its highest point, but being weary for a moment, she lay down by the wayside and, using her burden for a pillow, fell into that dreamless sleep that kisses down the eyelids.

Although Mommie Mac tried to shield me from the particular pain of losing my mother, she generally did not shy away from the topic of death. Like all of my Carolina kinfolk, she recognized that it was as natural as the changing of seasons or cycling of crops. My grandmother could easily use the words *corpse* and *pound cake* in the same sentence, as in: "Didn't Swanee Gilmore bring a brown-sugar pound cake when Uncle Ernest was a corpse?" (Translation: *What home-cooked dish did Swanee bring to the grieving family between the time of Ernest's death and his burial—when his body was still on view at the funeral home?*)

My grandparents came from large families, and it was not uncommon for one of their kin to have recently died or even to pass away during one of my visits. Although I didn't attend funerals, I was coming to learn that death was a fairly common occurrence in families with lots of older people. Assured that I would probably not die until I was very old, I viewed the experience as something that was far in the distance, mildly sad and strangely beautiful.

In 1957, I had not yet seen my mother's grave in Dallas, but I got plenty of hands-on experience with cemeteries and tombstones in North Carolina. For instance, my cousins and I frequently visited Uncle Sip's monument company. There, we watched workmen engrave granite or marble headstones, and we climbed on the display markers that filled a graveled yard. Some bore designs of flowers, doves, sunsets, or—for a baby—little lambs.

I also romped in real cemeteries when we rode "out in the country" to see my grandparents' old homeplaces and the rural churchyards where my ancestors were buried. Sometimes we attended Homecoming Sundays at those churches, where the morning service was followed by dinner-on-the-grounds.

Whether I was in North Carolina or Texas, both sets of my grandparents gave me a strong sense of my heritage. Down in South Texas, Grandmother Withers was passionate about genealogy and early on recited the names and stories of our forebears. Like my paternal grandparents, she and Granddaddy had come from very large families, and many of their siblings were still living—most within a hundred-mile radius of Baytown. We sometimes drove to visit these great-aunts and uncles, but it was not an easy feat to see all of them: their homes were not in a central location but were spread among various towns and cities.

A couple of times, we went up to the piney woods near Jasper, where a country church founded by my great-great-grandfather still stood. The family homeplace, however, had long ago burned to the ground.

The situation was different in North Carolina, where I had a much more visceral knowledge of "our people." Daddy and Mommie Mac each had ten siblings, and many still lived in or near Siler City. Visits were frequent, and Mommie Mac's house was the focal point for Sunday lunches. Uncle Sip and his wife, Margaret, always showed up, as did Aunt Ella and her family. We could usually count on several great-aunts and uncles and even a few second cousins, all of whom arrived bearing their own home-cooked dishes.

After we had devoured fried chicken, deviled eggs, caramel cakes, and chess pies, Great-Uncle Murph would fall asleep in a recliner and snore while all the womenfolk cleaned up the kitchen. Other relatives would gather on the porch or in the front parlor to visit until Aunt Kate (who was phobic about thunderstorms) said, "Murph, there's a cloud coming up. We need to start home."

By early evening, most of the older relatives had gathered their platters and casseroles and left, replaced by other cousins who had stopped by, bringing their own children for us to play with. The grown-ups relaxed outside in lawn chairs. If we were making ice cream, one of us kids sat on top of the churn while an adult hand-cranked the device. Sometimes we cut into one of Daddy Mac's homegrown watermelons.

Eventually, twilight deepened into what was called "the gloaming": that magical time when cicadas began to chirr and night flowers opened. Our bare legs sticky with watermelon juice, my cousins and I now loped after sluggish lightning bugs that idled around shrubs and hedges, easy prey for our mason jars or cupped hands. Nearby, mourning doves cooed while the evening star rose above distant pine tops—as ever, a beacon for the homesick or lost.

A stone's throw away, our elders made small talk and recounted stories of kinfolk both living and long dead. Surrounded by these recitations, we youngsters dove in and out of the green edges of our world, anchored by voices that assured us from whence we had come . . . and to whom we belonged.

24

Bug Hunt

WHEN SUMMERING WITH Mommie and Daddy Mac, I slept in what we called "the Little Room." Opening off the den, it was only large enough to hold a chest of drawers, a treadle sewing machine, and a double bed squeezed into one corner.

My grandparents would eventually install a window-unit air conditioner in the den; until then, summer days and nights could be quite uncomfortable. I recall lying in the Little Room on one especially hot and muggy night, so miserable that I could not fall asleep. It must have been fairly late because everyone else had gone to bed; the house was dark and quiet. As the mantle clock ticked loudly in the next room, I tossed and turned. A top sheet was all I could bear; I soon kicked even that covering into a ropey tangle near the bed's footboard. The clock chimed the quarter of some late hour. I rolled across the bed and face-first into a window screen that kept me from tumbling clear out into the backyard. There, I lay still for a while, sucking warm air through the mesh and wishing for a breeze that never came. By the time the clock struck another quarter hour, I had sat up and shed both my nightgown and underpants. This brought some relief, but my bladder was now full from the Pepsi-Cola I earlier swigged from a baby bottle.

I padded through the den and headed for the bathroom, which was located off an enclosed back porch. After taking care of business, I found myself even more wide awake. The bathroom's window was not a glass pane that lifted up and down but a solid wooden shutter that latched horizontally. For a few moments, I amused myself by banging the green shutter back and forth. Then I climbed onto the sink to examine whatever might be propped on the windowsill. I spotted two drinking glasses holding my grandparents' false teeth and a tin of denture powder (which, I discovered, had no particular taste). More appetizing was a dollop of Colgate toothpaste, which I sucked from the tube. Climbing down from the sink, I rummaged through a cabinet and liberally dusted myself with Mommie Mac's lavender talcum powder.

The sweet Colgate taste lingered in my mouth. Needing something tangy to offset it, I wended into the kitchen, where I stood naked in front of the refrigerator and spoon-fed myself some yellow mustard.

I then backtracked to the porch. Like the rest of Mommie Mac's house, this small room was neat as a pin with every object in its proper place. Cleaning supplies were stowed in a corner cupboard. Above the washing machine, a row of tomatoes ripened on a windowsill. A cane-bottomed chair rested against a wall, with my grandfather's straw hat hung on a nail above it. Daddy Mac's gardening shoes were perfectly aligned by the back door. Even paper sacks brimming with excess squash and cucumbers—from which Mommie Mac could easily grab a handful to carry to a neighbor or loved one—sat neatly arow against the wall. More than any other room, this porch had absorbed the aromas of my grandparents' house: fresh corn husks, roasting chicken, cedarwood, Pine-Sol cleaner. And the porch was as clean and well scrubbed as any other room in the house. I make this last point to defend my grandmother and to keep her spirit from deleting these next paragraphs from my computer. For when I recently told Aunt Ella that I was writing about cockroaches, she said, "Good Lord, Mother would roll over in her grave if you told anyone that she had *roaches!*"

But she did.

I saw the first one scuttle under the washing machine as soon as I pulled the string on an overhead light bulb. Now another raced toward the corner broom closet, and a third tried to hide behind the cane-bottomed chair. Rather than being afraid or disgusted, I was stirred by a sudden call to arms. My grandfather's heavy, box-style flashlight sat by the back door, and I selected it as my weapon of choice. I hefted the metal lantern with one hand and moved the chair with the other.

The cockroach dashed behind a sack of long-necked squash. I could have simply lifted the bag, but I spied a yardstick hanging on the wall. With this second weapon, I poked at the paper sack and flailed its sides until the insect scurried out. He was an especially big fellow, and I experienced a perverse joy as I slammed the flashlight down and smooshed him flat.

For a moment, I pictured that Blue-Pajama Girl on the funeral-home fan. I couldn't imagine *her* killing cockroaches.

But that thought was fleeting. Sliding the yardstick under the washing machine, I tried to rout even more critters. One made a run for the bathroom, and I whipped around. *Bang-BAM!* I bisected him with one slam of the lantern.

In retrospect, I'm not sure what motivated me to go on a Bug Hunt and derive such pleasure from crunching cockroaches into a porch floor. Except for pulling the glowing tails off lightning bugs to wear as "diamond rings," I had never in my life been cruel to animals. A psychologist might suggest that—as with my Tiny Tears doll—I was venting pent-up anger as I pounded my flashlight into the linoleum. I probably was. Maybe I was trying to be helpful to my grandparents by playing exterminator. Or perhaps I was simply creating a late-night amusement with whatever materials I could find.

Another enormous insect darted from a corner. I scrambled after it on my knees, flashlight raised and aimed.

Slam!

I pulverized the creature.

"What on *earth?*" My grandmother stood in the doorway wearing a long pink nightgown. Without her teeth, her lips had collapsed inward, making her words all mumbly. "Kathie, honey, what in the world are you doing?" Then she giggled. "Why, you're naked as a jaybird!"

"I was killing bugs for you," I explained as Mommie Mac led me into the bathroom to wash mustard from my face and lavender talc from my hair. Back in the Little Room, my grandmother set up an electric fan. She then coaxed me into my nightgown and lay down next to me on the bed.

"You and I are having a good time together this summer, aren't we?"

she asked, pulling me close. I snuggled into her bosom as if she were a giant pink teddy bear.

"Uh-huh," I said. "I like stomping bugs. And I like picking green beans."

"Ohhh," moaned my grandmother, "don't remind me of those beans!"

The two of us were referring to an incident that had occurred a few days earlier when I had misbehaved at Sunday lunch. My grandparents' wooden dining-room table was plain as could be, but on Sundays Mommie Mac fancied it up with a white tablecloth and pulled up extra chairs for visiting relatives. On this day, my plate had just been loaded with a chicken leg, roast beef, gravy, and half a dozen vegetables when I butted heads with one of the grown-ups. I was perhaps being scolded or maybe had been denied something I wanted. Whatever the case, it made me so mad that I just sat in silence, glaring across the table and clenching my teeth. Then, slowly and deliberately, I took hold of my dinner plate with both hands and—*whish!*—flipped it upside down, soaking the tablecloth with my greasy, mushy lunch.

Mommie Mac had never laid a hand on me, but Daddy Mac didn't hesitate to wield a yardstick or a switch (neither did Aunt Ella—had she been with us that day, she would have hauled me up by one arm and whaled the tar out of me). Without a word, my grandfather rose from the table and strode out the back door toward a peach tree, with Mommie Mac shuffling after him, calling, "George" (her Southern accent turned it into "*Jaw-age*"), "don't whip her—she didn't mean it!" But I did *too* mean it, and moments later my legs were being striped pink by a switch.

As always, I wailed. And as always, when it was over, Mommie Mac took me out to the porch swing and pulled me close. While I snuffled into her pillowy bosom, she asked, "You don't want to be a naughty little girl, do you?" When I answered "Yes!" she pretended to cry, whining like a puppy. I reached out to comfort her, and after a few moments, we both ended up grinning.

Eventually, I not only apologized, but I felt so bad about ruining Mommie Mac's tablecloth that I devised my own penance: when my grandmother lay down for her afternoon nap, I took pots and colanders and paper sacks from the kitchen, went out to the vegetable garden, and picked nearly every single pole bean—ready or not. In my mind, I was being a great help and saving Mommie Mac hours of backbreaking work. When I presented my haul to her later that day, she acted duly pleased . . . but for the rest of her life she would wince, recalling how it had taken her two days and nights to string, snap, cook, and can those beans.

"I like helping you," I now said as we nestled in bed.

"Yes, you're a big help," my grandmother agreed, suppressing another groan.

I reached out and stroked her soft, saggy face. "Mommie Mac," I asked in a sudden change of subject, "why do you have whiskers on your chin?"

"Well," she drawled, "I guess I'm just a silly old woman. No young boys care how I look." She chuckled and then whispered as if sharing a great secret: "Besides, I already *have* me a nice man!"

I burrowed closer. "Mommie Mac, do you love me?"

"Of course, I do, Snookie!"

We lay in silence, lulled by the droning fan.

"I was naked as a jaybird!" I sleepily announced. It was a new phrase for me, and I delighted in repeating it.

"You sure were."

"Mommie Mac?"

"Hmmm?"

"I love you too."

Ready to fly back to Texas

Mommie and Daddy Mac, Aunt Ella, and Cousin Susan (Greensboro Airport)

IV
Half-A-House

25

Playmates

THE FIRST ANNIVERSARY of Mother's death passed completely under my radar: after all, I could not even identify all the days of the week, much less the months of a year. Nor did I know how to tie my shoes, read a clock, recite the alphabet, or use a pair of safety scissors. Some of these skills I would master in kindergarten, which I began in the fall of 1957.

My class was held in a large room at our church and taught by a young woman named Bonnye Burnett. In this less pressured decade, we kids were not expected to read before the first grade, but we did learn to print our names. Beyond that, we mainly sang songs, listened to stories, and had Rest Time on our blue mats.

I knew some of my classmates from Wilshire and made new friends among those who went to church elsewhere. Sometimes I played well with other children; sometimes I didn't.

If the Doll Care or Housekeeping Centers grew tiresome, I might venture into the boys' territory. More often than not, they hunkered on the linoleum floor and manipulated wooden blocks of varied shapes and sizes. Standing off to the side, I waited patiently while they constructed a skyscraper or a long multi-car train. Then, just after the boys balanced a final spire or added a tail-end caboose, I shouted, *"DYNAMITE!"* (another word I had learned from Bo Brannon) and flung myself onto their creation, scattering blocks to the four walls.

It was, I would later realize, a near perfect metaphor for what had happened to my own world.

Throughout kindergarten, I would continue to have this penchant for perversity, but I was not always so intractable or coldhearted. After one of my classmates was absent for a few days, I learned that his mother had died, and I felt very sorry for him.

* * *

A few months earlier, an angel floated into my life in the form of my first true *girl* friend. Claire Ball was a year older than me, but we quickly became great buddies. Her parents, Ruby and Sterling, had joined Wilshire after Mother's death, and they lived several blocks south of us on Llano Avenue. Over the next couple of years, I would spend almost as much time at the Balls' house as I did at the Brannons'.

Other than enduring some rowdy teasing from Claire's preteen brother, Carl, I had wonderful times when I stayed with the Balls. As my first-ever best friend, Claire was someone with whom I could play dress-up, dolls, and Candy Land. She and her mother shared a dark-eyed, exotic beauty that hinted of Creole or Iberian blood somewhere in the family tree. Despite her pretty features and ebony curls, I was never jealous of Claire. She was not overprotected nor was she the kind of prissy girl who got bent out of shape over a scuffed knee or lost hair bow. Self-assured and even-tempered, she easily weathered my occasional snit fits and bad moods. As it turned out, I had very few of those around Claire, because she was just so much fun to be with.

Together, we held tea parties and played house/store/school/doctor/circus. Sometimes we concocted our own games. Claire owned a tiny rubber ball that bounced halfway around the world when you threw it. We would stand in her bedroom, toss the ball, and then watch as it hit a wall . . . boomeranged onto the toy chest . . . *boinged!* into a bedpost . . . and finally was deflected onto the vanity table, perhaps coming to rest next to a hairbrush. For some reason, the two of us found this to be hysterically funny. And so we invented the game Funny Ball, where the only object was to throw the ball, watch it careen around the room, and wonder, *Where will it end up? In a doll's lap? Inside a jewelry box? Beneath a windowsill?* When the ball finally lost momentum and stopped—no matter *where*—Claire and I would scream "FUNNY BALL!" and laugh until we gasped for air.

For the next few years, the words *Funny Ball* could set us to howling like hyenas.

So could the phrase "Toady Comody," which is what Claire and I named a little toad we found in her backyard one summer day. We put him in a coffee can and decided that I would get first dibs on being his guardian. I took the can back to our duplex, set it inside our screened porch . . . and then forgot all about it while Daddy and I went out of town for a few days. Meanwhile, the heat index in Dallas climbed to around 120 degrees. When we got back, I opened the can . . . and discovered a vignette too sad to relate.

Poor Toady Comody.

I don't recall watching much television at the Balls' house, but Claire and I were both fond of *Captain Kangaroo*, which was both educational and entertaining. The Captain interacted with several regular characters, such as Mr. Green Jeans. But Claire and I especially enjoyed those programs that featured The Banana Man. The Banana Man was a character that today's parents might keep *far* away from their kids. With a putty face and bird's-nest hair, he looked like he had slithered out of a skid row gutter. His trademark costume was a gigantic (and reputedly filthy), multipocketed overcoat from which he produced all manner of odd items. He squirted milk from the coat's lapel and extracted watermelons from suspiciously low places on his person. But his piéce de résistance was to pull endless ropes of bananas from his pockets, all the while singing a falsetto, *"Lahh-deeeee . . .* WOW!"

The routine was utterly nonsensical, with no moral or plot. But Claire and I rolled on the floor, holding our stomachs and laughing until we cried. Out of such bonds was our friendship forged.

* * *

In the autumn of 1957, I continued to spend occasional weekends with Ricky and Bo Brannon, where Saturday mornings still found the three of us belly down on the den floor, our eyes inches from the console television. As always, we squabbled over Crayolas while Tweety Bird outsmarted Sylvester the Cat and Wile E. Coyote plunged off cliffs. We also honed our poetic skills, singing ditties that were part of every kindergartener's repertoire:

> I'm Popeye the Sailor Man
> I live in the frying pan
> I turn on the heat
> And burn up my seat

"*Nuh*-uh, Bo! It goes like this: 'I'm Popeye the Sailor Man, I live in the garbage can.'"

"No! It's 'I eat all the worms and spit out the germs.'"

"Nuh-uh. It's 'I get all the switches and pull down my britches.'"

* * *

Sometimes the boys and I went out to the driveway's concrete apron and played House. Bo was always The Father: he simply put on an old fedora and went off to work, where his job entailed riding a tricycle and shooting cap pistols. Ricky clamored to be The Mother or The Big Sister—roles that allowed him to wear Sis's discarded crinolines. If Ricky was The Mother, then I was The Baby. If Ricky was The Big Sister, then I was The Mother.

Sometimes we played Wedding, with Ricky swanning down the driveway in petticoats and a makeshift veil as Bo and I serenaded:

> Here comes the bride,
> Big, fat, and wide;
> Stepped on a turtle,
> Down came her girdle!

Our little family might have been a bit dysfunctional, but we did have some good times together.

26

Half-A-House

DESPITE MY FORAYS into other homes, the bulk of my days and nights was still spent at 6005 Marquita Street. For over three years, the left side of our orange duplex would serve as my crash pad and playground, and it became a safe haven for Daddy and me when we had been too long apart. Oddly, I would have far fewer memories of life at the duplex (and with Annie Kaye) than I would of other settings. Instead of being vivid and varied, most of my Marquita Street recollections were rather bland. And that was not necessarily a bad thing, for I probably *needed* the stability of ho-hum routines and of days that blurred together with a comforting "sameness."

In my most recurring image, I see myself slouched in an upholstered living-room chair, feet dangling while I watch hours of television. In addition to preschool programs, I was fond of some newer sitcoms, such as *Leave It to*

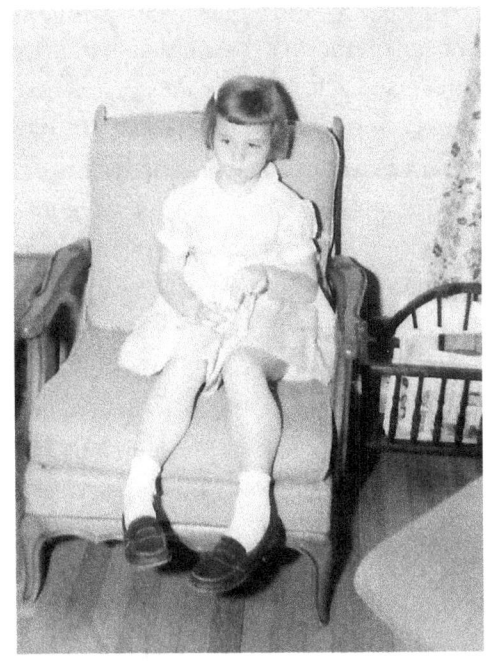

In my files, this photo is labelled "Sad Girl"

Beaver or *Our Miss Brooks*. I especially identified with *Bachelor Father*, in which John Forsythe and his teenage niece tried to navigate their wifeless, motherless world. While watching one of our three available channels, I snacked on Cracker Jack or shoestring potato sticks.

In yet another image, I am stretched out on the living-room floor, listening to a hi-fi record player that my father had acquired. Our collection of LPs was quite meager. Daddy had a couple of albums featuring stand-up comics, and I had a boxed set of children's Bible stories. Also around this time, someone gave me a recording of the Obernkirchen Children's Choir from Germany. Humming along to an upbeat "The Happy Wanderer" (and not minding at all that the words were foreign), I would study an album-cover photograph of these ruddy-faced orphans, marveling that they could look so cheerful when they had lost *both* parents.

Of course, I still kept my own record player up in my bedroom where, as in Lubbock, I spent hours in solitary play. Even when I went outside, I played alone for there were no other children on my block. More than anything else, I loved to make myself dizzy on the swing set that Daddy and a neighbor had assembled in our backyard. Legs pumping and head tilted far back, I sang songs or told knock-knock jokes to whomever I had chosen to be my Fantasy Mother of the Moment. Sometimes I described a funny scene I had witnessed or recited from memory the entire plot of a movie or television program I had seen.

I also liked to play Airline Stewardess. For this role, I soared high on a teeter-totter while making announcements to imaginary passengers: "Ladies and gentlemen, we are landing. Buckle your seat belt. And please chew some gum to unplug your ears."

During hot weather, Mrs. Ball sometimes took Claire and me to a swimming pool at nearby Llano Park, where an hour or so of baby-pool splashing was followed by grape sno-cones. At the duplex, a backyard water hose provided heat relief. Someone grabbed a camera one day when I had stripped down to my underwear and was using the garden hose to make mud pies. With my matted hair, bony ribs, ragged knickers, and dirt-caked body, I looked like a child who had been reared by wolves. Whenever I later looked at those snapshots—even as a five- or

"Uncivilized"

six-year-old—I would think of them as "My Uncivilized Pictures." No, I didn't yet know the word *uncivilized,* but I had a pretty good sense of its meaning. As an adult, I would realize that the photos simply captured a normal kid playing in the mud and getting messy. But as a child, I saw them as proof of my imagined decline from a lovable, well-tended, attractive little girl into an unkempt heathen who wallowed in muck.

* * *

In later years, my memories of life in our "half-a-house" duplex would be neither especially negative nor positive. When I revisited Dallas as an adult, I would not avoid Marquita Street, but neither would I go out of my way to drive by our old dwelling, for which I felt no great warmth or nostalgia.

In retrospect, the duplex strikes me as having been a utilitarian place where I ate, slept, played, watched television, and spent precious hours with my father.

Still, something was missing.

Although the house contained my mother's furniture and the few accessories she had unpacked, it seemed as hollow and plain as a cardboard box. Its edges were somehow too sharp, its corners too square, its floors too bare. Cafe curtains dressed the living room, but I can only remember venetian blinds in the upstairs windows. A few pictures or plaques hung on walls, but no family photographs.

As time passed, the duplex took on an aura more masculine than feminine. Candles and flowers were absent, as were lacy touches or even a hint of perfume. We rarely had company and did not entertain. Neighbors did not stop by for coffee, and the aromas of home cooking never teased our appetites.

We had a piano, but no one ever played it.

27

The Forever Staircase

IN EARLY 1957, Daddy had taken all of the sympathy cards, letters, and telegrams we received after Mother's death and had them professionally bound into two large volumes. The books were an extravagance, with a marbleized design on the interior covers and every piece of correspondence permanently affixed to high-quality paper. Stamped onto the calfskin bindings was the name JEAN. These volumes, weighty as encyclopedias, were stored in one of our small bookcases. I knew that they had to do with my mother, but I almost never looked at them. When I did, I saw dozens of sturdy yellow telegrams, handwritten messages on pastel stationery, and letters typed on everything from flimsy onionskin to thick ivory paper with embossed seals. Some letters bore the logos of the writer's business ("Mead's Fine Bread," "Pontiac," "First National Bank of Lubbock"). Many were headed by pictures of churches, universities, seminaries, and Baptist Student Unions across the state and nation. Had I been able to read, I would have seen that some were signed by ranchers, others by college presidents. One came from a preacher whose congregation met in a movie theater that boasted "100% Refrigerated Air."

On the dedication page, my father had typed:

January 16, 1957

Dear Kathie,

These letters tell the story of your mother. I sincerely
hope and pray that her personality and faith will be
reflected in your life.

Love,
Daddy

                              *   *   *

When I was four, family members had felt I was too young to be
exposed to caskets, funerals, and cemeteries. Over the next couple of
years, I gradually came to understand what happened to a mortal body
after death. I don't recall when or how this information was relayed or
by whom. But by the time I scampered over country-church tombstones
in North Carolina, I was quite aware of their purpose.

At some point, Daddy finally took me to Restland Cemetery to see
where my mother was buried. He rarely went there himself; he was not
the type to brood in a graveyard, and he fully believed that his wife's
spirit was elsewhere. But an older couple in our church always arranged
for a large wreath to be placed on the grave every Easter and Christmas;
thus twice a year—more as a gesture of appreciation than anything
else—we drove out to see it.

Mentally, I understood that Mother's earthly remains lay in that
place. Emotionally, I was still divorced from the experience. Oh, I felt a
vague sadness—the kind I might feel for anyone who had died or been
bereaved. But I could muster no deeply personal grief.

Instead, my pain was reserved for *other* people touched by tragedy. A
year or so after Mother's death, I was spending a day with the Brannons.
As usual, the television was on, tuned to the national news. Normally, I
paid no attention to such programs, but on this evening the newscaster
reported that a woman's frozen body had been found in the Rocky
Mountains. She had been lost for several days, and I overheard the
older Brannons discussing it. For some reason, that woman's tragic
end gripped my soul.

Later that evening, I listened to Debbie Reynolds singing her new
hit tune "Tammy" over Sis's radio. A sweet love song, it somehow got

all tangled up in my heart with the lost and frozen woman. Along with "Little April Shower," "Tammy" would become one of the saddest songs I had ever heard.

* * *

I seldom thought about my mother. I didn't obsess about her earthly remains and never pondered what her spirit might be doing in heaven. But I *did* sometimes contemplate the afterlife.

I had learned that in heaven, time went on forever, and everyone was very happy to spend all of eternity up there. When I tried to wrap my mind around the concept of "forever," I imagined a staircase that spiraled up through the clouds and then kept going on and on and on. For me, this was not a pleasant image. I mean, who would want to keep climbing forever and ever, without any hope of *arriving* somewhere? There would be nothing to look forward to. No birthday parties or Easter Bunny. No trick-or-treat or Texas State Fair. You just climbed endlessly into eternity, without even a chance to sit down and catch your breath.

If I dwelled too long on this notion, my brain got so dizzy that I had to stop and comfort myself with something earthly and solid—like a pop-bead bracelet, a glob of Silly Putty, or maybe that book where the Poky Little Puppy laps up a big bowl of chocolate custard.

28

Baytown

DURING THESE UNSETTLED YEARS, the homes of both my paternal and maternal grandparents became oases of unconditional love, acceptance, and security. I adored Grandmother and Granddaddy Withers as much as I did my father's parents, and I normally visited with them three or four times a year. Sometimes they drove to Dallas—usually en route to visit Aunt Winkie in Colorado—but their stay was not long; since Grandmother could not climb our duplex's steep staircase, other arrangements had to be made for overnight visits.

More often, I traveled to Baytown. Daddy and I always drove down for Christmas, and sometimes Thanksgiving. Once or twice, I hitched a ride with Dallas friends heading in that direction. Later in the decade, I flew to Houston on Braniff Airways's Electra turboprops (infamously grounded in the 1960s when their wings began to snap off midflight). And when I was even older, I would travel by train.

Baytown lies southeast of Houston, fifty miles north of Galveston. It was not directly on the Gulf of Mexico but abutted the Houston Ship Channel, the San Jacinto River, and Buffalo Bayou. Still, it was close enough to the coast that when a good breeze billowed inland, you got a whiff of salty air and shellfish—along with the stench of oil refineries. The ground in Baytown was like a wet sponge, and some of the houses were perched on low stilts, buying them a foot or two of protection during floods or hurricanes.

My grandparents lived right in town, not far from Main Street. Mother and Winkie had grown up a few blocks away on Humble Street, but when they were in college, Grandmother was diagnosed with a weak heart. The doctor forbade her to climb stairs, so my grandparents swapped their two-story clapboard for a one-level brick house on the corner of Lobit and Ashbel.

Unlike at Mommie Mac's, I didn't have many "back to nature" experiences on the Lobit Street property. True, the yard's Saint Augustine grass was a thick emerald cushion beneath my bare feet, and I did enjoy collecting tiny snails that clung to the house's bricks after a rain shower. These I stored in an empty Sucrets tin until they eventually died and someone asked, "What's that gosh-awful *smell?*" But my maternal grandparents had no vegetable or flower gardens, no cornstalks or cows, no bobwhites or tree swings. In fact, during the summer, it was just too darn hot to be outside.

On sweltering days, window-unit air conditioners turned the house into a cool, dark refuge where I spent most of my time. Built in the Craftsman style of the 1940s, it was a trove of inset shelves and bookcases, window seats, glass doorknobs, telephone nooks, and oddly placed alcoves.

The living room's rose-colored damask drapes complemented an antique love seat and matching chairs. Centered on one wall was a nineteenth-century pump organ with a four-octave range, yellowed keys, and two foot pedals that produced an emphysemic wheeze. We cousins enjoyed spinning around on its stool or smooshing down a handful of keys while another child worked the foot bellows. The instrument was too old to make decent music, but Grandmother used its shelves as an étagère to display knickknacks.

Grandmother herself oversaw the room from a high-backed vintage rocker. Each morning, Granddaddy helped her into a thin crepe dress and eased her feet into sequined slippers. She then cane-tapped down a hallway to the front of the house, sometimes pausing in the dining room to straighten one of the wall-hung china plates. Flowers or fruit had been painted onto some pieces. Others displayed the symbols of Granddaddy's Masonic lodge and Grandmother's Order of the Eastern Star, where she had once held the high position of Most Worthy Matron.

Grandmother would then move to the living room and lower

herself into the rocker. Although she still had fine tastes in furniture, her handicap had forced her to settle for some less glamorous accommodations, such as an aluminum TV tray that served as her chair-side desk and makeshift dining table.

Genealogy was Grandmother's favorite pastime, and almost all of her research was conducted with notebook paper, a pencil, and stamps. Using her good hand, she spent hours writing letters to cousins in East Texas and to courthouses in Georgia, rooting out family records. Some of this information had been compiled into lists or books; even when I was a gangly grade-schooler, Grandmother would coax me to sit on her lap while she inculcated me with family history, reminding me that I would be eligible to one day join the Daughters of the American Revolution and the United Daughters of the Confederacy. Recitations of names and dates might bore another child, but I lapped it up: just as in North Carolina, this dwelling was a place where I *knew* I belonged—a place where my baby pictures hung on walls, where my earliest years were fondly remembered and recounted, and where I felt a deep connection to long-dead forebears.

Grandmother often told me stories about my mother, and even as a young child, I sensed that she continued to grieve for her daughter. She said things like "Kathie, darling, your mother never lost her temper" (not quite true, I would later discover) or "Mary Jean was *always* kind to others." These idealized pronouncements sometimes induced better behavior if I was acting up. If they didn't, then Grandmother told me all about the devil—a disciplinary technique that would horrify modern parents but was sometimes used by those born in the Victorian era. I would stand wide-eyed as Grandmother described Satan's pitchfork, horns, and long tail with a stinger on the end. "And that stinger will *zap* you!" she said, playfully jabbing the tip of her cane at my leg. I jumped back.

"Does the stinger hurt worse than a penicillin shot?" I asked.

"A *hundred* times worse!"

I could imagine nothing more hellish than getting shots forever and ever. The image should have stopped any naughtiness, but I recall one day when I must have needed more persuasion. As I continued to act up,

Grandmother pointed to the front door. "The devil comes to get little girls who misbehave, and I just saw his horns in those high windows," she announced. I whirled around and looked up at the inset panes.

"There's no one there," I argued, turning back to the rocker.

"He *was* there just a second ago. I saw his horns sticking up in that glass! Look—there they are again!"

This time I was afraid to turn around. Instead, I ran to the kitchen where my grandfather was stirring a big pot of chicken and dumplings. When I told him who was after me, he immediately lowered the flame and took off his apron. "Where's that devil?" he demanded.

"At the front door!"

Without another word, Granddaddy strode out a side door. A couple of minutes later he returned, out of breath and wiping imaginary sweat from his brow. "Well," he panted, "I had to chase him nearly ten blocks— all the way down to Humble Street. But, sweetheart, that old devil is gone, and he won't be bothering you anymore."

It might seem that such an incident would be traumatic, but it wasn't. Instead, my grandfather's response made me feel greatly loved and very secure.

*   *   *

My visits to Baytown sometimes coincided with those of Aunt Winkie and her kids. Uncle Roger, a soft-spoken and bookish man, spent the late 1950s working on his doctoral degree in literature. His wife spent the same amount of time giving birth to almost one child per year. Their daughter, Leslie, was followed in quick succession by four boys.

When we all converged at the Lobit Street house, a baby was usually drooling on a quilt that had been spread across the living-room floor. We older cousins used the same space as a play mat, strewing our many toys on it. My cousins were a noisy, boisterous bunch. (Within a few years, they would keep emergency rooms hopping with their broken bones and gashed foreheads. As teenagers—while their father was president of a Baptist college in Texas—they once took the family station wagon for a joyride and somehow ended up in *Canada*.) Fortunately, my grandparents' house had a long enclosed side porch with plenty of space for romping around.

As far as I know, my grandparents didn't show favoritism when all of us kids were in Baytown. But when I visited by myself, they treated me like fragile cut glass. I was coddled, catered to, overly protected, and smothered with terms of endearment. And even when I was older, they would not let me lift a finger to help with housework—not even to carry an empty plate back to the kitchen ("No, no, darling! Granddaddy will get that for you!"). This Pampered Princess treatment did not always serve me well in other settings or in later life. But as a child, I savored it.

My grandparents also stuffed me with food, expressing their love through succulent meals and unlimited sweets. Ever since Grandmother had suffered her stroke, Granddaddy had been in charge of all housekeeping and cooking. Nothing could surpass his holiday turkey and dressing, but our everyday meals were just as good. And for a special treat, I was allowed to drink "coffee milk"—a little coffee mixed with lots of milk and sugar, served in a pale-green cup and saucer that made me feel very grown-up.

As in Siler City, I had no trouble amusing myself in Baytown. Of course, I had brought a few toys, and I always watched *Looney Tunes* when it was on TV. Otherwise, I was content to listen to Grandmother's stories, fool around on the organ, and collect snails. I also explored every nook, cranny, closet, drawer, and bookcase in the house.

My favorite space was the guest bedroom, with its shell-pink walls and antique furnishings. A four-poster bed angled from one corner, along with the step stool that helped boost guests onto its high mattress. An embroidered coral-and-green coverlet (dated "1848") accented the bed's white spread. Against a nearby wall stood the oversized pink crib that had been used for my mother, Aunt Winkie, and each of us cousins in turn. A marble-topped dresser and washstand filled other spaces, the latter accessorized with a china basin and pitcher.

At the bed's foot reposed a faded ivory trunk packed with memorabilia from Winkie's and Mother's childhood: baby photos, locks of toddler hair (my mother's had a gentle swirl, just like my own when it grew longer), a tattered teddy bear, crocheted booties and hand-smocked dresses, grade-school report cards, high-school scrapbooks. I loved to rummage through these artifacts. Sometimes when my head was buried deep under the trunk's lid, I would hear Grandmother's approaching footsteps. Using the cane for support, she stepped with her right leg, then dragged the useless left one. The living and dining rooms were carpeted, but Grandmother's movements were clearly audible on the hall's hardwood floor: *Tap* went the rubber-tipped cane. *Swish* came the slippered left foot: *tap . . . swish . . . tap . . . swish . . .*

"Kathie, darling," she would say at the bedroom's doorway, "be careful with those things. Grandmother has put them in there *just so,* and they are all that I have left of your mother." I would close a frayed baby book and refold the dresses as if they were sacred relics. Sometimes Grandmother stood beside me, reminiscing about each item.

When I was older, she explained that Mother's wedding dress had been saved for me, boxed and stored in a bedroom closet. But someone later opened the box to discover that the satin had completely *rusted* in the humid, salty air.

* * *

When I visited Baytown during warmer months, my grandparents and I almost always took a day trip to Galveston Island. With folding lawn chairs and a cooler packed with sandwiches and soft drinks, we set off in an unair-conditioned Ford whose vinyl seat covers smelled like Granddaddy's cigarettes and stuck to my bare legs. A couple of miles out of town, a white obelisk towered in the distance. It was taller than the Washington Monument and topped by a star, representing the Lone Star of Texas. When my parents and I had traveled to Baytown in earlier years, I always called it "Grandmommy's Monument," for along with "Grandmommy's Oil Wells," it signaled that we were getting close to her house.

The San Jacinto Monument actually commemorated the 1836 battle in which Texas won independence from Mexico. Like many folks in the eastern part of our state, Grandmother was more rooted in Old South gentility than in the West's rugged pioneer spirit. After all, some of her not-so-distant kin had fought in the Confederacy and bequeathed their antebellum memories. Her grandparents had migrated to Texas in the 1880s—traveling through New Orleans by Pullman train rather than across prairies in a covered wagon—and settled in Jasper County, whose sloped terrain and piney woods resembled their native Georgia.

Despite her Southern sensibilities, Grandmother was fiercely proud of the Lone Star State. Within a few years, she would regale me with an animated version of the Battle of San Jacinto. Punching the air with her good arm, she would describe how Sam Houston's Texans surprised "ol' Santa Anna" and his Mexican army during their siesta, causing them to skedaddle into Buffalo Bayou, where they were either shot or drowned. (Grandmother omitted the story of Santa Anna's foiled escape, when he disguised himself in the dress and bonnet of a visiting whore.)

On beach-trip days, we turned off onto a highway just south of the monument and soon entered a tunnel that burrowed under the Houston Ship Channel. Emerging near La Porte, we motored past gator grass, swamps, and thousands upon thousands of acres devoted to the petroleum industry. A refinery tower's oscillating, tear-shaped flame might prompt Grandmother to recall a time years earlier when she had been riding a bus in Houston. She had sat in front of two women, one of whom was discussing her horde of small children.

"What do you do to settle all them babies down when they's fussy at night?" asked the woman's companion.

"Well," said the mother, "I just turns up the gas jest a little bit, and them childrens drops right off to sleep."

It was one of Grandmother's favorite stories, but I was still too young to understand why she found it so funny.

As we got closer to the coast, I gawked at every puddle-sized body of water and pestered, "Is that the ocean?"

"No," Grandmother explained, "it's just an inlet . . . or bayou . . . or part of the channel . . ."

Just past Texas City, the Ford mounted a causeway-spanning drawbridge and a few minutes later rumbled onto Galveston Island. Granddaddy navigated the town's palm-lined streets, cruising by houses whose louvered windows and lolling bougainvillea seem more fitted for New Orleans than ride-'em-cowboy Texas.

Galveston had done an admirable job of rebuilding after the

Hurricane of 1900 pretty much scrubbed it off the map. One of the storm's legacies was an eighteen-foot-high seawall, and it was into this concrete-topped barrier that we eventually dead-ended. Granddaddy found a parking space beside some stone steps, and seconds later I was out of the car and gaping at the panoramic Gulf of Mexico. Since I had little knowledge of geography, to me it was just "the ocean."

Excited as I was to finally be there, something about all of that endless water was a bit scary. It was not the kind of fright that kept me anchored to dry land, but my stomach fluttered when I gazed at this gray expanse that went on and on and on. Grandmother told me that it eventually bumped up against other shores, but I could not see—or even imagine—that far over the horizon. The gulf reminded me of a picture in my *Childcraft* volume on "The World Around Us." It was a photograph of a pelican perched on a post against a backdrop of navy-blue ocean. Later, I would understand that the piling was attached to a pier connected to land. But in the photo, it seemed that the bird was stranded out in the middle of nowhere, surrounded by water that had no beginning and no end. If I looked at the picture too long, I got scared and had to turn the page.

The gulf affected me the same way, but only if I stood by the seawall and looked far out to where it smudged into the sky. It was not so bad when I was closer in, near sand pails and towels and other people.

Once my grandparents were situated on the beach, I would shed the playclothes covering my swimsuit and dash down to the shore, squealing as a rim of incoming surf overtook my feet. I would later encounter writers who likened the Gulf of Mexico to lukewarm brown dishwater. But since I had never laid eyes on turquoise seas or sugar-white sands, I found our own coast to be quite satisfactory. Of course, after a storm, seaweed sometimes slimed around my toes, but I really didn't mind. No longer as fearful as I had been at four, I scampered in and out of a shorebreak where the waves were mere tuffets of foam, as gentle as the water in a baby's wading pool.

Grandmother sat in her lawn chair farther up on the dry sand, while my grandfather stood guard closer to the water. Wearing tan trousers, a straw hat, and a short-sleeved shirt that flapped in the breeze, he paralleled my movements inch by inch, foot by foot.

"Edward!" my grandmother frequently called in a panicky tone. "Watch her! She's going out too *far*!"

The water was barely up to my ankles.

Constantly worried that an undertow would sweep me off to Florida, my grandparents rested easier when I sat near the shoreline and played in the sand. Using a Donald Duck pail and shovel that we had purchased earlier, I built cockeyed turrets and surrounded them with moats. I dug for shells, storing the tiny ones in a Sucrets tin. I watched sandpipers stitch the beach as they raced toward pools left by outgoing waves, trying to catch tiny mollusks before they could squiggle back into the muck.

At lunchtime, we ate our sandwiches and tossed extra bread to the seagulls.

More often than not, rain clouds chased us homeward by midafternoon; sometimes, though, we would eat supper at a local restaurant and not start back until sunset. Years later, I can picture myself on one of these return journeys, sitting on a towel to catch the sand that still filled every crevice of my body. Pressed to my ear was a large conch shell that Granddaddy had bought me at a gift shop. When I asked Grandmother about its hollow roar, she explained that the shell had once lived in the ocean depths, and the sound was simply a *memory* of its former home.

Temporarily satisfied by this explanation, I took a long draw of Grapette soda and, with my mouth ringed in purple, joined Grandmother in one of her favorite songs:

> Oh, it was down in Louisiana,
> Just about a mile from Texarkana,
> In them old cotton fields back home.

Outside the car's open windows, a refinery's yellow-blue flames slid by, filling the swampland with their pungent odor. It was a smell despised by most everyone on earth, but I would always associate it with love. I soon grew drowsy and lay down in the back seat. As the Ford rocked through the night, my body remembered the rhythm of waves and the surf's muted roar. It remembered Grandmother calling out from her lawn chair and Granddaddy pacing back and forth on the beach, both of them guarding me as tenderly as they might a cherished pearl.

29

1958: High Hopes

IN 1957, DADDY AND I CELEBRATED our second Christmas together, this time with a *pink* tree twinkling above my Betsy Wetsy doll, Lincoln Logs, and Suzy Homemaker housekeeping set with its miniature dish drainer and tiny box of S.O.S. soap pads. At Wilshire, the Youth Department presented a "Living Nativity" on the sanctuary's front lawn: for several nights, a spotlight illuminated a tableau of the holy family, wise men, shepherds . . . and *live* sheep whose *baa*s punctuated carols piped through a PA system. The scene was striking enough to stop traffic along Abrams Road. What was most striking to *me* was to see Sis Brownlee dressed as Mary and silently adoring a Baby Jesus, when I was more accustomed to watching her lip-synch "Hound Dog."

Although Elvis was still the King, 1958 was ushered in by a spate of new tunes, such as Buddy Holly's "Peggy Sue" and Jerry Lee Lewis's "Great Balls of Fire." Both were endlessly played over Sis's radio, soon to be followed by other hits from Bobby Darin, Pat Boone, Ricky Nelson, and the Everly Brothers. We preschoolers enjoyed singing Perry Como's "Catch a Falling Star":

> Catch a falling star
> And put it in your pocket,
> Save it for a rainy day.

This phase of my childhood also took place against a continuous backdrop of commercials that jingled from the Brannons' television set:

Brylcreem, a little dab'll do ya!

Winston tastes good, like a (clap, clap) cigarette should!

See the USA in your Chevrolet!

Bo enjoyed imitating a Dr Pepper commercial in which a beatnik took a big swig of the soft drink and declared, "Frosty, man—*frosty!*"

This youngest Brannon was still incorrigible, and I was convinced that he would grow up to be a robber. Once, Bo told me that he had lifted a manhole cover and peed on top of a man's head.

* * *

Daddy still traveled frequently, and he usually brought me a small present upon his return. At some point, he began giving me ceramic "birthstone" angels: each five-inch-tall figurine depicted a haloed girl dressed in the color of a particular gemstone. I displayed these angels on a shelf, and my collection grew until I would eventually have one for all twelve months.

Meanwhile, real-life angels continued to care for me in their Dallas homes. In later years, people would give me pitying looks when I told of being farmed out to various families. However, the only downside of these sleepovers was the initial parting from Daddy; occasionally I would cry softly into a pillow at night because I missed him so badly. As for the visits themselves, I was well cared for and never mistreated . . . unless you count the times Bo Brannon tried to beat me up or lock me in a closet. If I was naughty, my guardians attempted to calmly correct my behavior, but none ever hollered at me or raised a hand to my backside.

My sojourns greatly broadened my world, allowing me to see how other families lived. I not only had enjoyable times in various homes, but I was exposed to new experiences. For instance, Mr. and Mrs. Connolly Baldwin's only child was an adolescent boy with severe cerebral palsy. Once I got past the initial surprise of meeting Terry, I was completely comfortable around him. The Baldwins' huge old Swiss Avenue home had a carpeted landing halfway up the grand staircase. Here, I played

House with small objects that Mrs. Baldwin had helped me scrounge up: matchboxes for tables, toothpaste caps for vases, nail-polish bottles for lamps. The landing was large enough to hold Terry's wheelchair, and he spent hours watching me play. I learned that I could easily entertain Terry with the Three Stooges impersonations or pratfalls down the stairs. And when I made monkey faces, he laughed so hard he almost toppled out of his wheelchair.

Sometimes I stayed with Mrs. Orena Miller, whose elderly mother lived with her. Mrs. Bussey was almost ninety and bedridden. But her mind was still sharp, and she often asked me to play at the foot of her bed while she sat propped against pillows, a shawl around her shoulders. Whether I fed my doll or created pictures with my Popeye Colorforms, Mrs. Bussey loved to watch me as much as Terry Baldwin did.

I had missed out on many types of knowledge that a mother might teach her small daughter, but other ladies helped to fill in some of those gaps. Mrs. Baldwin let me sit at her vanity table and uncap dozens of lipstick tubes. I really didn't want to make up my own face, but I was entranced by the endless shades of red and pink and orange, whose names Mrs. Baldwin read aloud. I learned from Mrs. Flavel Chastain how long it took to fry chicken and make cream gravy. Orena Miller taught me how to shell pecans, and Durene Sinclair explained where babies came from.

At the Brannons', I learned about important current events . . . such as Elizabeth Taylor's scandalous affair with singer Eddie Fisher. "How *could* she?" cried Sis. "How *could* he?" exclaimed Myrtle. Along with the whole country, the two of them were incensed that Fisher had abandoned his wife, Debbie Reynolds—America's "sweetheart" and the mother of two small children—for that violet-eyed vixen. And had it not been for the Brannons, I might have never known that Bobby Darin was dating Sandra Dee or that Jerry Lee Lewis had secretly married his teenage cousin.

I still enjoyed going over to Claire's house. She was now a first grader, and I was awed by her talk of teachers and classroom gossip. She also taught me how to play less babyish games, such as jacks, pick-up sticks, and the card games Go Fish and Old Maid. Sometimes Claire talked like a beatnik. If her mother called to her, she would answer, "You rang?"

Like Claire, I was maturing, but in fits and starts. For one thing, I had finally quit drinking from baby bottles, although I kept them around just to look at. At the same time, my "impulse control" still needed improvement. Once, when Aunt Winkie was visiting us, I had been playing outside with three-year-old Leslie. When it was time to go inside, the two of us stood on the porch steps and tussled over who was going to open the back door. In my entire childhood, I was never physically aggressive toward another youngster . . . except for Leslie. Something about my little cousin just brought out the devil in me. On that day, I was so enraged that I shoved Leslie off the porch steps and into a rosebush; she was wearing a sunsuit, and thorns raked her exposed back.

Seconds later, Aunt Winkie was out on the porch, where she managed to grab her screaming child with one hand and wallop me with the other. Then she carried Leslie to the upstairs bathroom and made me tag along. My aunt sat on the toilet, put my cousin face down on her lap, and began to dab alcohol over a dozen bloody scratches. Leslie wailed even louder.

Still snuffling from the spanking, I tried to sneak off to my bedroom, but Aunt Winkie ordered me back. "You're going to stand right here and watch," she said, continuing to disinfect her daughter's wounds. "Do you see how *much* this is hurting her?"

I gulped and nodded.

"Are you *sorry* that you did this to Leslie?'

"Yes," I mumbled.

But I was not one bit sorry.

* * *

In April, my sixth birthday party was held at nearby Llano Park. Just like the previous year, it was supervised by Mrs. Brannon, Sis, and Annie Kay. My most memorable gift was a bicycle with training wheels. The party's most memorable event occurred when Ricky Brannon, showing off his acrobatic tricks, hung upside down from a moving swing and busted his head open.

I was at an age where I was contemplating future occupations. Like most little girls, I assumed that I would one day be a mother and take care of my babies and my house. Sometimes I fantasized about being an airline hostess or a nurse. The latter had nothing to do with compassion for sick people or a desire to care for them. It had more to do with the little white uniform and cap that my Aunt Ella had sewn for me. It probably also served as an emotional outlet, allowing me to sadistically give my dolls the same painful "injections" that I had endured.

For years, I had played with toy nurse kits, which came with candy pills and harmless plastic equipment. But right after I turned six, a doctor in a local church heard about my career aspirations; he gave me a shoebox packed with *real* medical supplies and instruments—including *real* glass syringes with long needles.

I carried this box of treasures on one commercial flight that I took with Daddy. Bless his heart, my father did the best he could to look after me, but I would later wonder *where* his head had been when he let me take out those "toys" and show them to another little girl I had met on the plane. We must have been in some rough air because several grown-ups (including the girl's mother) were making frequent use of their barf bags. My new friend and I gave these passengers only cursory glances as we created a play area for ourselves by a bulkhead. There, we sat on the floor, screwing a needle onto one of the syringes and pretending to give each other shots while the plane bucked around at twelve thousand feet.

No one paid us any mind. And if one of us *had* accidentally bayoneted the other, it is doubtful that our parents would have sued each other or the airline. They likely would have just scolded us, saying, "You need to be more careful with those things!"

The 1950s might not have been the safest decade for kids, but it certainly was a *polite* era.

30

Beyond The Sunset

IN LATE AUGUST OF 1958, Mrs. Brannon accompanied me to Robert
E. Lee Elementary School for First-Grade Orientation. Ricky was not
with us because the Brannons lived in a different district, and he would
attend Stonewall Jackson Elementary (many of our city's schools were
named for heroic Texans, but the Confederacy was still revered by many
older Dallasites).

Robert E. Lee was several blocks from our duplex, in a neighborhood
where the surrounding houses were older, the trees shadier, the
sidewalks more buckled. When I thought of this school in later years,
the two words that would come to mind were *old* and *dark*. Unlike the
streamlined school buildings of recent years, Robert E. Lee was a somber
two-story edifice with high ceilings, brown lockers, cast-iron radiators,
and mahogany-colored wood for doors, window trim, and transoms.
Dallas schools would not be air-conditioned until 1970; before that,
teachers could only lower the transoms with long poles and pray for
some circulating air. Many of the teachers themselves seemed as ancient
as the building with their saggy bosoms and heavy orthopedic shoes.

None of this dampened my spirits on Orientation Day, for I had long
been eager to start school. My only moment of fear occurred when we
six-year-olds were herded to the cafeteria during a tour of the building.
As several white-uniformed women lined up to greet us, my heart caught
in my throat: I was afraid that these cafeteria workers were *nurses* who
were going to give us booster shots.

I had actually already been to Dr. Spegal's office for a physical exam and the required inoculations. At this visit, my pediatrician had jotted down some "reminders" for Daddy regarding my care:

- Two hours of outdoor play each day in good weather
- 1 Tbs. cod liver oil each day
- Limit TV viewing
- To bed by 8 p.m.
- Steady and *consistent* discipline

Other school preparations had been more pleasurable. A few weeks earlier, my grandparents and Aunt Winkie had taken me to Foley's Department Store in Houston, where I was outfitted with new shoes and several school dresses. Normally I hated shopping, but this time I *was* excited about getting a fresh wardrobe. Back in Dallas, Mrs. Brannon and I went to a drugstore, where I selected a red book satchel and other supplies on a mimeographed list: fat Number 2 pencils, Elmer's glue, crayons, manila paper . . .

From the first day, I loved everything about school, including my grandmotherly teacher who was firm but kind. When it came to learning, I had long been like a bucking bronco rarin' to be loosed into the arena of academia. My *Dick and Jane* reader thrilled me, as did the pulpy Big Chief writing pad in which I penciled letters, numbers, and— eventually—actual words and sentences.

I was generally better behaved in class than I was in some other places. Maybe it had something to do with the more formal structure of a *real* school, where we sat in neat rows, raised our hands to speak, and received report cards. Also, if you were truly bad, you risked being sent to Mr. Lichtenwald, the largely unseen principal who kept a spanking paddle in his office.

Despite my normally good behavior, I did go through a stubborn phase of refusing to stand when we pledged allegiance to the flag. I sat in the middle of the room, so either Mrs. Basden didn't notice or she decided to let my rebellion slide. But a classmate named Stella didn't ignore it. Stella was a loud, flouncy girl who wore extra-stiff petticoats and spoke with a pronounced lisp. Her desk was in front of mine. Whenever I remained seated during the pledge, Stella would whirl around, her crinolines nearly smacking me in the face, and chide, "Gah, Kathie! Don't you have any re-*thpect* for the *thlag*?"

At six, I had already been slotted into the social pecking order that I would hold for years: a position somewhere in the middle (and at times, lower-middle) of our class caste system. I was never on the very bottom with kids like Dorcas Wiggins, who got teased because she slobbered and wore "chubby" sizes. But neither did I effortlessly hobnob with the most popular girls. For one thing, I *was* an eccentric child. And the fact that I was motherless further stigmatized me, as if I had cooties. In this pre-divorce era, it was seen as "unnatural" for me to be raised by a single parent, or to make Mother's Day flower baskets for my *father*. None of this was overtly stated, and I was never teased because of my domestic situation. But then, as now, kids were experts at sniffing out anything that marked another child as an oddity.

All the same, I *did* become friends with several girls and even a few boys. Almost all of the boys in my class were pretty goofy, but Peter Evans seemed more serious than most. He was also a prodigy with Crayolas: his artwork looked like Rembrandt's compared to the rest of our stick-figure pictures.

One day, we read a story about Willy Bear, and Mrs. Basden then instructed us to draw and color a scene from the story. Twenty minutes later, she walked by our desks, nodding at lopsided flowers and drunken birds. But when she got to Peter, she stopped and gasped. Our teacher gingerly took his sheet of manila paper and held it up. "Boys and girls!" she enthused. "Look at what Peter has done!" We saw that our classmate had not only drawn a very convincing likeness of a bear but had depicted Willy sitting on a log, his legs as casually *crossed* as any human's while he read a newspaper. Oh, how we oohed and aahed—as much over the fine picture as from realizing that such talent was in our midst!

Peter sat behind me, and a few minutes later the two of us started clowning around, playfully grabbing at items on each other's desks. While we were giggling and squirming, Peter's Willy Bear drawing somehow got caught between our desks (it was mostly *my* fault), and someone's desk moved (I think it was mine). *Rrrippp!* went a large corner of the masterpiece.

Peter immediately raised his hand. "Mrs. Basden, Kathie tore my picture!" he tattled with an air of prim innocence.

Mrs. Basden walked over. Speechless, she picked up the ruined drawing. She then took my hand and led me out to the hallway. "Why," she asked, pointing to the terrible evidence, "did you do something like this?"

"It was an accident," I mumbled. "I didn't mean to." My voice was barely audible, my head lowered in shame. At that moment, there was not a drop of maverick blood in my veins. I was humiliated, frightened, and trying hard not to cry.

"You know," my teacher said, "I really ought to send you to Mr. Lichtenwald for this."

My heart galloped. Our principal, with his dark suits and jet-black hair, looked like a powerful tycoon. He was probably a very nice man who cared about children, but for me, he was a larger-than-life figure whom it was best to avoid. Students dreaded being sent to Mr. Lichtenwald's office, for he was known to have paddled seventh-grade boys as big as Carl Ball. And each day his godlike voice came over the PA system, sternly reminding us not to roughhouse in the hallways or turn our lunchroom straws into peashooters.

In those days, we had Morning Devotions over the intercom, which involved a couple of students reading a Bible passage or inspirational thought and reciting a short prayer. Sometimes a religious song would be played on the office phonograph and piped through the speakers. One morning, we listened to a baritone solo of "Beyond the Sunset," a song about that "blissful morning" when our earthly toils will end, and we will rejoin our Savior and departed loved ones.

A few classmates later swore that it had been Mr. Lichtenwald *himself* singing over the intercom.

It never occurred to me that our principal had selected an odd song for elementary students. For one thing, what "toil" did we have in our lives beyond completing spelling worksheets and moving our bikes out of the driveway? I certainly didn't understand all the words, but I did grasp that the song was about dying and going to heaven. It reminded me of a sympathy card pasted into one of the JEAN books. I rarely looked through those two volumes, but this large and lovely card was hard to miss, with its scalloped gilt edges and a picture of a magnificent clipper ship sailing into a pink-and-gold twilight. Much later, I would read the poem inside, which described a group of weeping mourners who cry, "There she's gone!" while loved ones on a distant shore exclaim, "Here she comes!" The "Sunset" song was like that card—both sad and beautiful.

An even sadder song had recently hit the radio airwaves. Performed by The Kingston Trio, it was about a man who was going to be hung:

> Hang down your head, Tom Dooley,
> Hang down your head and cry;
> Hang down your head, Tom Dooley,
> Poor boy, you're bound to die.

I heard it all the time at the Brannons'; it was so catchy that even Ricky and Bo went around chanting it. I liked the ballad too, although it made me feel so sorry for Tom Dooley that my stomach seemed weighted with rocks.

And that was how I felt standing in the hallway with Mrs. Basden, awaiting my own sentencing. An eternity passed while she studied Peter's torn picture. Finally, she sighed. "Okay, Kathie," she said, "go on back to your desk. But I expect you to apologize to Peter, and I want you to be more respectful of other people's property."

Unlike poor Tom Dooley, I had been reprieved. I wanted to cry with relief, but didn't. At some point, I had made a vow never to cry at school . . . and I would not break that vow until a November day in 1963, when President Kennedy visited our city.

* * *

Every October, the Dallas public schools closed for a whole day so that students could enjoy the State Fair of Texas. I usually went with the Brannons, but in 1958 I tagged along with the Shocklee family, whose daughter Martha was in my Sunday school class.

The fairgrounds themselves were enormous, encompassing the Cotton Bowl stadium, a music hall for staged productions, acres of agricultural buildings, and one of the largest midways in the nation. The fair's iconic emblem was Big Tex, a fifty-two-foot-tall cowboy who greeted visitors at the venue's entrance. Clad in denim jeans, a red-and-blue shirt, a bandana, and a Stetson hat, Big Tex waved a mechanical arm and moved his lips, booming out a friendly "Howdy, folks!"

My 1958 fairground visit was like those of other years. Ushered by her parents, Martha and I cruised a midway redolent with corn dogs and buttery popcorn, mixed with a fetid odor from livestock pens. We ate caramel apples, drank Dr Pepper from waxy red-striped cups, and devoured cotton candy that turned our mouths a shocking pink. Peanut shells crunched under our sneakers as we passed straw-hatted barkers: "Step right up, ladies and gentlemen, boys and girls!" Heeding their staccato invitations, we tossed nickels, hoping to win an oversized teddy bear or pistol-shaped ashtray. We swiveled giant tongs inside a box full of plush animals but never could get them to grab hold of anything. We gawked at a Fat Lady and watched a chicken frenetically plink a toy piano. I gave wide berth to the shooting galleries and their loud *cracks!*, where air rifles toppled rows of fake yellow ducks.

Martha's teenage sister, Mickey, and her boyfriend had come with us on that day, although they put distance between themselves and the elder Shocklees. As we neared the carnival rides, they went their own way, eager to tempt fate on the Calypso, Caterpillar, and Moon Rocket. But Martha and I had no desire to risk whiplash on a Tilt-a-Whirl or dangle from a giant Ferris wheel. We younger girls were quite content with the baby fare, happy enough to put-put in slow circles on little motorcycles or glide up and down on carousel horses. Through the calliope music, we could hear the distant clatter of cars mounting a wooden roller coaster, followed by a unison shriek as they plunged almost straight down.

Later, Martha and I met up with Mickey and her boyfriend. They let us tag along for a while and even took us on the Tunnel of Love ride, where we floated in boatlike cars. We sat behind them and giggled whenever they kissed.

* * *

The following Monday morning, I walked into my classroom and noticed an empty desk near the bulletin board where cheery autumn leaves drifted from construction-paper trees. The desk belonged to Robin O'Leary, an elfin, snaggletoothed girl with reddish-gold hair. I did not know Robin well but she seemed sweet, and we had recently smiled at each other on the swing set.

When the bell rang, Mrs. Basden closed the door and crossed to her desk. A couple of children near the front raised their hands and began excitedly telling our teacher something that I couldn't hear.

"I *know*!" she responded, her eyes widening. "When I opened my newspaper yesterday and saw the article, I couldn't *believe* it!"

Mrs. Basden then announced that our classmate Robin had been killed in a car accident over the weekend.

I don't recall how much detail she provided—and how much I gleaned from first-grade gossip—but it seemed that Robin, her parents, and her older sister had spent the previous Friday at the State Fair. They were leaving the fairgrounds that evening when a drunk driver hit their car, and Robin was thrown out. Her parents and sister were not badly injured, but Robin was killed instantly.

At recess, one of my classmates claimed to have been there and seen Robin lying on the pavement. (I would always picture her lying directly beneath Big Tex, sightlessly staring at his red-and-blue shirt while he kept up a steady, "Howdy, folks!")

"Was she crying?" someone asked.

"Yes," the boy somberly told us. "There was a tear coming out of her eye, because she was sad that she died."

* * *

I would eventually transfer to another school district after third grade, and these earlier classmates completely disappeared from my life.

I remembered many of their names, physical features, and personality traits, but in my mind, they would be forever frozen at six, seven, and eight years old. These children and I also went to different high schools. A half century later, when the Internet let me access their Woodrow Wilson High 1970 Yearbook and Class Reunion photos, I was astonished at how many faces looked *exactly* as I had held them in my memory. I also found it hard to believe that these former classmates had experienced Beatlemania, the Kennedy assassination, or the hippie movement . . . for I could not imagine them in any world beyond *Dick and Jane* readers or playground jungle gyms.

Robin O'Leary, of course, never grew up at all. As an adult, I rarely thought of this phantom child on the swing set; when I did, she seemed such a distant dream that I half wondered if I had conjured her from my overactive imagination. Shortly after rediscovering my Robert E. Lee classmates on the Internet, I did another cyber search: within a few minutes, I located the *Dallas Morning News* article about Robin's 1958 death, as well as her obituary. I had not been aware that her father was a principal at another elementary school, but almost every other detail from my memory had been correct. The O'Leary family *was* leaving the fairgrounds on that Friday (although the accident had occurred on a residential street several blocks away). In that era before cars were equipped with seat belts, Robin *had* been ejected from the vehicle. And a drunk driver was indeed charged with manslaughter. The only thing I got wrong was my classmate's final resting place. I had long believed that this was Hillcrest Cemetery off Northwest Highway, and for years I thought of Robin whenever we drove past it. Now I learned that she had actually been interred at Restland, where my mother was buried.

Caught up in the past, I next found an online obituary for Harold Lichtenwald, who had died in 2009. The article noted that in addition to serving as principal of two Dallas schools, Mr. Lichtenwald enjoyed singing and had directed the music at a couple of area churches.

A final bit of research revealed that the song "Tom Dooley" had peaked on the charts within a week of Robin's death.

That evening, as I sat in the glow of cyberspace, several of my disjointed memories began to meld and make sense. First, I better understood why "Tom Dooley," even decades later, gripped me with an out-of-proportion sadness. Second, I realized that Mr. Lichtenwald had probably been acquainted with Robin O'Leary's father and must have felt a strong kinship with this fellow principal. When Robin died, he would have grieved, not just for the loss of a student but for the daughter of a colleague. It also seemed likely that Mr. Lichtenwald had selected "Beyond the Sunset" as a tribute to Robin shortly after her death.

And, yes, it probably *was* his own rich baritone that rose a cappella through the speakers on that long-ago autumn morning, heartfelt and haunting, to lament a fallen child.

V

Preacher's Kid

31

Feeding The Flock

"Dang nabbit! . . . Dad gummit! . . . I'll be dog!"

Daddy let loose a string of preacher-style curses as he yanked a baking sheet from the oven and dropped it onto the stovetop, almost upending a saucepan of green beans. Standing in our kitchen doorway, I watched smoke billow from the aluminum sheet holding a charred row of Swanson's fish sticks. My father raised a small window over the sink. Using a pot holder that I had made for him in Vacation Bible School, he flapped at the smoke. Both of us coughed.

I commented that Jesus was a much better cook than Daddy was. After all, He didn't burn up *His* two little fishes and ruin supper for that crowd of people on the hillside. Daddy sighed and said he reckoned Jesus didn't.

Our predicament was unfortunate on this late afternoon in mid-December. My father usually pulled off frozen fish sticks like a master chef, but he had been distracted lately—perhaps because he was still adjusting to a brand-new job.

Several months earlier, Ralph Langley had resigned as Wilshire's pastor and moved to Houston to serve in another church. My father not only delivered occasional sermons during the interim, but he also sat on Wilshire's Pulpit Search Committee, whose task it was to find a new minister. What Daddy didn't know was that by autumn, the committee was secretly meeting behind his back and considering *him* for the full-time position. With a mixture of embarrassment and gratitude, he accepted their nomination; the congregation voted its approval, and

4316 Abrams, Dallas, Texas   November 30, 1958   Vol. 3, No. 47

Welcome Pastor!

"Our waiting is over! Our prayers are answered. May we renew our dedication to the Lord and increase our efforts in His name as we welcome the leadership of our new pastor."   Asa Newsom, Jr., Chairman, Board of Deacons.

"The entire Sunday School pledges its support and prayers to our new pastor and we are looking forward to a new era of spiritual leadership and growth." Vondyl Willis, Sunday School Superintendent.

"Welcome, Pastor! The Training Union pledges you its complete cooperation in every phase of our work in developing a more consecrated and better trained membership for advancing the cause of Christ at Wilshire. Call on us!" Pat Managan, Training Union Director.

The drawing at the top of this bulletin depicts Wilshire as members envisioned it in the future. (In 1958, the church facilities were much smaller.)

on November 11, 1958, my father became pastor of his own church.

Daddy was now staying much closer to home, so it would seem that he might be able to concentrate on his cooking. But for whatever reason, our supper was now in the trash can, and the two of us had to be up at the church in half an hour for a committee meeting. Since this was a weeknight, with no regular church activities or services, Daddy would normally have gotten a babysitter or dropped me off at someone's house to play, but he had promised that if I behaved during his meeting, we would later go Christmas caroling on a bus that the church had chartered.

I had been thrilled with this proposition. Not only was I excited about riding on a bus, but I knew that many members of Wilshire's Youth Department would participate in the outing. I *adored* teenagers and had been begging Daddy for quite some time to marry Peggy Jo Plunkett, whose ponytail and glittery teeth braces were, in my opinion, irresistible assets. My father argued that she was only fifteen, and once when I asked if she could babysit me, I heard him mumble that Peggy Jo didn't have enough sense to babysit an *ant* farm.

Daddy was now rooting around in the pantry, shuffling tins and boxes. I declined the can of soup he offered to heat up, opting instead for some Sugar Smacks cereal. Opening the refrigerator, Daddy uttered another "dang nabbit" when he saw that the milkman hadn't come that morning. Then he noticed a clock and said oops, he had to hurry upstairs to dress and shave, and he was very sorry but could I please just eat my cereal straight from the box? I might also want some of those canned green beans that he had warmed up, or maybe an apple . . . and, yes, I could wear the playclothes I had on, but after I ate, I should be sure to run a comb through my hair and wash my hands.

The sky was the color of sugarplums by the time Daddy backed our fin-tailed Chevy from the driveway. I slouched in the passenger seat, bundled into a hooded coat and wearing a Cracker Jack–prize ring on one ungloved finger. Dad fiddled with the car's heater and asked if I had gotten enough supper. And had I remembered to eat some of the green beans in the saucepan?

"Uh-huh," I lied, telling him that I had forked up a few. In truth, not a single green bean had supplemented my handful of Sugar Smacks, which I had scooped straight from the box. My half-filled stomach rumbled as we cruised past our neighbors' winter-yellowed yards. We turned north on Skillman and began to pass side streets whose signs I was learning to decipher: *Monticello, Mercedes, Morningside*. These same names, I knew, appeared throughout Wilshire's membership directory, and up and down those blocks lived many good folks who had helped us during the past few years, often sheltering me under their rooftops.

Somewhere around Kenwood Avenue, my stomach let out an especially loud growl. Daddy suggested that he could drop me off at the Sinclairs, where I could eat supper and then play with David. Or we could stop at the Shocklees. During his short tenure as pastor, my father had fed his flock well, and he knew that most parishioners would gladly reciprocate by dishing up a hot meal and entertaining me for a few hours—just as they had been doing all along.

I declined the offer. Yes, I *was* hungry, but I also wanted to go caroling. And truth be told, I was even more possessive of Daddy's time and attention than I had been during his traveling days. As we came to the Skillman stoplight, Daddy reminded me that we would be coming back to the church later for cookies and hot chocolate. And he said that if I was still hungry after that, then the two of us could go to the Waffle House for bacon and eggs.

Both sounded like excellent propositions.

A few minutes later, my father pulled into Wilshire's parking lot and a space labeled PASTOR. Before I could escape, he took a comb from his pocket and ran it through my short hair. Then he called out as I bolted from the car and raced toward the educational building, once again reminding me to wash my hands.

Half an hour later I sat at the church secretary's desk, a small bottle of ink before me and a fountain pen between sugar-sticky fingers. Uncapping the pen, I dipped its nib into the bottle, lifted a lever, and siphoned thick blue ink into the pen's core. I then hunched over a sheet of typing paper and printed:

Dear Daddy,

How are you? I miss you when you are gone but you are here so I do not miss you now.

My father, along with a few other grown-ups, was only steps away in his PASTOR'S STUDY, behind a door that I felt had been closed far too long. For the past twenty minutes I had rummaged through desk drawers and played secretary. I had created a paper-clip necklace, hummed

Christmas songs, and spun myself silly in the swivel chair. But with the wall clock's hands apparently frozen, I was growing both restless and increasingly hungry. I reread my letter and considered adding another couple of sentences:

> When will your stupid committee meeting be over? I want to go caroling and have refreshments!

Unsure of how to spell the longer words, I settled for a simple,

> Love,
> Kathie McIver

I folded the paper, walked across the cramped reception area, and slid it under the study's door. A chuckle or two drifted from the inner office, but the voices quickly resumed their low, serious drone. Annoyed that no one was going to invite me in to discuss budgets and building programs or to exchange knock-knock jokes, I huffed out to the main hallway. There, I paused for only a moment before my feet began to move out of pure habit, off to go exploring.

At the time, Wilshire's facilities were quite compact, with no inch of space wasted. The crazy-quilt floor plan was as familiar to me as my own house, and I regularly revisited every alcove, cubby, and odd-shaped room. On this night, hunger determined my route, for our church had plenty of food, and my foraging skills were keen.

A dozen steps brought me to the Toddler Nursery, whose high doorknob I tiptoed to turn. I snapped on the light and, ignoring low shelves full of pull toys, crossed to a cupboard where I knew the teachers kept a box of butter cookies. The cookies were flower shaped, with a hole in the middle. Taking two from the easily reachable box, I placed one on each pinky finger and alternately nibbled the "petals."

In this fashion I shuffled through a utility area to the Infant Nursery. Here, I would find no food, but I always enjoyed perusing the room's handful of cribs. None had built-in toys, but what wonderful items the teachers had attached to their railings: a mobile of twirling butterflies, cup-shaped bells in sherbet colors, miniature fish floating in a tube of clear liquid, and my favorite—a string of pastel *sheep,* each with tiny beads that rattled inside their plastic bodies. These flimsy creatures would never have passed future child-safety standards, but they were so pretty that I was often tempted to "sheep-nap" them. On this night, I gave each a perfunctory spin before heading back to the hallway, a trail of crumbs and inky fingerprints in my wake.

Down the corridor I came to Nina Knox's Preschool Nursery where, when I was younger, I had stayed during worship services. Nina's hair was still swirled into a silver bun, and every time I saw her, she still knelt to hug me and coo, "Jesus loves sweet Kathie." For a moment I longed to dally in Nina's room, perhaps reworking some puzzles or playing with the wooden mailbox shape sorter. But I was on a mission—and it took little time for me to find the Ritz crackers stored in an upper cupboard.

They helped to fill my stomach, but now I was thirsty. Realizing that I had no nickel for the Dr Pepper machine tucked under a stairwell, I settled for a long drink at a water fountain and then moved on down the hallway, detouring through a maze of rooms just behind the sanctuary. First, I poked my head into the closet-sized library, and then the choir room with its two tiers of twenty or so chairs. In an anteroom, I brushed my hand along a row of lilac choir robes, wondering which of the lady singers might consider marrying Daddy and me, just in case Peggy Jo didn't work out.

Next, I cut through the Fellowship Hall to the adjacent kitchen, where I opened an industrial-sized refrigerator and spotted several condiments. My favorite was French salad dressing, which at Wednesday evening suppers was poured into small bowls and placed at intervals on the long tables. It was my habit to wait until everyone had finished their meal and left the room, then make my way along the tables and slurp leftover dressing from the bowls. On this night, I just grabbed a Wishbone bottle from the refrigerator, unscrewed the cap, and guzzled. After chasing the tangy liquid with a big swig of Worcestershire sauce, I pulled out a bottle of Lord's Supper grape juice . . . but put it back quickly when I heard footsteps. They probably belonged to Denver, the janitor, and I knew he would tell me to get my cotton-pickin' head out of that icebox. I really didn't want to make Denver mad, because I was trying to get him to marry Annie Kay.

I ducked out to the hall and climbed a staircase to the second floor. Both sides of the corridor were lined with Sunday school classrooms, including my own Primary Department. At least twice a week I ventured into this empty room after worship services, usually because Daddy was spending way too long chatting with people and I was bored out of my skull. My ritual on this night was the same as always: I walked over to an upright piano, where I tried to two-finger "Chopsticks." I passed by the teacher's storytelling easel and paused to sniff some Magic Markers. I spun a record player's turntable and studied a picture of Jesus sitting on a hillside, surrounded by Suffer the Little Children. Finally, it was on to a row of wall-hung cabinets, where I located a four-pack of Play-Doh. Normally we used the clay to mold baskets for Baby Moses or animals for Noah's ark . . . but it was also good to eat. I opened the pink-lidded can, broke off a hunk, and popped it in my mouth. It was salty and succulent—a perfect last course for my makeshift meal.

* * *

A half hour later, around thirty of us carolers boarded a chartered bus that idled in the parking lot. While parishioners of all ages had turned out, the Youth Department had a large contingent, as did the College and Career Department, whose members included university students and unmarried professionals. In future decades, churches would refer to the latter as "singles" (putting the image in my mind of processed cheese slices). In 1958, Wilshire's Career class had no divorced people and only a few confirmed "old maids." Most members were young adults, many of them women biding their time between college graduation and wedding bells.

Most of this group were sitting at the front of the bus, and from my seat midway back, I could hear them joking around with Daddy. As pastor, my father did not stand on formality. Like other Baptist ministers, he wore no starched collar, and he preferred to be called "Bruce" as opposed to a stuffy "Reverend." Daddy was also quite good-looking for a preacher. By that, I mean that he didn't resemble some of those sissified

Although Daddy and I are not pictured here, this might have been the caroling excursion when I got sick on the bus.

Bible-thumpers who sported narrow ties and wire-rimmed glasses and either plastered their hair with a gallon of oil or poufed it up like a girl's. No, Daddy might have been short of stature and walked with a slight limp, but his face was still boyishly handsome, and his blue-gray eyes undoubtedly melted many a heart.

I had chosen to sit farther back, where I could soak up attention from the teenagers. I teased Dean Miller about his ducktail hairdo and asked Peggy Jo Plunkett to show me how the rubber bands hooked onto her teeth braces. When the bus bucked into gear, causing Fred Davis to fall into Charla Grey's lap, I laughed so hard I nearly wet my pants. The motor coach rumbled from the parking lot and horseshoed south onto Abrams Road, heading toward the older sections of Dallas. Instead of visiting hospitals or rest homes, we would be stopping at the private residences of Wilshire's elderly or homebound members—otherwise known as "shut-ins." And since most of the congregation lived within a three- or four-mile radius, our route would not cover any great distances.

A few minutes later we gathered in the front yard of Mrs. Lummie

Hathcox, Wilshire's oldest member. "Mother Hathcox" had grown up in East Texas just after the last Comanches were driven from the warpath, when a few aging settlers could still remember Stephen F. Austin and General Sam Houston. On Mother's Day, our church always presented Mrs. Hathcox with a corsage for having borne the most children. Now, she and her daughter nodded politely at their front door as we sang several selections, concluding with a robust "We Wish You a Merry Christmas." Throughout the caroling, I had kept an eye on Daddy, who stood across the yard. He was having a jolly time with the College and Career group, and I hoped he might ask one of the women for a date—perhaps Julia Woodrum, who played the sanctuary's piano, or Ellen Porter, a stewardess for Braniff Airlines.

When we reboarded the bus, I accepted Daddy's proposal to join him up front for the next leg of the trip. All of the seats were taken, so Raynelle Coe offered to let me sit in her lap. As soon as I settled onto her slack-clad long legs, the bus jolted forward and swung again onto Abrams. Everyone around us was discussing which carols we might sing at our next stop, and Raynelle asked what my favorite Christmas song was. I ticked off several and then, warming to the topic, announced that I also liked an Easter hymn called "Up from the Gravy and Rolls."

Raynelle and a few other eavesdroppers said they had never heard of it. To refresh their memory, I sang it for them:

> Up from the gravy and rolls,
> With a mighty trumpet on his nose!

Everyone laughed. Then, from just across the aisle, Daddy told me that the words were actually, "Up from the grave He arose/with a mighty triumph o'er His foes." He said it was about Jesus rising on Easter morning.

Yes, I had learned about the resurrection at church, but I was convinced that *my* lyrics also made sense: after all, Daddy and I were usually invited to someone's house for Easter Sunday lunch, and they almost always served gravy and hot rolls. Of course, that second line about the nose trumpet was rather strange, but so were a few other hymns—such as the one where a man drops his "robe of flesh" and flies buck naked through the air, shouting, "Farewell, farewell, sweet hour of prayer!"

Raynelle had chuckled along with the others, but now she told me not to feel bad. She said that when she was my age, she had thought there was a hymn called "Bringing in the Sheets"—like off a clothesline.

I told her that was silly, because everyone knows that the song is about "Bringing in the *Sheep*."

Instead of correcting my misnomer of "sheaves," Raynelle gave me an affectionate squeeze. I had never considered Raynelle as a potential mate for Daddy and me, because unlike Julia and Ellen, she was not especially pretty. But who cared if her figure was lanky, her face pockmarked, her teeth big, and her eyes framed by thick glasses? Raynelle was nice to me. She called me "sweetie," and she had admired my Cracker Jack ring and blotted ink stains from my nose. Now, with both arms wrapped around me and her chin resting on top of my head, she asked what Santa might bring on Christmas Eve. "A Ginny doll," I told her. "A Hula-Hoop. An airline-stewardess outfit that comes with a cap, travel bag, and pin-on wings . . ."

My voice trailed off because I was suddenly beginning to flag. Maybe it was the hypnotic motion of the bus or the hum of voices around us. Maybe I was intoxicated by diesel fumes or having a delayed reaction from huffing Magic Markers. But I was suddenly very tired. Sensing this, Raynelle pulled me closer. I nuzzled into a coat that was soft and warm and hinted of woodsy perfume.

Behind us, the bobby-soxers had launched into a chorus of "Rockin' Robin," and even though they were not supposed to dance, I could hear fingers snapping and penny loafers tapping. None of this seemed to bother the older crowd up front. I half listened as my father told one of his trademark stories. It was one I had heard before, but when everyone howled at the punch line, I just smiled. I was plumb laughed out, sung out, talked out.

I was also "snacked" out. Thus far, the bus ride had been pleasant. But the big front window was almost under my nose, and I felt woozy whenever I glanced through it. The sensation worsened when the bus, rolling toward Gaston Avenue, began to move up and down, up and down. Dallas might look utterly flat from a distance, but parts of the city slope into declivities or rise on gentle mounds. This was especially the case around White Rock Lake and in the Lakewood neighborhood, where streets could make drunken loops around creek banks.

Just when I thought my stomach was going to do a complete somersault, we turned onto La Vista Drive and pulled up to another house. Everyone began to file off the bus. I dawdled, half heartedly searching for the dinky plastic ring I had dropped moments earlier.

Daddy and Raynelle asked if I was coming.

I told them to go on ahead, that I would be along in a minute. By the time I finally located the bauble, the driver and I were the only ones left on board. I stood up. Although the bus was no longer moving, my insides continued to sway. I took two steps forward and paused to clutch a seat back. My head spun with images of Hula-Hoops and Rockin' Robins, gravy and rolls, and that Sweet Hour guy who flings off his bathrobe and goes sailing through the sky.

The Worcestershire sauce was suddenly at the back of my throat.

I gulped.

The driver got up from his seat and reached toward me, asking, "Little girl, are you okay?"

Two seconds later, my supper was all over his shoes.

It did not take long for a few people, including Daddy, to answer the poor man's distress call. A flurry of handkerchiefs and tissues soon appeared, along with a cup of water. Women gathered around me, motherly hands patting my back and palming my forehead. "I'm fine," I told them truthfully, for I was feeling oh-so much better! There was a bit of concern that I might have some internal bleeding until Daddy quizzed me about what I had been eating.

"*Play*-Doh?" he exclaimed. "Bright *pink* Play-Doh?"

He then assured everyone that I didn't seem to be all that sick. Still, it seemed best to get me home as soon as possible. The next thing I knew, Raynelle was offering to go back to the duplex with me and babysit so that Daddy could continue with the group and enjoy the post-caroling party. Like any good parent, he protested. I might have protested too, except that I was thrilled at the idea of having Raynelle babysit me for the first time ever. "Please?" I begged. My father hemmed and hawed, and I whined until he finally gave in.

For a couple of minutes, logistics were discussed, and someone pointed out that one of our stops would be on Concho Street. Wasn't that only a few blocks from Marquita? Could the driver perhaps make an extra stop?

Moments later, the bus detoured over to Marquita and dropped Raynelle and me right at our duplex. Daddy walked with us to unlock the door, again asking if I wanted him to stay. Not only did I want my father to *go*, but as I hugged him goodbye, I whispered that maybe after the party, he could ask Julia out for coffee. Or take Ellen to a movie. Of course, Raynelle was also a prospect, and Peggy Jo wasn't entirely out of the running—but it was important that we cover all our bases.

And so on that cold December night, I cheerfully sent Daddy away, hoping that he could find a wife . . . and happy that I could borrow a "mother" for a couple of hours.

32

Theology 101

Dear Daddy,

I knoe what you preched about you preched about poeple
eating each other up, and I dont knoe the last letter of the
sentuts but that is what you said.

I HAVE NO IDEA WHAT MY FATHER said in his sermon on that day (nor do
I recall what *letter* and *sentuts* had to do with anything), but his anecdote
must have been colorful enough to grab my attention. Normally, I didn't
do much listening when Daddy preached. Whether I sat with a surrogate
family or by myself in the front pew, I spent most church services with
library books, pencil and paper, or a Sunday school quarterly, in which
I could draw mustaches on all the disciples or give Jesus a cigar.

I also enjoyed playing a long-running trick on my father. Before the
service, I would sometimes place a penciled note on the pulpit:

Dear Daddy,

I ran away from church.

The first time this happened, the congregation saw my father's
panicked expression as he looked all around the sanctuary. After a few
minutes, I poked my head over a balcony railing, behind which I had
been hiding. I grinned and waved at Daddy. I was probably scolded

afterward, but it must have been such a gentle reprimand that I can't recall it. My father still disciplined and occasionally spanked me . . . but not nearly as much as he had before Mother died.

Years later, some older church members would remember me as being a "sweet little girl." Perhaps I *was* at times. But I'm sure that many others were just too polite to declare that I could also be a spoiled brat. Baptists are a convivial bunch, and folks at Wilshire enjoyed standing around after the services to socialize. At those times, I made an utter nuisance of myself. Running up and down the aisles, I pestered, teased, bothered, interrupted, and pawed at people. I threw myself at the organist, shrieking, "*Curly!*" (he resembled one of the Three Stooges). I told the same jokes over and over, and hiked my dress to show off ruffled petticoats.

My father was not a dictatorial pastor: he led and inspired his congregants to be co-ministers, and he rarely pulled rank. Still, I saw Daddy as the "boss" of the church and felt this gave me license to do pretty much anything I wanted inside Wilshire's walls. One of the worst things I ever did fell into the category of Blatant Dishonesty. In my primary Sunday school class, we were given the chance to memorize a certain number of Bible verses and thus earn an award-style ribbon. When we had accumulated six ribbons, we could exchange them for a picture book. Although I was a whiz at memorization, I devised an easier way to get hold of those colorful ribbons. One Sunday morning, I gathered several classmates and led them downstairs to Daddy's empty office, where a large candy jar sat on one bookshelf. From this container, I passed out Brach's caramels, Bit-O-Honeys, and Hershey's kisses. In return for the candy, the children gave me their ribbons, which I then traded for a book. Surely the teachers knew that something fishy was going on, but I don't think I was ever scolded.

And that was the problem. The adults at Wilshire were very reluctant to chastise or discipline me. I can remember only one time when someone seriously called my hand after I misbehaved. I had been rude to Mrs. Gussie Womble one Sunday, and she not only marched straight to Daddy, but she gave him the names of two other ladies I had sassed. Back at home, Daddy did not spank me. Instead, he sat me down for a serious talk, during which I saw how disappointed he was. The next evening, he drove me to the homes of all three ladies, and I had to ring their doorbells and apologize. I did feel bad about disappointing Daddy, but I was really *not* sorry for sassing the women—especially old tattletale Gussie.

Though it might sound like I was an uncaring child, I was not totally heartless. I would never have intentionally hurt another person's feelings (although, in my opinion, teasing and mouthing off to grown-ups didn't quite fall into that category). Admittedly, I was less concerned about the feelings of God and Jesus who, according to my grandmothers, cried when I misbehaved. God seemed so remote and all-powerful that I doubted my snit fits could harm Him. And while I now knew most details of the crucifixion, the event was so ancient that I couldn't muster a great deal of pity for our Savior. To be honest, I felt much sorrier for Buddy Holly, Ritchie Valens, and The Big Bopper, who were killed in a 1959 plane crash. And, oh! Those poor space monkeys! Both Russia and America were launching rocket ships with dogs and monkeys inside, and sometimes the animals died. On the TV news, I once saw footage of scientists closing the door of a space capsule while this little monkey stared out the door's window. He had no idea that he was about to be blasted into outer space—perhaps forever—but he still looked so confused and frightened that my heart nearly broke for him.

* * *

Within a few years, I would come to better comprehend and accept Jesus' sacrificial death on the cross; after formally professing my belief, I would be baptized and officially entered into church membership. And while I still had many questions, my theology would not be nearly as tangled as it was when I was six.

For instance, as a first grader, I believed that baptism caused a somewhat strange metamorphosis in those who chose to be immersed. As in most Baptist churches, Wilshire's baptistry was behind the choir loft. Many a time, I watched a white-robed, newly professed Christian descend some steps into the rib-high water. Daddy would gently lower the candidate's upper torso backward . . . and then lift it from the water while quoting this scripture: "Buried with [Christ] through baptism . . . raised . . . [to] walk in newness of life" (Romans 6:4). Except that I heard the last phrase as "*eunuchs* of life." I wasn't really sure what a eunuch was, but I had heard about one in Sunday school, and he didn't seem all that scary or bad. I had certainly never noticed any Wilshire members looking or acting different after being baptized, so if this rite *did* turn you into a eunuch, that was fine by me.

Around this same time, I had my first exposure to "Comparative Religion." As the pastor, Daddy often visited hospitalized church members, and I sometimes tagged along. Since I was too young to go above the first floor, I hung out in the lobby, entertaining myself with books or crayons until he returned. The two hospitals we most frequently visited were Baylor and Saint Paul's. I did not like the latter, which was a Catholic institution and reminded me of those penicillin-bearing nuns back in Lubbock. Saint Paul's lobby was filled with spooky-looking statues of saints, who probably had long hypodermic needles hidden beneath their marble robes. Baylor, on the other hand, was a Baptist hospital. By my reasoning, Baptists were generally nice people . . . and thus they did *not* give shots. Daddy said this wasn't true, but I still maintained that Baptists would never be so cruel to a little child.

I recall a particular conversation that my father and I had one day when we were headed to Saint Paul's. I must have been talking about my "shot" theory, because Daddy said that Catholics, like Baptists, were good people who loved God and Jesus, and who helped others. Even if that was true, I argued, their church services were just plain weird. I had never been to one myself, but my classmate Vanessa Vanderpool *had*. She reported that the preacher wore a dress, the ladies played with their necklaces, and right in the middle of everything, the Popsicle Man showed up and rang a bell.

Daddy did his best to explain the robes, rosaries, and rituals. He told me that Catholic pastors were called "priests," and he said that they sang parts of the service.

"The preacher *sings*?" I asked, incredulous.

I knew that such a practice would be disastrous at Wilshire.

And I reminded Daddy once again that he needed to stand *far* away from the microphone during the hymns, because everyone could *hear* him.

* * *

As a child, I never had a Burning Bush encounter or a mystical revelation from the Almighty, but I *did* learn about God's love as I watched other people . . . including my father. Although Daddy was always willing to answer my theological questions, he never got preachy with me (or with others) or peppered casual conversations with Bible verses. What I saw instead was a pastor who took a deep and sincere interest in the everyday lives of his parishioners, of those outside of our church, and even of total strangers. I watched as my father drove an elderly woman to visit her husband in a nursing home and eavesdropped as he telephoned a child to express concern for her injured pet chicken. I sometimes went with Daddy when he visited the homebound, sick, or bereaved, witnessing the way he tenderly held their hands, prayed, and comforted. I later learned that in the earliest days of desegregation, he bucked Southern Baptist tradition and insisted that Wilshire be open to people of *all* races. My father was not perfect: for one thing, he gave so much of himself to the ministry that he was sometimes short-tempered at home. But he always apologized; and if my naughtiness had been a factor, he—like a gracious God—was quick to reconcile and forgive.

The members of Wilshire also had clay feet. Although the church was spared any major infighting, I would later learn that Daddy sometimes had to deal with petty disagreements, difficult personalities, and the very occasional parishioner whose sins had destroyed a marriage, career, or reputation. (When outsiders complained that churches were full of hypocrites, my father had a standard response: "Come on in—there's room for one more!")

Imperfect as Wilshire's congregation was, they were a prism for God's light and a catalyst of His love. From a young age, I observed these saints and sinners sharing their joys, laughing together, and bearing one another's burdens. And just as they cared for their own, they also reached out to those less fortunate. They gave generously to mission offerings and to the church itself . . . but I was equally impressed when they purchased a washing machine for a needy widow or a new pair of eyeglasses for an impoverished grandfather.

Daddy and I were often on the receiving end of unasked for blessings in the form of material goods, deep discounts, or pro bono services from Wilshire's many professionals. But perhaps the greatest gift the church gave us was the freedom to be ourselves. My father had always deplored the media's portrayal of ministers as dour, stiff-collared, sepulchral-toned pontificators. Fortunately, the folks at Wilshire did not force him into such a mold nor did they demand unrealistic perfection (and they knew better than to put *me* on a pedestal!).

Through the years, Wilshire members reached out to Daddy and me with friendship, compassion, generosity, forgiveness, and unconditional love. And such examples taught me far more than a whole year's worth of Sunday school lessons or sermons.

My father greets parishioners after a service.

Every one of Wilshire's staff members had a role in raising me.

*Daddy clowning around with fellow staff members Bill O'Brien
(Minister of Music) and Bob Feather (Minister of Education).*

33

Secretary

DURING MY 1959 SUMMER VISIT to North Carolina, Uncle Sip took my cousins and me out in the countryside one day to visit a farm. While we were inside the barn, Sip suddenly released a raging, ripsnorting bull from its pen. With this massive creature charging close behind, we three kids managed to vault some wooden slats into another stall. There, we sprawled in the hay-strewn mud with Elsie the Cow staring at us.

Back in Dallas, my second-grade school year began with a social studies unit on "Farms." After my summer experience with Sip and the bull, our classroom display of toy tractors, barns, and plastic animals seemed dull and unrealistically pristine. Compared to the previous year, I would recall very little about second grade except for those farm toys and a middle-aged teacher who left barely a ripple in my memory. Surviving report cards show that I made good progress in all subjects, although this teacher once wrote that "Kathie is often careless with her supplies and frequently forgets her pencil." ("Thank you for bringing this problem to my attention," my father responded. "We will work on correcting it.")

During our years together, Daddy saved nearly every piece of paper related to my school or church activities. Into a large file folder went report cards, invitations to father/daughter picnics, and information sheets about Blue Birds (a junior version of the Camp Fire Girls) and Brownies (a forerunner to the Girl Scouts). I opted to join the former, because I liked their red/white/navy uniforms. My Blue Bird troop met on Wednesday afternoons, and I could then wear my uniform to Wilshire's midweek services and act like a big shot.

The file folder also bulged with dozens of letters that I had written to Daddy. Some were printed in pencil or ink; others I had pecked out on Dorothy Russell's typewriter while my father did whatever grown-ups do in church meetings. All were rife with misspellings and typographical errors. Some were accompanied by drawings—particularly of airplanes, about which I was passionate.

I still daydreamed about my future as an airline stewardess or a nurse, but by age seven, I knew that my *true* calling was to become "Daddy's Secretary." The appeal of such a career was threefold. First, I saw clerical work as a very tangible way in which I could assist my father, keeping his life running as smoothly as it now did with Dorothy's help. Second, I loved all materials and equipment used by secretaries, especially the accoutrements of writing. If I was sometimes negligent about my own school supplies, this was probably because they *bored* me. After all, what lowly pencil could compete with intricate fountain pens or bottles of iridescent blue or black ink? (Green, red, and turquoise hues were also sold, but most users stuck with conservative colors.) I also loved the professional-looking letterhead on Wilshire's stationery; I crookedly rolled these sheets into Dorothy's typewriter and then clacked away with my index fingers. I didn't yet change the machine's ribbon or use carbon sheets to make copies, but I sometimes fiddled with an eraser whose attached brush could whisk stray flecks from the paper. Finally, secretarial work dovetailed with my aptitude for words and language. I rarely composed make-believe stories, but I loved to observe and record the world around me. By the time I was eight, I would be writing voluminous letters to loved ones; at nine, I began a lifelong habit of keeping a diary.

But at seven, almost all of my communiqués were directed to Daddy and contained only three or four sentences. I wasn't quite sure what *other* secretaries wrote about, but my own missives consisted of newsy tidbits, requests for money, and epic professions of love.

* * *

Dear Daddy,

I love you. I want you to be my daddy. I knoe I have said this
befor.
I will give you this letter if you give me a pinny.

* * *

Dear Daddy,

Brenda and her mother want me to go to the zoo and swiming
with them. So you do not have to take me. You can work.

* * *

Dear Daddy,

You dont have to give me a pinny.

* * *

Dear Bruce

I love you. I do not like this trip. I want to be in Dallas. Do you
like this trip? Do you want to be home?

* * *

Dear Daddy,

I love you a lot. But I do not miss you now. But I do miss you
when you are out of town. I need 6¢. I am trying to make this
letter as long as I can. Good By. I love you and I always will
From Kathie McIver

* * *

Dear Daddy

I miss you so much. I love you. I sent this letter befor I left

home so I dont know how my flyt was. It is a long way to
Grandmothers. Do you miss me?

* * *

Dear Bruce

I love you very much. But I do not miss you. I miss you when
you are away. And when I am sleeping. What did you do at
Feloship? Is this a long letter? Never forget that I love you all
the time. Good By. From Kathie McIver
See how fast I can tipe?

* * *

To R.V.E. Bruce McIver,
From Me, Worlds fastist tiper,
Kathie McIver

* * *

Dear Bruce,

I love you. When are you going to give me 6¢? I want to go see
Tom Thumb [the movie].

* * *

Dear Daddy,

I did not know where my gloves were at church. But I found
them. When are you going to give me 6¢? Lets go home cause I
cant think of any thing else to say.

* * *

Dear Bruce,

You do not have to give me 6¢ and you never will.

Wilshire Baptist Church

4316 Abrams Road

Dallas, Texas

Rev. Bruce McIver, *Pastor*
Church Office: TA 4-4531
Residence: TA 7-3439

Dear Daddy

I love you <u>very</u> much.

But I do not miss you now.
  But I do miss you when you are out of town.
You do not have to give me 6¢
But when are you going to put my 50$ in the Bank?
Mail Grand mother and granddaddys letter.
When I gett a 4¢ Stamp.
When aer we going to get our Christmas tree?
We do not go to Biue___ Birds Wed.
Friday week at Blue__birds,   We are going to have
a party. We give gifes to us.
We do not put who it is from.
Do you think my Repot Card was good?
I have yo go now.

    Good by.
I love you

   To R.V.E.   Bruce McIver

From

Miss. Kathie Mc   McIver

    Merry Christmas

34

There's Within My Heart a Melody

There's Joy in our hearts
Because of Christmas . .

and You !

☆

KATHIE and BRUCE McIVER

THROUGH THE YEARS, I had occasionally messed around on Mother's upright piano, her metronome ticking away while I pretended to play "music." The day finally came when my pecking and banging turned into actual tunes, for I began taking lessons in September of 1959. Decades later, I would learn that my Grandparents Withers were paying for the weekly instruction. They had asked Daddy to find a reputable teacher, and he was referred to Mrs. E. J. Hammann, an older woman who lived near my school. Each Tuesday after school, I walked to her house for an enjoyable lesson on her Steinway baby grand.

Although I was a klutz at most everything else, piano-playing came as naturally to me as breathing. From my very first song—"Here we start on middle C/Making music easily!"—I raced through the pieces so quickly that I was soon working out of multiple books. Each Saturday I liked to replay every song I had learned since September. Almost as appealing as the music were the colorful stickers that Mrs. Hammann affixed to each page after I had learned a piece: I earned quite a few autumn leaves, jack-o'-lanterns, Pilgrims, candy canes, and Christmas wreaths.

I still stayed with the Brannons occasionally, but while I always brought my music books, I found it hard to practice on the upright piano in their living room. One of my early pieces had been a song called "Indian Tom-Toms," in which the left hand hammered the same two-note chord over and over. Bo Brannon *loved* that piece. Whenever I tried to practice anything else, he came up behind me and hissed, "No! Play the Tom-Tom song!" If I ignored him, he would punch my arm and threaten to beat me up. More than once I arrived at my piano lesson with a black-and-blue arm and my assigned pieces unrehearsed.

I couldn't imagine ever being as good as Julia Woodrum, one of our church pianists, who could play five and six notes *at the same time.* Every Sunday her arms cascaded up and down the keyboard to create swirling arpeggios and fancy chords while the congregation sang:

> There's within my heart a melody,
> Jesus whispers sweet and low:
> "Fear not, I am with thee, peace, be still,"
> In all of life's ebb and flow.

I often sat in the front pew, where I could watch Anita's high-heeled foot operate the damper pedal. Mrs. Hammann said that I would be able to play like that someday if I just kept practicing and stuck with my lessons. After all, she said, even Van Cliburn had to start *somewhere.*

I knew about Van Cliburn. Every American did—including lots of kids. He was a concert pianist from Kilgore, Texas, who had recently gone over to Russia and won the International Tchaikovsky Piano Concerto Competition. Normally, Americans wouldn't have given a fig about a classical musician. But with the Cold War ratcheting up, U.S. citizens had been elated when Cliburn beat Russian pianists on their own cultural turf. Gloating merged with propaganda, and for the first (and probably last) time ever, our country feted a concert pianist with a ticker-tape parade in New York City.

I had recently overheard my father telling some friends about the time he was preaching a revival in Kilgore. "The pianist for our services," he recalled, "was a curly-headed teenage boy who seemed like a big sissy. His mama was always nearby, and she really had him tied to her apron strings. All of us on the revival team used to snicker and make fun of him behind his back. But by gum"—here Dad slowly shook his head—"could that kid *ever* play the piano!"

At seven, I was not only learning how to read music, but I was also learning how to tell a good story.

35

All Around The Town

Chestnuts roasting on an open fire . . .

Silent night, holy night . . .

You'll wonder where the yellow went
When you brush your teeth with Pepsodent!

CAROLS AND COMMERCIALS jingled through the Chevy's radio as Daddy fiddled with the dial, trying to find a station to his liking. It was Christmas Eve morning in 1959, and the two of us had just left the duplex to run a few errands.

Along Marquita Street, rainbow lights outlined the eaves or windows of several houses. I asked Daddy if we could put lights on the *outside* of our house next year. He mumbled, "Hmm?" and I had to repeat the question. Then he said, "We'll see." He was probably envisioning tangled cords, an upended ladder, and himself sprawled in the juniper bushes. Or maybe his mind was just a million miles away, for he had been much more distracted than usual during the past few days.

At the end of our block we turned south onto Skillman, and began passing residential streets whose names I had memorized: Vanderbilt, Goodwin, Vickery, Llano, Velasco. Daddy continued to navigate the radio, perhaps seeking the latest sports scores. Dallas would not have a pro football team until 1960, when the Cowboys replaced the Dallas Texans. Instead, all attention was on the NFL championship game, in

which the New York Giants would face Johnny Unitas of the Baltimore
Colts. In college football, Texas and Syracuse were scheduled to play
in the upcoming Cotton Bowl.

My father might have finally settled on KRLD, which always relayed
the latest global or national news. The topics on that day could have
concerned most any recent event. During the autumn of 1959, Fidel
Castro had seized control of Cuba's government; North Vietnam had
invaded Korea; and Senator John F. Kennedy had begun planning a
presidential campaign. The last surviving Confederate soldier had died.
Hawaii was now the fiftieth state. The Dodgers won the World Series,
the first Xerox copier was marketed, and American Airlines inaugurated
"jet service" for some transcontinental routes. On a visit to the United
States, Soviet Premier Nikita Khrushchev had been highly miffed at
being denied entrance to Disneyland.

We soon came to the Skillman shopping strip and parked at Brewer's
Drugstore. Daddy needed a few toiletries for our upcoming Christmas
Day trip to Baytown, and I convinced him that I needed a new coloring
book. As we returned to the car with our packages, I glanced somewhat
wistfully at Ashburn's Ice Cream Parlor down on the corner, where
Daddy occasionally took me after Sunday or Wednesday-night church.
The small storefront was as cold and clean as fresh snow.

Dressed in his uniform of a crisp white shirt and paper hat, a young
man always stood behind a gleaming showcase. My teeth would chatter
as I watched him draw a silver dipper through tubs of confections, trying
to decide whether I should forego a scoop of chocolate-chip for the
more exotic lime sherbet or pink-striped peppermint.

Today, however, our next stop would be Baylor Hospital, where my
father planned to visit a couple of patients who were too sick to be
discharged for the holidays. We turned left onto La Vista Drive and
headed south through one of the city's older neighborhoods ("old," in
Dallas, generally referred to any building that had stood for at least fifty
years). Then Daddy turned onto Gaston Avenue. Paralleling Gaston was
Swiss Avenue: a broad, tree-canopied boulevard whose early twentieth-
century mansions were set far back from the street. In one of these grand
old homes, Daddy and I had shared several Thanksgiving dinners with

Dr. and Mrs. Walter Patton, who were Wilshire members.

Like Swiss Avenue, Gaston had once been lined with older homes, but many were now partitioned into apartments or boarding houses. Others had been razed, replaced by swanky apartment complexes whose names—Bali Hai, Sand 'n' Surf, Shangri-La—made residents think they were in the South Seas instead of on a landlocked prairie. Our church's membership included many young single adults, and quite a few of them lived in those Gaston Avenue complexes. As always, I was trolling for any unattached woman who would agree to cast her lot with us. When we drove past the El Tropicana, I suggested that Daddy might want to date two of its tenants: secretary Rosemary Jones or schoolteacher Ernestine Griggs.

Daddy mumbled, "We'll see," which was his standard response whenever I brought up marital prospects.

A few blocks farther down we turned into Baylor's parking lot, and my father guided the Chevy into a space reserved for CLERGY. Earlier in the day I had nagged Daddy to let me open just one present, because no—I didn't think I *could* hold my horses until evening. He had shuffled through the gifts piled beneath our tree and handed me a flat package. Inside was a brand-new book, *The Story of Babar*, which I had brought along lest I grew bored with errand-running. Now, with book in hand, I followed Daddy into the George W. Truett Building, named for the renowned pastor of Dallas's First Baptist Church. Baylor would eventually mushroom into a medical megapolis, but at the time Truett was its primary facility.

Inside Baylor's lobby, whose only statue was a dignified bust of Dr. Truett, Daddy fished a nickel from his pocket and told me that he would be back as soon as he could. As soon as he disappeared behind the elevator doors, I walked over to the gift shop and blew my coin on a roll of cherry Life Savers. Then I found a marble bench, where I sat for the next half hour, crunching candy as I read about the orphaned baby elephant who grows up to find love.

By the time my father returned, I had finished the rather lengthy book. *Twice.*

This surprised Daddy, but he was actually getting used to my knack for speed-reading. During the fall term, I had participated in a school-wide contest to see who could read the most library books. I didn't win first prize, but my very respectable grand total was thirty-seven, some of which (as Daddy liked to brag) were written at a fourth-grade level.

It was close to noon when we left the hospital, and our stomachs growled. I suggested that we get some lunch at a nearby Waffle House or maybe Sammy's Italian restaurant on Ross Avenue. Instead, Daddy proposed that we go to Keller's Drive-In and maybe pick up Claire on the way, which I thought was a splendid idea. We backtracked to the Balls' house on Llano, and Ruby agreed that Claire could come with us, so long as she was back in time to go visit her Mee-Maw.

A few minutes later, Claire scrambled into the back seat, where I eagerly joined her. Before Daddy had driven two blocks, we girls were bouncing our rumps on the back seat and singing Alvin and the Chipmunks' "The Chipmunk Song (Christmas Don't Be Late)," which was a big hit. Whenever I heard the record at the Brannons' house, Bo told me that *Sis* was singing, and I believed him. Claire and I now squeaked the words in little "mouse" voices, springing up and down to the rhythm, until Daddy told us to simmer down because we were making him a nervous wreck.

We tried, but it was hard. Not only were we excited about Christmas but also about the prospect of eating at Keller's. Fast-food chains were still scarce in Dallas, so it was quite a treat for us to frequent one of the city's most popular drive-ins.

Our church was not far from Keller's, and Daddy said that he wanted to swing by the office to check his mail and messages. This was long before the era of answering machines, but a secretary might have fielded recent calls and left memos on Daddy's desk. A few minutes later, having zigzagged over to Abrams Road, we pulled into the church parking lot. Except for one or two cars, it was empty. Most staff members were gone for the holiday, and Wilshire would not hold Christmas Eve services until several years later.

Normally, the staff stayed quite busy, for our church was still growing apace. With membership topping 1,200, the modest sanctuary and educational facilities were strained beyond capacity. Two Sunday-morning worship services continued to be held, and several Sunday school classes were now forced to meet off-site. Playground equipment rose from the large empty field, but by springtime, a row of surveyors' flags would flutter across a back portion, marking the ground to be broken for yet more expansion.

Once out of the car, Claire and I raced to the swings, ignoring Daddy's caveat that he would "only be a minute." There, we pumped ourselves high while singing some favorite songs: "Jingle Bells," "Away in a Manger," "The Purple People Eater," and "Jesus Was Born in the City of David." The latter we had learned in our Primary Choir, which had performed during a recent church service. For some long-forgotten reason, I had refused to participate. A teacher told me that we would later be rewarded with a shiny red apple, but I retorted that if I wanted an apple, all I had to do was open our refrigerator and get one from the vegetable bin.

A few minutes later, Daddy called to Claire and me from a side door, his arms overflowing with packages that had been left on his desk. Most contained homemade treats—cookies and cakes, candies and nuts, jellies and breads—that would soon join the other edible gifts on our kitchen counters. Claire and I were happy to help him carry the treats back to the car.

After we left the church, Daddy turned north onto Abrams Road. After crossing Lovers Lane (another thoroughfare that had retained its rural name), he stopped at a red light on Northwest Highway. Off to the west, the Park Cities and Preston Hollow neighborhoods were rapidly expanding; to the east, new houses were springing up in what would become the massive Lake Highlands subdivision. Northwest Highway itself was now lined with far more car dealerships, barbershops, dry cleaners, and restaurants than when we had moved to Dallas in 1956. Nevertheless, had we continued straight north, the city limits would have quickly seemed far behind us.

* * *

That was the direction Daddy and I had taken a few days earlier, when we drove out to Restland Cemetery to look at the holiday wreath

*My friend Claire is in the center, and the two of us are
watching a mirimba player at a church fellowship.*

that friends always placed on Mother's grave. For that excursion, we
had followed Greenville Avenue, which would one day be a congested
artery but was currently just a two-lane road that passed empty fields
and even an occasional farm. Restland lay a few miles beyond Northwest
Highway, a bucolic enclave surrounded by undeveloped prairie land.
Daddy had turned into the main entrance and slowly wound through
a maze of tree-shaded lanes. In some ways, the place didn't seem like a
regular cemetery, because all of Restland's grave markers lay flat. But
we could still see vases of flowers dotting grassy areas, each partitioned
by neatly trimmed hedges or trees and designated by its own roadside
placard: Garden of Memories, Serenity, Whispering Waters, Baby Land.

Daddy had stopped the car at a sign that read "Woodlands," and the
two of us got out. We crossed to a far end of the section, near a border
of closely packed trees. My father went straight to Mother's small, flat
headstone. Off to the side, a tripod supported a large green wreath
festooned with red bows and golden bells. Daddy fondled a sprig of
evergreen, said something about the arrangement being "very nice,"
and reminded me that we needed to thank Mr. and Mrs. Coker for
providing it.

On this beautiful day, live oaks swayed in a light breeze and a brook burbled behind the trees (two decades later, that thick curtain of oaks would mute traffic from the new LBJ Freeway, which would pass less than a mile away). I cannot recall what, if anything, Daddy and I talked about as we stood at the gravesite. For the most part, I was still emotionally disconnected from my mother's death: like a distant observer, I viewed it as something that was vaguely sad and far away . . . but I felt no specific grief nor did I consciously miss her. As for Daddy, he willingly responded to my growing curiosity about caskets, mausoleums, and funerals (I had never been to one, but Daddy had conducted a fair number of services for older Wilshire members). Still, when it came to Mother, Daddy never discussed his personal—or our mutual—grief. He rarely reminisced about her, perhaps fearing that this would hinder the progress we had made in "getting on with our lives."

And for better or worse, we had done just that. I have no idea what Daddy had been thinking as he and I walked back to the car on that day. But being a typical seven-year-old, my thoughts had probably already turned from cemeteries to sleigh bells . . . and to the toys that I hoped Santa was preparing in his workshop.

*   *   *

Claire and I were now deep into this very topic as we waited for the green light on Northwest Highway. For the next couple of minutes we discussed the merits of Easy-Bake Ovens and Patti Playpal dolls. We critiqued a machine that molded plastic trinkets for charm bracelets (a rip-off that reputedly broke after two days), a child-sized typewriter (I had a *real* one in Dorothy's office), and Hasbro's Sno-Cone Maker (Daddy said no).

When the light changed, my father turned right on Northwest Highway and almost immediately pulled into Keller's, where he nosed into a parking space. A waitress appeared outside the Chevy, and Daddy interrupted us girls long enough to take lunch orders.

A few minutes later, the carhop hooked a tray onto Daddy's lowered window, and he began distributing hamburgers, Tater Tots, and mugs of root beer. For the next little while, Claire and I were relatively quiet, occupied with unwrapping and eating our food. Then I lobbed a Tater Tot, which bounced off the seat back and landed in Claire's root beer. I looked at her and spoke two words that were guaranteed to send us into gales of laughter: "Funny Ball!" The phrase was a private joke, for we were the only two people on the planet who could visualize that stupid little ball caroming all over Claire's bedroom and landing in the oddest places.

We hooted and clutched our stomachs.

"Banana Man!" Claire shot back after she had caught her breath. The image of Captain Kangaroo's skanky, falsetto-voiced clown triggered another spasm of hysteria.

"Toady Comody!" I snorted, and Claire choked on her food.

"Please, girls!" said Daddy. "We're *eating*."

He finally distracted us by describing his boyhood Christmases. He told us how he selected and chopped down his own tree from some nearby woods. He recalled his delight over finding hard candies and a single orange in his stocking. When he reenacted his failure as one of the singing "We Three Kings," Claire laughed so hard that she fell over on top of me, and we squashed a loaf of Mrs. Viola Hickerson's cranberry-nut bread.

Daddy told us to settle down, but he didn't sound all that mad. Then he said that we needed to finish our food so Claire could get back home in time to go visit her Mee-Maw. He asked us to pick up the Tater Tots we had dropped on the floor. And a half century later, I can still hear his voice reminding us to use our napkins because we had mustard all *over* our faces and hands.

36

Dear Santa

BACK AT THE duplex, I hunkered beneath our Christmas tree with my new coloring book, occasionally reaching over to adjust an ornament. This was the year I had finally agreed to a traditional green pine, and I did have to admit that it looked very pretty and smelled even better than the spray-painted ones. While coloring, I daydreamed about the three items I hoped to find beneath the tree on Christmas morning:

- A geography book
- A Toni Home Permanent doll
- A doll-sized playpen

My book request had come about because I wanted to imitate Wilshire's teenage girls, who often brought their school texts to Wednesday-evening activities. Almost always, these tomes were wrapped in brown-paper covers that bore the school's name and a picture of its mascot. A few teens attended Hillcrest or other high schools, but the majority went to Woodrow Wilson. A few weeks earlier, I had asked Peggy Jo Plunkett what one of her school books was about, and she said, "Geography." I rolled the syllables around on my tongue—*gee-OG-rah-fee*—and found the sound delectable. I had no idea what the word meant but associated it with penny loafers, football "spirit ribbons" that you pinned to your sweater, teeth braces, and other trappings of teenage girls. I could not *wait* to become a teenager myself and had been pestering Daddy to buy me a geography book. When he procrastinated,

I sent my request to the North Pole. (I *would* receive a type of geography book the following morning, although it was written for grade-schoolers and titled *Children of Far-Off Lands*. It was not at all heavy, nor did it have a Woodrow Wilson Wildcat on the cover. But it was still a good book, and I liked it well enough.)

Along with the book, I felt sure that Santa was also bringing the Toni Home Permanent doll. I was not normally attracted to fashion dolls (such as the just-released Barbie), and I cared not a whit for stylish clothes. But I *was* fascinated by TV ads that showed Toni's miniature hair rollers, itsy curling papers, and bottles of fake solution. This would be the first year that I hadn't asked for a baby doll—a decision I feared I might later regret. To compensate, my third "Santa Request" was for a doll-sized playpen that I had seen at Sears, which I could use for my other babies.

Thus caught up in fantasies and waxy colors, I passed one of the longest afternoons of the year. I don't recall what Daddy and I ate for supper, but even if it was our usual poached eggs or beef potpies, the desserts filling our kitchen counters would have made the meal seem sumptuous. Soon, darkness fell, and while the radio spun holiday tunes, we dove into the loot beneath our tree. My father might have sat beside me, but since it was increasingly difficult for him to sit/squat/kneel on the floor, he likely stayed in his contour chair while I brought his packages to him. Someone had helped me purchase my own gift for Daddy, although I don't remember what it might have been. From relatives, close friends, and even a few church members, he probably received shirts, ties, cuff links, and maybe a nice ballpoint pen that didn't need to be refilled with bottled ink. And this may have been the year that his brother Sip, with unintended irony, sent him Dale Carnegie's best-selling book *How to Win Friends and Influence People*.

My memory is equally vague about most of my own presents, guessing that they included games, craft kits, clothes, and Tinker Bell toiletries. I do know that I asked for and received a pair of footed pajamas: such sleepwear was far too babyish for a seven-year-old, but I missed the sensation of being totally swaddled from head to toe and feared that I would soon outgrow the largest size.

However, my memory is clear about one final gift lying beneath the tree, almost buried under discarded ribbons and bows and shredded wrapping paper. Daddy had brought it home from the church office a couple of days earlier, where an elderly member (whose name I have long forgotten) had dropped it off. One afternoon, I had squeezed the package. Its unboxed contents felt soft, hinting at something totally useless—like clothing. Busy as I now was with new playthings, I had pretty much forgotten about this last gift until Daddy pointed it out from across the room.

With no great expectations, I reached back under the tree and extracted the tissue-wrapped, loaf-sized package. Placing it in my lap, I loosened its ribbon, which easily slipped off. I thumb-punched the tissue paper and saw fabric: something pink and powder-puff soft. I wondered if it might be slippers or a knitted scarf . . . and then I tore the paper away to reveal a beautiful store-bought doll.

A *baby* doll!

Only eight inches long, she was swathed in a pink flannel sleeper and lay on a matching, lace-trimmed blanket. With her eyes squeezed shut and little fists tightly clenched, she looked exactly like a sleeping newborn. Then I discovered a windup key on her back and gave it a few turns. The doll began to languidly stretch as Brahms's "Lullaby" chimed from a hidden music box.

I thought I had been transported straight to heaven.

From across the room, Daddy asked me what I had gotten. "A doll," I told him, my tone as understated as if the package had contained a pile of underwear. Having long ago learned to suppress many of my emotions, I was not a child who turned cartwheels or squealed with delight upon receiving a nice gift. But as I quietly cradled the musical baby doll, I was bursting with silent joy.

＊　＊　＊

Later that night—after Daddy and I had discarded crumpled wrapping paper, set Santa's milk and cookies on the piano bench, carted my new toys and clothes upstairs, and crammed some last-minute items into my suitcase . . . after I had donned the yellow-footed pajamas, said my prayers, kissed Daddy goodnight, and then tossed and turned because I was too keyed up to sleep . . . after all of this, I knelt at my bedroom window and improvised a favorite carol to our city's skyline glittering in the distance.

> O little town of Daa-llas,
> How still we see thee lie.

It didn't matter that no sheep grazed along Central Expressway or that the nearest lowing cattle were over in the Fort Worth stockyards. For this was *still* Christmas Eve: a magical time when angels sang, animals talked, and dolls moved with the turn of a key. It was a time when I could spy a star twinkling above the Republic National Bank Building and fully believe it to be the *very* one that had guided the wise men to Baby Jesus.

Like Jesus, my new doll had no crib for a bed, so I had laid her on the lid of my toy chest. Actually, it wasn't exactly true that she had *no* place to sleep. When I was a toddler, Daddy Mac had cobbled a doll bed for me, which I still had. It was not a crib, just a small wooden bed with an inset vinyl chair cushion for a mattress. While I appreciated the effort my grandfather had put into it, the piece was not especially colorful or pretty, and I mainly used it as a resting spot for stuffed animals. But the playpen I had requested from Santa would be truly lovely, with pink rails accented by pale-blue spinning balls. Granted, it wasn't a true crib, but it would still be a perfect place for the new baby to sleep. And Santa would appreciate that the playpen was collapsible and would easily fit into his sack.

Some of my classmates had been saying that there was no such thing as Santa Claus—that it was really your *parents* who put toys under the tree. I wasn't yet ready to give up my long-held belief in elves and reindeer, but I *had* been thinking about some of my friends' objections. For instance, how could Santa go around the entire world and visit every house in a single night?

As a seasoned air traveler, I hit upon the most logical solution: the sleigh was powered by *jet engines*. I had run this theory past Daddy, and he said that if Russia could blast Sputnik into outer space, then he reckoned Santa could also use rockets or jets.

I was thinking about this as I continued to gaze out the window, wondering if I might be able to spot the sleigh as it approached Dallas. For now, all I could see was a single stationary star above skyscrapers.

But . . . *wait!*

What was that red blinking thing off to the right? Could it be Rudolph's nose? I watched for a few more seconds . . . until the light climbed higher in the sky, turned away, and grew smaller. Disappointed, I figured that had just been a plane taking off from Love Field. Still, the scene did inspire me to compose another carol:

> Jingle bells, jingle bells,
> Jingle all the way!
> Oh, what fun it is to ride
> In a Delta Airlines sleigh!

While I kept vigil at my window, Daddy might have been watching TV down in the living room or listening to carols on the radio. Perhaps he was straightening up the kitchen, maybe enjoying a slice of some parishioner's banana-nut bread.

But I also wonder if, on that Christmas Eve, my father might have taken some moments to simply meditate . . . to ponder the end of another year and the end of a decade that had brought so many cataclysmic changes to his life. Although Daddy rarely wrote in his journal anymore, he *had* penned several entries through the years. I wonder if he might have leafed through the blue-bound ledger and reflected upon some of his more recent musings:

DAD'S JOURNAL
....

These past few years have changed my entire perspective on life. Most of us live on a shallow, superficial

level, and know very little of the deeper experiences
the Lord has for us. In some ways I'm grateful for this
"stewardship of sorrow." It has taught me some lessons I
needed to learn, and I doubt that I would have faced up to
them had not Jean died.

* * *

I'm afraid that I'm prone to leave the thoroughfares of
life and travel the well-worn path of distraction. Finances,
security, health, social life. Shall I seek to find a companion,
a mate, a Mother for Kathie, or is it the Lord's will for us to
be as we are? I do not know the answers. But Lord, I would
not make a mistake for all the world. I would not get ahead
of your plan and purpose.

* * *

Lord, Make Kathie strong and healthy, loving and
gentle, sincere and dedicated. Bless her personality that
it may reflect Thy love and peace. Grant to me, Lord, the
assurance that she will be watched over by Thy spirit. Help
me to be the kind of father that she can love and respect—
and that you can bless.

* * *

Upstairs, I remained at my post, singing and scanning the night
sky. Finally, just as my knees were beginning to hurt, another light slid
into the window frame, this one clearly *descending*. I couldn't say for
sure that it was a sleigh, but as each red pulse brought it closer, I grew
jittery with excitement.

Knowing that it would be best for me to be fast asleep when Santa
opened our front door, I stood up, turned back the bedcovers, and
climbed between the sheets. If the light was Rudolph's nose, I knew that
the sleigh would probably stop first at Claire's house . . . then Martha's
. . . then mine.

Or would it?

Santa had never failed me in the past, so long as I kept my wish list down to three or four items that were not overly extravagant. But now, a niggling doubt threatened my peace of mind. I began to remember first one transgression and then another . . . until I could catalog a whole year's worth of naughty behavior. I recalled how I had bribed my Sunday school classmates to give me their Bible-verse ribbons. How I had sassed Gussie Womble and refused to sing with the Primary Choir at church or pledge allegiance to the school flag. And then there was that time I yanked a bath mat out from under Cousin Leslie just as she got out of the tub.

It was probably these worries that spurred my next action. I climbed out of bed, and padded out to the landing. I usually liked the scritchy sound of my pajama's plastic feet, but now I was trying to be as quiet as possible. At the top of the staircase, I stood for a moment and listened. Daddy was not watching television, reading, or writing in his journal. Instead, it sounded like he was talking to someone. Sitting down on the top stair, I softly butt-bumped down each riser, trying to make myself invisible until the last possible moment. I skirted the heating grate and edged into the living room.

Daddy was indeed sitting in his contour chair with the rotary telephone in his lap. He covered the receiver long enough to ask what on earth I was doing out of bed. I muttered that I had something I needed to do. Instead of grilling me, Daddy resumed his conversation, which consisted of some chuckles and whispers. I walked past him to the desk, where I located a notepad. Opening a drawer, I contemplated a bottle of fountain-pen ink. (It was the same cobalt blue as those stained glass windows back in San Marcos, but I would not consciously make this connection for many years. Instead, I simply saw it as an enchanting color that seemed linked to something far, far back in my past.) I really wanted to use a fountain pen but didn't relish being scolded for making a mess. And I also knew that I needed to hurry because Santa was rocketing ever closer to our duplex.

Settling for a pencil from the same drawer, I bent over the notepad and printed:

Dear Santa,

I've been good.

From Kathie McIver

I tore the paper from the notepad and carried it over to the piano bench, where I had already left a glass of milk and a plate of Mrs. Sylvia Arnold's star-shaped cookies. I placed the note beside the cookies.

I had started toward the stairs when a sudden afterthought caused me to pause. With pencil still in hand, I returned to the piano-bench note, where I knelt to add a final sentence:

And please put something for my daddy.

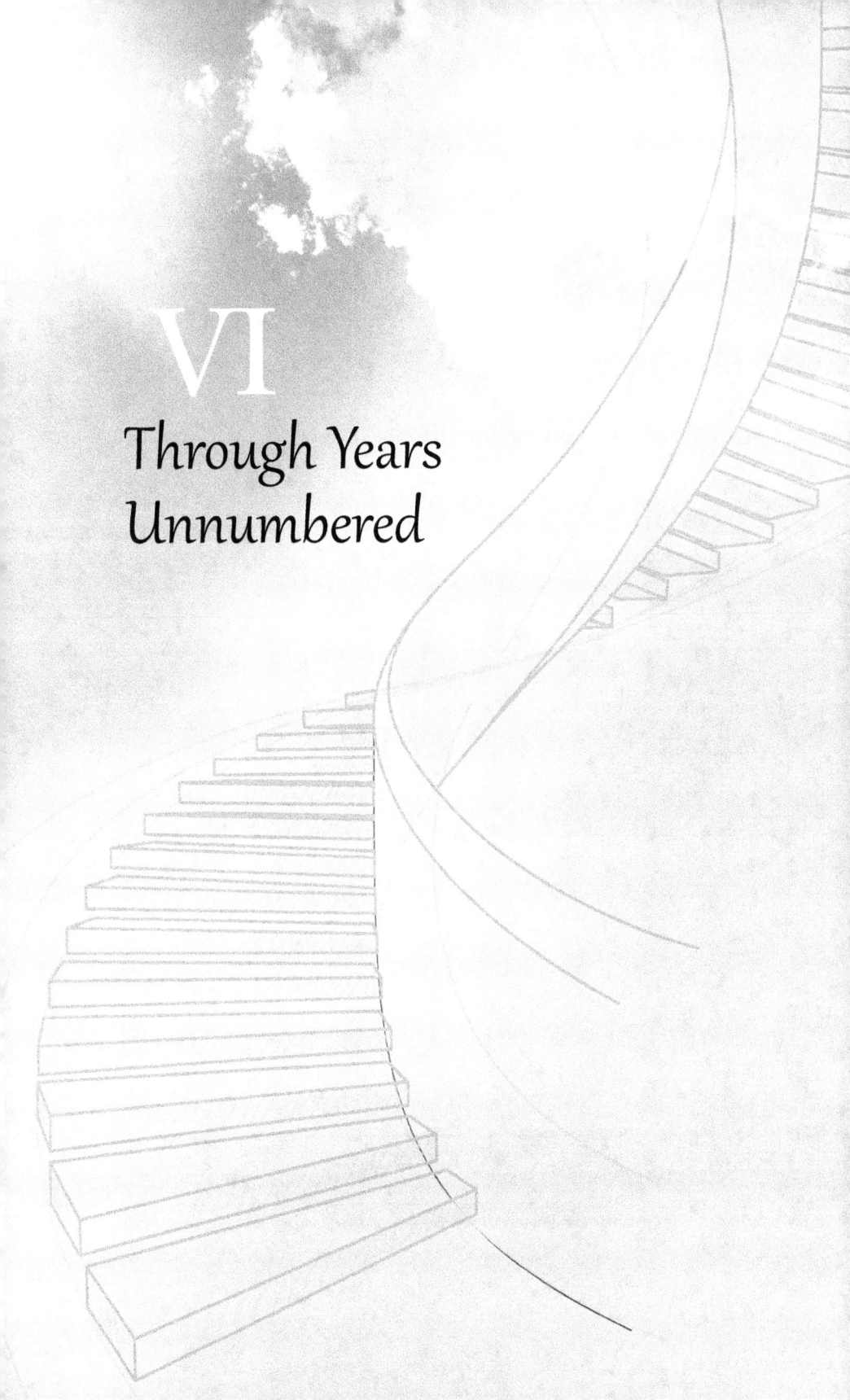

VI
Through Years
Unnumbered

37

We Are Family

ON CHRISTMAS EVE OF 1959, Santa *did* bring something for Daddy—and for me as well. Her name was Lawanna Jane House, and she swooped into our lives in the twinkling of an eye.

Two weeks earlier, a friend had tricked Daddy into a blind date with Lawanna, a twenty-five-year-old student at Southwestern Seminary. Yes, I recognized that my father had been more distracted than usual, but I had no clue that he had fallen hopelessly in love or was running up our phone bill with long-distance calls to Fort Worth. Nor did I know that on Christmas Eve, he had phoned Lawanna at her parents' house in Alabama . . . and proposed.

After accepting, an equally lovestruck Lawanna soon returned to Dallas, where she and Daddy spent their second date going to see the movie *Ben-Hur* and their third watching a New Year's Day football game at the Cotton Bowl.

When Daddy sprang the news that I would finally be getting a mother, I immediately sat down and wrote my Grandparents Withers:

Dear Grandmother and Granddaddy,

Guess what? We are getting married!

I forgot to tell them my new mom's name because I barely knew it myself, nor did I know much else about her. Daddy had arranged for Lawanna to babysit me one evening so that we could become better

Lawanna Jane House

acquainted, and I liked her as well as I did any sitter.

I was quite excited over wedding preparations and was fitted for a turquoise junior bridesmaid dress.

The February wedding took place at Wilshire, officiated by the patriarchal Dr. Forrest Feezor, a retired pastor whom my father greatly admired.

Immediately after Dad and Lawanna returned from their honeymoon to Padre Island, we moved into a somewhat larger rental house on Martel Avenue, a few blocks north of the duplex. Our old living room furniture was given to Annie Kaye (a romance with Denver never worked out, but she *did* end up marrying another Wilshire custodian).

I felt no particular sentiment over losing my birth mother's furniture. I was too excited about our new streamlined sofa and sleek, contemporary tables and chairs. *Contemporary* was a word that I quickly learned from Lawanna, and it could not have been more appropriate. After all, "we three" had gotten married at the beginning of a brand-new decade during which spaceships sat poised on launch pads and Jackie Kennedy would soon make Mamie Eisenhower seem frumpy and

I am standing next to Lawanna as "we" get married. Why am I glum? I am tired, my feet hurt, and I want some cake!

obsolete. The 1950s were over, and Lawanna was the perfect person to steer us into a new era.

Our Martel Avenue house had been built decades earlier, but everything in it seemed modern—from the wall-to-wall carpet to the console stereo, a wedding gift from Wilshire's congregation. Lawanna brought music back into our lives, augmenting our scant record collection with lush melodies from the Mantova Chamber Orchestra as well as soundtracks from such relatively recent movies as *The King and I* and *South Pacific*. Even now, I cannot think of the Martel house without hearing an exuberant "Shall We Dance?" or a dreamy "Bali Hai."

Daddy and I were also pleased to discover that Lawanna was an excellent cook of both country-style meals and more exotic dishes.

* * *

All of this might sound like a happily-ever-after ending for our family . . . and for this memoir.

But rest assured that life was hardly a fairy tale during our early days as a new family.

Sometimes Lawanna and I got along.

Much of the time we did *not.*

At nearly eight years old, I had spent over three years dreaming up an Ideal Mother who, like June Cleaver, would coddle me through every waking moment and croon me to sleep at night. What I got instead was an often flustered and frazzled Lucille Ball who would soon be pea green with morning sickness.

In fairness to Lawanna, she was confronting challenges that tested her own illusions of domestic bliss. Back in November of 1959, she had been a spiritually fervent but fun-loving bachelorette; mere weeks away from earning a graduate degree in Religious Education, she was eager to work as a church youth director. Less than six months later, she had married a widower ten years her senior (Dad was thirty-five; Lawanna, twenty-five), moved to a new house and city, become a preacher's wife, inherited a bratty seven-year-old . . . and almost immediately gotten pregnant.

Lawanna was not only burdened by these stressors, but she arrived on our doorstep with few parenting skills or positive role models: while she and her own mother loved each other, their relationship had always been contentious, and sparks usually flew when they got together. That did not mean that my new mother lacked love or affection. But although a maternal instinct *did* lie deep within her heart, expressing it was a hit-or-miss affair.

With me, it was all too often a "miss." The reasons for this were complex, but one of the most obvious was a simple clash of personalities. Lawanna and I were like oil and water. I tended to be morose and moody. ("Are we sure she's not *Sip's* child?" my parents would ask themselves.) By contrast, Lawanna was a high-spirited whirl of manic energy. And while I repressed my feelings, my new mom easily vented hers. Thin-skinned, I interpreted *any* yelling, scolding, snapping, or criticism as blatant rejection.

We squabbled over everything from my refusal to eat vegetables to whether the ruffles on my panties should be worn in the front or back.

Despite such tensions and fumbles, I *do* credit both Daddy and Lawanna for helping the three of us bond as a family, especially during those earliest months. We enjoyed outings, filmed home movies, took a cross-country road trip, got a dog. Daddy even tried to institute family devotions at breakfast: that lasted about two weeks, until Lawanna and I got so tickled over an Old Testament guy named "Peleg" that Daddy finally closed the Bible and gave up.

In such ways, we McIvers strove to carve out a new family unit. During the early months of 1960, the three of us groped, stumbled, backtracked, fell on our faces, and occasionally hit pay dirt as we felt our way down an unfamiliar road, unaided by any professional advice or "how-to" manuals. But through sharing new experiences and creating our first "family" memories, we slowly began to meld.

For the first few weeks of their marriage, I had called my new mom either "Lawanna" or, more often, nothing at all. One spring day, my parents and I were strolling through downtown Dallas. I lagged behind on the sidewalk because I had been suddenly enthralled by a store-window display. Whatever it was excited me so much that I raced toward my parents, crying, "Mama! Daddy! Come look at this!"

No one made a big deal out of it (which would have embarrassed me), but Lawanna noted the date in her wedding book and wrote, "Kathie called me 'Mama' today!"

She would later recall the exact moment when she knew that she had fully accepted me as her daughter. It occurred shortly after I began third grade. Noticing how I squinted at the blackboard, a teacher advised my parents to take me to an eye doctor. Less than one week later, I left an ophthalmologist's office with a diagnosis of "nearsightedness" and a prescription for glasses. Later that same day, my parents were trying to determine from whom I had inherited my bad eyes.

"I dunno," mused Daddy. "Two of my uncles *did* go blind, but that might have been from bad hooch back during Prohibition."

Lawanna was thoughtful for a moment and then said—as serious as mud—"Well, I can't recall any of the Houses or Gorhams needing anything stronger than reading glasses, so I know she didn't get it from *my* side of the family."

38

Growing Pains

IN THE SUMMER OF 1960, my parents announced that I was going to be a big sister. As a younger child, I might have been resentful, but at eight, I was overjoyed.

During the next months, I vicariously participated in nearly every aspect of my sibling's arrival. Mom answered my facts-of-life questions and let me open gifts at a baby shower; together, we threaded satin ribbons through a bassinet, prepared a layette, and discussed names. I eventually learned so much about pregnancy and childbirth (the details of which I freely shared with both friends and perfect strangers) that one of the neighborhood mothers wouldn't let me play with her daughter anymore.

Shannon Paige was born in January of 1961. "Are you sure they gave you the right one?" I asked Mom when I first saw my sister's red, squinched face. But I was soon enamored with this living doll, who smelled of warm milk and talcum powder, and who fit so snugly into my arms as I sat in an easy chair.

When the baby was a few weeks old, we dressed her in a crocheted outfit and shawl and took her to church for the first time. Proud as punch, I was allowed to carry my sister down Wilshire's hallway to a just-completed educational wing, where she would be the first infant "displayed" in the nursery's brand-new maple cradle.

In April of 1962, just as I was beginning to teach a toddling Shannon her nursery rhymes and ABCs, our family grew to five with the birth of Maureen, who was nicknamed "Renie."

With my sister Shannon

By then, we had purchased a newer three-bedroom house on Rutgers Drive—still close to the church but in another school district. Claire and her family moved to Fort Worth, but I made other close friends at Dan D. Rogers Elementary School and at Wilshire, whose membership steadily increased. I continued to take piano lessons and was active in Blue Birds and other church organizations.

Once my sisters were born, I took care of them so proficiently that babysitters were almost unnecessary. Mom needed every bit of help she could get. She now had two babies in diapers (*cloth* diapers that had to be wrung out, laundered, and then dried on a backyard clothesline). Even worse was that the girls were almost constantly sick with one thing or another, and they generously shared every sniffle, virus, and ear infection. On one memorable day when they were toddlers, they shared a bottle of baby aspirin. It was nearly impossible for Mom to single-handedly take both girls to the pediatrician, so I often came along to help tote diaper bags and babies.

In fact, I so often lugged babies on my hip that by the age of ten, I had nearly thrown it out of joint. But my parents were even more concerned about my shoulders, which had developed a severe forward slump. An orthopedist could find no obvious cause for this deformity and simply assigned daily exercises. I rarely did them, but within a year or so, the problem resolved on its own.

In hindsight, I think that I was experiencing "growing pains," both physically and psychologically. An early onset of puberty had caused me to suddenly shoot up a head taller than most of my nine- and ten-year-old friends. Self-conscious, I deliberately stooped so that my height would be more in line with that of my peers. Psychologically, I sensed that my childhood was rapidly receding; like someone dangling from a cliff top, I hung on for dear life, clutching at anything that might hold adolescence at bay. Although I had sometimes yearned to be a teenager, this was mainly because I wanted to emulate those Wilshire girls who still fawned over me; in truth, a much stronger part of me longed to remain a little girl.

My over-the-top regression involved moving a few of my sisters' toddler toys into my bedroom and writing reams of poems about fairies and elves. I certainly didn't believe in the creatures and normally gave them little thought. But I was creating a facade—both for myself and others—whose message was clear: fairies belonged to the world of children. And despite my physical growth spurt and big-sister duties, I was *still* a child. (It would be another decade before we discovered the 1953 tape recording, and I heard my mother's voice: "What do you do when you go to Sleepytown? Can you say, 'Play with the fairies?'" At the time, I literally gasped, "My Lord, *she* put those creatures into my head!" While I had no memory of the Sleepytown scenario, I recognized that on a deeply subconscious level, I had never forgotten it.)

I hung around with Debbie Ferguson, whose tastes were as babyish as mine. Debbie was an adopted only child whose overprotective mother made a big fuss over her skinned knees and taped her crayoned pictures to the refrigerator. She dressed her daughter in pinafores and buckled the straps on her Sunday shoes, even though Debbie was quite capable of doing this herself (for that matter, both of us were getting too old for pinafores and Mary Jane shoes). Mrs. Ferguson was the kind of woman who made me want to hork and roll my eyes. But at the same time, I secretly craved her nurturing . . . for I was getting far too little of it at my own house.

This is no great family secret. In later years, my parents would freely confess that during those chaotic "early" days, their attention was so focused on babies and illnesses (including their own—Mom suffered from debilitating migraines, while Dad was in constant pain), their time and energy so sapped by church duties, their household so often in disarray, that there was almost nothing left over for me. Nor was it apparent that I *needed* attention: independent and self-sufficient, I never had to be reminded to do my homework or practice the piano, and I could easily amuse myself with a Nancy Drew mystery book or a solo game of Parcheesi. The latter I played while listening to my parents' record of Tchaikovsky's *1812 Overture*. According to my self-made rules, the goal of the game was to get all four colors of men around the board before the kettledrum "cannons" went off in the symphony's finale. If I failed to do this, then—by my reckoning—Russia would drop an atomic bomb on Dallas.

We children of the Cold War could easily get our adrenaline pumping with such not-so-far-fetched fantasies.

39

Turmoil And Grace

By the time I was eleven, I had done a 180-degree turn and was finally ready to become a preteen. I now listened to Top 40 hits, wore penny loafers, and tried in vain to roll my hair into a bouffant "bubble" or perfectly symmetrical "flip." I swooned over The Beatles and scorned adults who had never heard of The Kinks or Herman's Hermits.

Lawanna and I continued to bicker on a daily basis. As the Queen of Passive-Aggression, I found powerful weapons in my bad attitudes, silence, facial expressions, and snide quips. Hurtful words were lobbed back and forth.

And where was Daddy at those times? Well, he was busy with church duties or perhaps out in the small office attached to our freestanding garage. He was often tired, stressed, and in physical pain. If he walked into the house during a verbal skirmish, he didn't care *who* started it or *what* the issue was: he wanted the bickering stopped. NOW!

Despite these stresses, my adolescence was filled with close friendships and many happy times. I participated in Camp Fire Girls, choral groups, church activities, and summer camps; at fourteen, I joined the drill team at Ben Franklin Junior High; along with eighty other girls, I donned a red satin short-skirted uniform and marched, danced, and high-kicked across football fields on Friday nights. My appearance had also improved with the help of contact lenses and orthodontic braces.

Although I enjoyed social activities, I was a voracious reader and still treasured quiet time in my bedroom. I never developed an interest in

The McIvers, 1967

writing fiction, but I began to keep detailed diaries, typing hundreds of pages during my teenage years. For variety, I sometimes handwrote my entries. Ink pens and spiral-bound notebooks always accompanied me to camp and on church youth trips. And I documented nearly every mile of our family's annual road trips to Alabama and North Carolina. (Grandmother Withers died when I was twelve, but for several more years, I continued to visit Granddaddy in Baytown.)

* * *

In 1968, my parents custom-built their "dream house"—orange shag carpet and all—northeast of White Rock Lake, and I became one of 3,500 students at Bryan Adams High. At first, I had been excited about transferring to this new school. But by the beginning of my junior year I felt lost in the crowd, unable to fit into any group or make close friends.

Then, during my junior year at Bryan Adams, I became close friends with a Jewish girl who steered me into the school's large Speech and Debate Department, where I was involved both junior and senior year. There, I found my niche as I participated in numerous local and out-of-town tournaments, winning a fair number of trophies and awards. Unlike the stereotypical "wild" preacher's kid, I kept my behavior pretty much in check. By the age of seventeen, however, I began to rebel intellectually, mimicking my nonconformist Speech Department friends.

Socially, I was also having more difficulty at church. I had always hung around with the older teens, and once they graduated, I discovered that I didn't fit in as well with my own age group. Many of my former grade-school peers from Wilshire had moved away, and the "new" kids who took their place quickly formed their own cliques. For the first time ever, I felt snubbed at church and found myself on the *outside* looking in. (With the benefit of hindsight, I—like most people—wish that I could go back and redo some of those rougher patches of my youth. How I regret having been so thin-skinned, self-centered, and resentful! How I wish that I had simply been a *nicer*, more self-assured person. But achieving such ideals is easier said than done—especially when you're a teenager.)

After high-school graduation, I bypassed Baylor University for the more liberal Austin College, a Presbyterian school in Sherman, Texas. My junior and senior years were spent at a similar institution: Guilford College in Greensboro, North Carolina.

In 1974, I graduated from Guilford with a BA in English; two years later, I earned a Piano Performance degree from Greensboro College. The music degree had been a total fluke. Yes, I had continued to study piano with Mrs. Hammann through my junior year of high school and had frequently accompanied both school and church choirs. And yes, I was quite aware of my birth mother's keyboard skills and realized that I had inherited some of her talent. But I had never felt a compulsion to follow in her footsteps.

The "fluke" came about in 1972 when, through a series of near-magical coincidences, I landed a summer job at a performing arts

I call this photo "Hippie at the Piano"

camp for girls in western Massachusetts. There, I spent many happy
hours accompanying ballet classes and theatrical productions. When
I transferred to Guilford College, I did not want to stop playing; while
working on an English degree, I resumed my piano studies at nearby
Greensboro College and served as accompanist for Guilford's choir.
Soon, I was immersed in music courses and, in 1976, ended up with a
second degree.

For the next several years, I lived in Greensboro, giving private piano
lessons, playing for ballet classes at the North Carolina School of the
Arts, and returning to the Massachusetts camp for several summers.

* * *

Lest it seem that my career path was smooth, well-marked, and clearly
lit, that was not always the case. And if that road was sometimes bumpy,
my *emotional* journey into adulthood was downright turbulent.

Major problems had first arisen when, at sixteen, I was walloped by depression. When it showed no signs of abating, my parents consulted a psychiatrist, whom I began seeing weekly. At that time, medications were not readily available to treat depression. The only thing my doctor could do was to prescribe Valium and let me chat with him each Wednesday afternoon.

The depression followed me to college where, safely away from home, I freely vented a long pent-up anger (this was, after all, the era of "If it feels good, *do* it!"). But instead of being healthy, my expressions were all too often excessive and inappropriate. With door slams, screams, and curses, I lashed out at the whole world, losing friends and destroying relationships in the process.

During my later college years, music—as well as my delightful summers in Massachusetts—lifted my spirits and helped to keep me on a more even keel. A healing antidote during difficult times, it proved to be a true "gift of grace."

After graduation, however, I was once again gripped with new waves of emotional pain. Realizing that my problems were not going to resolve on their own, I rationed part of my meager income to pay for five years of therapy with a psychologist—first one, and later another. My "issues" were numerous, and I will not rehash them here: not only would they fill another book, but I am no longer as willing to bare every corner of my soul as I might have been during the era of "confessional memoirs" (nor would I burden my worst enemy with such reading!).

Suffice it to say that my counselors and I invested a great deal of energy plumbing the depths of my psyche. Outside of their offices, I spent hours dissecting my feelings in oversized journals: such intensive self-focus was quite trendy during the "Me" Decade of the 1970s.

Some of my problems might have arisen even if I had *not* lost a parent in early childhood. Others, however, undoubtedly stemmed from my birth mother's death. With this in mind, I tried over and over to recall those crucial days in 1956, hoping to unearth some powerful but deeply repressed memory. After all, isn't that the way it works in the movies? In *The Three Faces of Eve* or *Sybil*, the title character struggles with debilitating neuroses until hypnosis helps her to remember some original trauma . . . and—*ta-da!*—find instant healing.

Despite my efforts, such a dramatic moment did not happen for me. What *did* happen was that one of my overly maternal therapists moved to a distant city. I had known for months about this impending separation and had done what I could to prepare for it, including lining up a new counselor. Still, when the "loss" actually occurred, I was surprised by the intensity of my reactions. I screamed with rage, sobbed with grief, and dry heaved for days, unable to eat. Terrified over being abandoned, I visibly trembled.

"The world has ended," I wrote in my journal.

Over the next few days, I somehow managed to function, following schedules and routines. But as I ran errands and taught piano lessons, a mechanical refrain got stuck in my head: "There's been a death . . . there's been a death . . . there's been a death."

But there was no funeral.

No burial.

No flowers or casseroles or Hallmark cards appropriate for my situation.

The term "Post-Traumatic Stress Disorder" had not yet entered the mainstream vocabulary. Still, I intuited what was happening: that in 1978, I was being sucker punched by every emotion I had *not* felt in 1956.

My subsequent work with another therapist was not especially beneficial, and I grew increasingly despondent. Finally, I was referred to a psychiatrist, who diagnosed me with "major depression." This was in 1983, when psychotropic drugs were just coming into widespread use to treat biochemical imbalances. Abandoning "talk therapy," I substituted Elavil—a small white pill that proved to be almost miraculously effective. Two weeks after taking my first dose, I woke up one morning and thought, *So* this *is what it feels like to be happy. I had* forgotten*!*

Elavil was by no means a magic bullet that solved all of my problems . . . or even kept my mood consistently sunny. But it did help to level my emotions so that I could more easily change my unhealthy thinking and behaviors. The latter did not occur overnight. But gradually, I began to accept both myself and God's love *for* me. I learned to quit blaming others for my problems; to better control my anger; to be kinder, more loving, and less self-centered. These attitude shifts took years to achieve (to this day, I still struggle with some of them) and were not without setbacks.

But like my adolescent friendships and my music, that white pill was nothing short of *grace*.

40

To Everything A Season

WHETHER I WAS racking up college degrees, playing for ballet classes, or trying to unravel my neuroses, I returned to Dallas and my parents' home at least twice a year. (Dad and Mom also made occasional trips to North Carolina to visit his parents and to see me. Daddy Mac died in 1976; Mommie Mac later moved to Greensboro, where she lived with Aunt Ella until her passing at ninety-four.)

My father continued to pastor Wilshire, whose membership eventually grew to 3,600. Within the Baptist denomination, he accepted leadership roles at the state and national level. He served as a trustee of Baylor Hospital and was awarded an honorary doctorate by Baylor University (always modest, he equated it with "a curl in a pig's tail"). He toured the world and wrote books.

Mom was almost as active as Dad. Once my sisters were older, she was appointed to the Baptist Home Mission Board and hosted a TV talk show on a Christian network out of Fort Worth. Like Dad, she gained a reputation as a good storyteller; the two of them frequently traveled— jointly or independently—to speak at various venues.

During the late 1970s and the 1980s, the Southern Baptist Convention was fractured by theological and sociological differences, as well as leadership styles. In 1988, Wilshire voted to leave the convention and affiliate with the more moderate Cooperative Baptist Fellowship. This transition had been painful, and the drawn-out denominational conflicts undoubtedly contributed to my father's health problems.

Daddy not only endured relentless orthopedic pain, but stress had weakened his heart: he underwent his first coronary bypass in 1972, and another in 1988. Still, he had access to some of the finest doctors and medical facilities in the nation, and they kept him ticking along far longer than any of us would have thought possible.

Our household did not always offer a peaceful retreat for my father. It was, in short, a *zoo*. The telephone rang off the wall. People constantly came and went, while Mom rushed around trying to do ten things at once. As teenagers, my sisters were far more . . . well, *adventurous* than I had been, and their escapades would become legendary in our neighborhood. In the 1970s my parents had installed a backyard swimming pool so that Daddy could more easily exercise; during the summers, it was filled with teens. Sometimes *dozens* of them. These were the same kids—and later college students—who felt perfectly free to raid our fridge, walk on the furniture, call my parents by their first names, and send our poodle Napoleon ("Mr. Nappy McIver") a subscription to *Playboy* magazine. This was the way Mom and Dad wanted it: tired and stressed as they might have been, they enjoyed Shannon and Renie's friends, and created a welcoming environment for them.

Our home was not without arguments, tears, grumbling, and occasionally slammed doors. But the walls of 10825 Ridge Spring Drive also absorbed laughter and love, along with savory kitchen aromas and a myriad of sounds: swimming-pool splashes, a poodle's tinkling tags, adults baby-talking to this same poodle, crackling flames from a rock-wall fireplace, boisterous whoops and shouts during any televised Dallas Cowboy game.

And when the decibel level grew too loud, you might have seen my father slowly ambling toward the back door, a plaid tam on his head and cane in hand, mumbling to no one in particular, "Ya'll excuse me. I think I'll go over to Scotland and wander the moors for a while . . ."

Had Daddy and I foreseen such images back in 1959, we would have shaken our heads in amazement.

* * *

Much as I had once dreamed of marriage and motherhood, these milestones did not come to pass. For several years, this was a soul-

Mom and Dad in the Scottish heather

Dad, Shannon, Maureen (Renie), and Mom

crushing disappointment, but I later realized that being single gave me the solitude and independence I have always craved. It also gave me the freedom to uproot myself in 1983 and return to my home state.

Needing a more stable full-time job with benefits, I had returned to Dallas, where for two years I clerked at Baylor Hospital in the ICUs (and, yes, Baptists *do* give shots). The work was interesting, but it was a "dead-end" position.

My Aunt Winkie and Uncle Roger, who were by then living in Houston, had long encouraged me to consider a graduate degree in English. In 1985, they gifted me with a two-week "Literary Tour of the British Isles"—led by the director of Texas A&M's Graduate English Department, who just *happened* to be a close friend of Uncle Roger's. If my kinfolk had an ulterior motive, it worked. Awed by Canterbury Cathedral and Wordsworth's Lake District, smitten with Shakespeare's Cotswolds and the Highlands of Sir Walter Scott, I was inspired to reenter academia and resume a study of literature. Before our return flight had touched the Texas tarmac, Dr. Burt had offered me a teaching assistantship at Texas A&M.

Two months later I moved to College Station to begin graduate studies. While working on a master's degree in English, I taught Freshman Composition. The moment I first set foot in a classroom and faced thirty undergraduates, I knew that I had found my true calling. Three years later, diploma in hand, I was hired by nearby Blinn College, where I spent the next twelve years teaching Composition, as well as British and American Literature.

Once I moved to College Station, I was only a three-hour car trip from Big D and made occasional jaunts to see my family. Both of my sisters had graduated from Baylor, and each had married at Wilshire, with Dad officiating. Renie's husband, John McCarthy, came from a long line of Irish Catholics. When she asked Daddy to perform the ceremony, he was silent for a moment and then said, "Renie, I will marry you on one condition: for the sake of John and his family, I insist that you *also* have a priest present to bless the vows."

That was my father: loving, wise, and far more tolerant than many would expect from a Baptist minister.

In 1990, Shannon and George Allen gave my parents their first grandchild, Emily Paige. Mom had long wanted to be called "Grandmum," as is common in England; when Emily began talking, she heard everyone call Dad "Bruce," and she quickly tagged him "Goose."

And thus it was that my parents became "Grandmum and Goose" to all five of their grandchildren: Emily and Drew Allen; and Alexandra (Ali), John Francis, and Kyle McCarthy. Shannon and George lived in Houston for several years before relocating to Calgary, Canada. John's career in pharmaceuticals took him and Renie all over the country, and ultimately to Delaware. Despite the distances, my parents managed to visit with the McCarthys every few months, and they saw young Emily even more frequently when she still lived in Texas.

Over the years, the style of our Ridge Spring Drive house had morphed from Brady Bunch Contemporary into Homey Traditional. The great room's orange shag carpet gave way to a soft colonial blue, and—after a decade of Nappy's accidents—a thick-ribbed ecru. The kitchen's avocado-green appliances were now eggshell white. Gone was nearly every piece of '60s-era furniture, replaced by wingback chairs, overstuffed sofas, and even some sturdy antiques.

A vintage drugstore display case housed everything from our baby bootees and locks of hair to far older relics from long-deceased forebears. After Nappy went to Doggie Heaven (where, Dad claimed, he was probably hiking his leg on the Pearly Gates), Mom even showcased his collar and tags and poodle sweater.

This, then, was the house that the five grandchildren loved to visit and grew to cherish, much as I had my own grandparents' homes. It was a place where we McIvers had created our own traditions, where the walls held stories and nearly every object triggered a memory.

And just as the house had mellowed, so had my parents. Lawanna would always be high spirited and youthful, but she also knew how to cuddle and coddle and nurture. Over the years, she had *learned* to be a mother . . . and now an affectionate "Grandmum."

In 1986, Daddy became Wilshire's Pastor Emeritus—a mostly honorary title that allowed him to relinquish virtually all responsibilities to George Mason, the younger man hired to be senior pastor. Unlike in many churches, the transition was blessedly smooth, and George and my father became the best of friends. During the first few years of his retirement, Dad occasionally preached at Wilshire and for a time served another church as interim pastor. He also wrote. His first book, *Stories I Couldn't Tell While I Was a Pastor*, was followed by a sequel, *Just as Long as I'm Riding Up Front* (with a hearse on the cover). Both recounted humorous, touching, and inspiring anecdotes about our family and about his decades at Wilshire. Another book, *Riding the Wind of God*, was a more scholarly account of the Youth Revival Movement of the 1940s.

Beset as he was by health problems, my father still made ample time for his grandchildren. His physical activity was limited, but he loved to read (or tell) them stories and to share in their fantasy play. One of my favorite mental images comes from a day when I drove Daddy and four-year-old Emily to Love Field Airport so that he could escort her back to Houston, then return to Dallas on the same plane. I dropped them off at Southwest Airlines Departures and would forever remember the picture they presented as they headed inside: Goose's left hand tenderly clasping Emily's own . . . and his right hand clutching a Little Mermaid suitcase filled with a few clothes—and a *lot* of Barbie dolls. The scene made me smile as I recalled those bittersweet years when Daddy and I had no one but each other.

Grandmum and "Goose" with their five grandkids

41

Getting Well In the Broken Places

BACK IN COLLEGE STATION I stayed continually busy grading papers and devising lesson plans. The pace was often grueling, but I enjoyed working with students and socializing with fellow faculty members.

I was still taking an antidepressant, necessitating biannual "medication checks." At various times, I was encouraged to try newer drugs as they became available, and I usually found them to be quite effective. I had not received counseling since 1980, but in 1995, I consulted a psychologist to help me deal with some temporary difficulties. The two of us were a good "fit." Under Dr. T's guidance, I changed some self-defeating attitudes, gained a great deal of insight, and continued to mature.

I had long ago given up any hope of recovering some lost memory or repressed feelings associated with my birth mother's death. ("It's not that you repressed any emotions *after* they arose," Dr. T theorized. "At four, you never allowed those emotions to surface in the *first* place—for they would have been unbearable.") And I no longer believed that all of my adult problems stemmed from her death. At the same time, however, I realized that the early loss of a parent had profoundly affected my emotions. I likened that traumatic event to a black hole: I could not see, touch, feel, or recall in any depth, but I knew it was there because of the tremendous force it exerted on everything around it. In my own case, its power was most apparent whenever I experienced real or perceived rejection.

Yet another effect became apparent to me one day when I watched my four-year-old niece Emily trying to color a picture. She was having trouble and began whining for her mother, Shannon, who was nearby but preoccupied with something else. Finally, Emily threw her crayon across the kitchen table and put her head down on the coloring book, weeping in frustration. "What on earth is wrong?" asked Shannon, walking over to the table.

"It's too *hard!*" cried Emily. "I need you to *help* me!"

In an instant, I was transported back to that hot summer day in 1956 when I couldn't get my toy truck to budge and had wailed for my own mother.

I thought of the numerous times, as an adult, when I still succumbed to that same helplessness and frustration. It didn't take much to send me into a tailspin: tax forms, technology, trying on clothes (after two hours of shopping, I *still* need a tranquilizer and a nap). Yes, all adults experience stress, but my reactions were often over-the-top childish. To this day, whenever I catch myself having an "It's too *hard!*" spasm, I think, *Kate, you are acting just like a four-year-old.*

I began to recognize that in many ways, the wrenching loss of my mother *did* leave me emotionally "stuck" at four. This did not excuse some of my attitudes or juvenile behaviors, but it did help to explain them.

✻   ✻   ✻

Although I rarely thought of my birth mother, I occasionally amused myself by wondering what she might think if she suddenly returned to our high-tech world of the 1990s. She would certainly marvel at microwave ovens, home computers, and telephone answering machines. Barcode scanners would amaze her, as would housewives who wore *blue jeans* to do their grocery shopping! And how shocked she would be to hear a store's PA system routinely playing Elvis Presley and rock 'n' roll tunes that had been judged "sinful" in her era. But times change, and I imagined that Mother (like her dear friend Melba, who rejoiced when Baylor University finally lifted its dance ban in 1996) would quickly adjust.

I sometimes wondered what parts of our modern world *would* have been familiar to my mother as she viewed it from a 1956 vantage point. For instance, would she have recognized televised reruns of *I Love Lucy, Father Knows Best,* or *The Adventures of Ozzie and Harriet?* Absolutely! But not *Leave It to Beaver,* which didn't premiere until 1957, or *The Donna Reed Show* in 1958. She probably knew that Liza Minnelli was Judy Garland's little girl but had no inkling that this child would become famous in her own right. She might have seen the film version of *Oklahoma!* (1955) but not *The Sound of Music* (1965).

Upon learning that John F. Kennedy had been assassinated, would she have recognized his name? Almost certainly, for JFK was a popular young senator in the mid-1950s, and his marriage to Jacqueline Bouvier had dominated society columns.

I once asked Daddy if my mother ever flew on an airplane. Yes, he said. She once accompanied him to a convention in Missouri.

* * *

One evening when I was well into middle age, I was sitting on my living room sofa in College Station, grading a stack of essays. I paid little attention to a droning TV, for I was preoccupied with grammatical errors, convoluted sentence structures, and two cats who thought my red pen was a toy. But after a half hour or so, something onscreen caught my interest. It was a documentary on the paranormal "signs" or visitations that some people have received from deceased loved ones. I had never been particularly psychic myself nor had I experienced any clear messages from the Other Side. Still, I was completely open to the possibility of afterlife communication.

That evening's program featured the case of a three-year-old child who regularly "saw" and conversed with a grandfather who had died years before she was born. The parents stressed that they rarely spoke of this grandfather and that the little girl had never seen a picture of him, yet she recounted details and mannerisms that she could not possibly have known except through a personal encounter.

My pen had been poised over a student's essay, but I now set it aside, along with the stack of papers. Giving my full attention to the television, I watched a small girl race to playground equipment, giggling and chatting with some unseen presence. She seated herself in a swing that began to sway in graceful arcs as she urged invisible hands to push her "higher!" In an instant, I was mentally transported back to our Lubbock yard, where my mother was hanging damp sheets on a clothesline as I sat in a tree swing and called, "Come *push* me!"

Against this tableau the TV host provided commentary: "Some people," he explained, "believe that spirits are more likely to visit children instead of adults because small children are far more sensitive to and accepting of such encounters."

Oh yeah? I suddenly snapped. *And what about* me*? Did I just fall through the cracks?*

My snarky response was so unexpected and intense that it took me by surprise.

As the host continued his narration, my vision was drawn to a nearby bookcase where, alongside other large tomes, I had shelved the two volumes of JEAN letters that Daddy had passed on to me. I rarely opened those calfskin books, but a few days earlier, something had prompted me to revisit them. Many of those letters and sympathy cards were still fresh in my mind:

I came to know you and Jean at a time of personal distress in my own life. I shared some very personal experiences with her, and she always instilled in my heart the peace that passes understanding. She walked with Jesus, and radiated his spirit and love.

* * *

I feel I have lost a dear friend whose quiet but radiant, humble, and consistent Christian faith has long been an inspiration. Hers was a rare and beautiful character.

* * *

Jean was pianist for the Negro mission in Waco when I preached there. She was always so willing to serve the Lord.

* * *

She gave me so many practical tips on how to be a Christian wife and mother.

* * *

Bruce, I want you to know that Jean was instrumental in encouraging me to no longer delay an answer to my call [to the ministry].

As I now recalled these testaments to Mother's faith, I found myself deeply moved—not by pride or piety or sorrow . . . but by *anger*. The emotion took hold like a small but intense pinprick, then grew larger and more painful until I cried out, "*WHY?*"

I wailed it loudly enough to startle my cats. They bolted across the room and then stared at me, wide-eyed and confused. I had learned years earlier that cats are greatly upset by shouting or weeping, especially if they are not used to hearing such things.

"It's okay," I told them in a calmer tone. "Mommy's all right." Reassured, the kitties went about their business, and I turned back to the TV. But I could no longer focus on the program. Its images and sounds faded in my mind, crowded out by a fury that demanded expression. This time, in deference to the cats, I kept my mouth shut. But behind sealed lips and clamped teeth, I let fly with angry, sarcastic thoughts:

> *Mother, I'm just delighted that you were oh-so-perfect here on earth, and that you're up there flittin' around with the angels and your fellow saints, and that you can stand around the throne singing eternal hosannas forever and ever. I think it's hunky-dory that in your spare time, you and God "go through the field together," and that you hold hands and talk "as good friends should and do." But, Mother, when I called you on that toy telephone*
> *WHY.*
> *DID.*
> *YOU.*

NOT.

ANSWER ME?

You don't DO that to a four-year-old! It's just plain MEAN! Good God, Mother, I didn't even know how to tie my shoes!

By now, my chest was heaving, and while tears did not flow in a torrent of grief, they trickled in an anger that was finally directed at the correct source.

Or *sources.*

Even now, I'm not sure if I was more furious with my mother or with God, for I don't know who decides about heavenly visitations between loved ones. As an adult, I understand that such contact might not have been in my best interest (since preschoolers cannot easily separate fantasy from reality, "hearing from" or "seeing" Mother might have just confused me, amplified my grief, or delayed my adjustment to the loss).

But on that night in College Station, I was reacting on a much more primal level—as a small child who didn't give a fig about theology, buried Bibles, hobnobbing saints, or holy platitudes. Still crying soundlessly, I continued to unleash my mental tirade:

Look, Mother, I know you couldn't control getting sick and dying. But what makes me so spitting mad is that you could have chosen to answer that telephone! You, of all people, knew how ultrasensitive I was and how receptive I would have been. It's just flat-out cruel to ignore someone—but especially your own child! And if God kept you from answering me, then He was mean, because He'd rather walk through the meadows with you than care about a little girl's feelings!

I had been close to hyperventilating, but as I sat there, my breathing gradually slowed. My chest stopped heaving, and my pulse calmed. Finally, my tears were spent, and so was I.

A commercial jingled on the television, and one of the kitties meowed. I got up and went into the kitchen to feed him. I wasn't sure how to process all of the emotions that had just wrung me out. Nor did I receive any clear answers to the questions I had hurled upward.

However, while I was popping the lid off a can of Friskies, I did have a "vision" of sorts. It was just a quick mental flash, but in my mind's eye I suddenly saw the pink-and-white angel rattle that I had stumbled upon shortly after Mother's death.

I had not thought of it in decades.

Now, I wondered: *Could my mother have been sending me a message after all? Could that little cherub have been her version of "Pennies from Heaven"?*

Bereaved adults might find solace in hymns and scriptures and eulogies, but perhaps Mother had known that what I needed was a *toy*. Something pretty and pink and beribboned. Something tangible that I could hold in my hands and tie to a crib. A *perfect* toy that might bring some moments of comfort and pleasure.

It made perfect sense. Still, part of my mind scoffed at the notion: *It's silly to read so much into what was probably just a coincidence.*

But then I recalled a saying that I had read somewhere: "Coincidences are just Providence in disguise."

* * *

Would my life have been any different had I *not* tuned in to that television program when I did?

I don't know.

I do know that within a week of my silent tantrum, I had two unexpectedly healing dreams. In the first, I learned that, unbeknownst to our family, my mother had never died in 1956; in fact, she had been living in Dallas for the past forty years! When she and I were reunited in the dream, I confronted her with a mixture of joy and irritation: "Why on earth didn't you drop by our house and see us?" I asked. "Or at least *call?* Our number was right there in the phone book!"

"Well," Mother answered, "it was because Daddy-Boy had remarried, and you all now had another family. It would not have been appropriate for me to intrude in your lives. But rest assured, I *have* been around and have watched you through all of these years."

If this first dream brought comfort, the second dramatically altered my perceptions. In the latter, I traveled to heaven where I found not winged angels, pearly gates, or streets of gold but rather a plain kitchen table where sat several young women, including my mother. What a grand time they seemed to be having as they laughed and chatted like friendly neighbors at a coffee klatch! The women were youthful and lovely in their casual but becoming housedresses and short hairstyles of the mid-1950s.

Suddenly, I joined them, taking a seat across the table from my mother. I was quite aware of being in her presence, but in a manner that was dramatically different. For in the dream, I was no longer a small child still traumatized by the severing of a primal bond but rather a grown woman enjoying the camaraderie of other women.

In retrospect, I realized that Mother and I never had the chance to relate as adults. As a narcissistic preschooler, I would have viewed my birth mother as little more than a nurturer who met my bottomless needs. In the months before her death, I was just beginning to "detach" from her—to see her as a separate person whom I could imitate and admire. (I had even taken to calling her "Jean" once in a while, which I thought very clever.) Still, her life ended before I know her as a fully developed and unique individual in her own right. What were her particular quirks and habits and tastes? What were her favorite foods? The funniest joke she ever heard? Her most embarrassing moment? Her favorite composer? Author? What were her greatest hopes and desires?

This second dream proved to be especially cathartic, for it revealed a pleasant and far more fulfilling way of relating to my mother. And it gave me hope that the two of us *will* one day become reacquainted over a cup of coffee . . . like close friends who have been too long apart.

42

In The Sweet By And By

In May of 2000, I moved back to North Carolina, for whose soaring pines, hazy foothills, and crisp autumns I had never quit longing. This was not an impulsive uprooting but one that I had carefully planned.

Despite the rewards of teaching, fifteen years in the classroom (including summers) had taken a heavy toll. I was physically and mentally sapped. It wasn't so much the lecturing, conferencing, and lesson planning that depleted me—although I did find it increasingly difficult to multitask as I aged. Rather, it was the nonstop grading of hundreds of compositions and research papers. The problem was my own OCD-level of perfectionism. Week after week, I tediously corrected every grammatical and mechanical error, pounced upon every logical fallacy or half-baked notion, groped through drunkenly organized paragraphs . . . all of this while simultaneously offering suggestions, encouragement, and praise. Then, I would lie awake at night fretting over whether to give a particular essay a C-plus or a B-minus.

Because I devoted such excessive time and attention to each paper, I was always late in returning them. This, in turn, threw us off the syllabus, which exacerbated my stress. It got so that I would literally throw up when faced with stacks of unmarked papers.

For some time, I had contemplated returning to North Carolina, and the yen grew stronger with each passing year. I considered a similar teaching job in the Tar Heel State, but not only was the pay significantly less than I was making in Texas, I was just plum "burned out" from grading papers. With rose-colored glasses, I convinced myself that I could resume my first career as an itinerant piano teacher and make a decent living.

My parents were initially horrified when I announced that at age forty-eight, I was not only planning to leave a secure teaching career and return to a life of freelancing, but I was cashing in my retirement to finance the move and transition. Mom eventually came to champion my decision; I think she recognized that I was truly on the verge of a nervous collapse. Dad, while outwardly supportive, remained quite concerned.

Nevertheless, I hired a moving van, put my kitties in my Toyota, and made the cross-country trek. Once in Greensboro, I stayed with my Aunt Ella and Uncle Bill until I found a suitable apartment. Their Baptist church immediately hired me as accompanist, and I began to recruit a few piano students, knowing that more would follow in the fall. I continued to be optimistic that a music career (perhaps supplemented with some freelance editing) would allow me to both fully support myself *and* compensate for lost benefits.

The Good Lord knew better.

During my second week in Greensboro, I had driven out to our local airport—the same one I had flown into as a child. As a college student, I had sometimes enjoyed sitting in the observation deck and watching the planes come and go. It was an "escape" back then, as it was now. Although I had financial padding, I knew it would not last forever. I had decided that it wouldn't hurt to look for some supplemental work. And so on that early-June morning, I scolded myself: "Kate, you need to be pounding the pavement for a part-time job . . . *not* out here at the airport watching planes take off!"

The Piedmont Triad International Airport was almost unrecognizable from the one I used to frequent. The runways were the same, but the original terminal was long gone, replaced by a larger and more modern facility. The old observation deck no longer existed. After driving around to locate the best vantage point for plane-watching, I ended up in a remote parking lot near the end of one runway. There, I met two Parking Department managers who just happened to be out there repairing a broken gate. We chatted for several minutes, and I told them about my recent move and future plans. Finally, we said our goodbyes. The managers walked off toward their van . . . but suddenly stopped and came back. Was there any chance, they wondered, that I might be interested in a part-time job in a parking booth? They were pretty desperate for extra help and assured me I would have lots of free time to read, watch TV, or even write on my personal laptop.

Well . . . why not? I told them that I *would* be interested, just as long as the job didn't interfere with my church obligations.

I formally applied and was quickly hired.

"I can just hear Daddy's groans," I told Aunt Ella, "when he learns that I've chucked my graduate degree to sit in a parking booth!"

Upon hearing the news, Daddy was actually relieved. "I'm not worried about her now," he told Mom. "She's going to be okay."

* * *

I was working in one of those parking booths on the morning of December 22, 2001, and my heart was breaking.

My father had suffered from congestive heart failure for several years, and his condition had worsened since my move to Greensboro eighteen months earlier. My sisters and I had quickly been summoned to Dallas the previous July, when it seemed that his death was imminent. But by the time we arrived, Daddy had rebounded. "What are we gonna do?" we asked ourselves at the DFW airport, where our planes had landed within minutes of each other. "If we all show up at once, he'll get worried!" Finally, realizing that Dad's birthday was only days away, we decided to stop at a party-supply store on the way to Baylor Hospital. Half an hour later, we trooped into his room bearing balloons, noisemakers, and a colorful banner. "Surprise!" we cried. "We're here to celebrate your birthday a week early!" Dad stared at us. "No, you're not," he said, seeing right through our scheme. "You're here for my *funeral!*"

Dad was discharged, and we once again visited when I flew home for Thanksgiving. Then, as Christmas approached, my father took a turn for the worse and was rehospitalized. Through the years, his doctors had treated his weak heart with periodic infusions of some miracle medicine, but they—and he—knew that at some point, the infusions would no longer be effective.

That time came during the third week of December.

Pastor George Mason had phoned me the previous night to relay the news. After receiving a grim verdict from the cardiologist, my parents had decided to discontinue aggressive treatment. Dad was going to be discharged from the hospital on this day—December 22—and essentially sent home to die.

On that morning, my father was not literally on his deathbed; instead of ashen, semiconscious, and gasping for breath, he was up and dressed, joking and laughing with a string of visitors. Mom was at the beauty salon, after which she would pick Dad up and take him home. When she had phoned Daddy earlier, he told her how unhappy he was with his bland, low-sodium hospital breakfast. He normally kept a contraband packet of salt with him but had searched everywhere and couldn't find it. "Where's that damned salt?" he muttered over the phone. (Those would be his last words to Mom. A few days later, she would discover the tiny packet hidden inside his Bible.)

No one knew how long my father would live once he was home. He could pass away in a few days . . . or a few weeks. Once we received word of his condition, my sisters and I began making plane reservations to fly to Dallas. My reservation was for the day after Christmas, so I went ahead and worked my Saturday shift at the airport.

Aunt Ella—Dad's sister—was flying to Dallas that very morning to "nurse him to the end." I was working on the top level of the parking garage, and around 10 a.m., I watched her jet spear upward into the cold blue sky.

Because of 9/11, the airport had temporarily lost its metered parking at the terminal. Short-term customers were using the garage, and I was extremely busy exiting drivers who had just picked up loved ones flying in for Christmas. Nearly every vehicle was full of holiday cheer and gaily wrapped packages. I did my best to smile as I interacted with drivers: *Good morning! . . . Two dollars, please . . . Thank you . . . Have a wonderful holiday! . . . That will be one dollar . . . Thank you . . . Merry Christmas! . . . No, I won't have to work—I'll be spending Christmas in Texas . . .*

My motions were robotic, my merriment false. Even as I continued these routine tasks, my thoughts began to rise upward and outward, spanning the hundreds of miles between my parking booth and my father's room at Baylor Hospital. I found myself silently expressing sentiments that went something like this:

Daddy, I want to thank you for all you have meant to me, all you have given me through your example, wisdom, and love. I will do my best to live in a way that will make you proud. I will be kinder and more sensitive to others. I will continue your legacy of storytelling. And I will do everything in my power to have a good relationship with Mother.

I was most emphatic about this last pledge. A few years earlier, Daddy and I had been discussing Lawanna one day, and I voiced a thoughtless criticism. Dad was silent for a moment. Then, his voice choking, he slowly spoke: "I don't know any other person who has loved you as *much* as Lawanna has."

And an arrow flew straight to my heart.

Dad's comment stayed with me, allowing me to finally acknowledge and *accept* this deeply maternal love. My relationship with Mom did not change overnight, but it began to steadily improve.

However, as Dad's health declined, I occasionally wondered if Lawanna and I might regress, growing more distant once he was no longer around to "hold the family together." Although this seemed unlikely, I had enough of a niggling doubt to concern me.

I did not want my father to be burdened by these same doubts during his final days. *Please don't fret about this, Daddy,* I silently messaged on the morning of December 22. *I love Lawanna with all my heart and promise to be good to her. I will do my best to cause her no worries or tension, because I don't want* you *to be worried about us.*

As I continued to wait on customers, I struggled with mixed feelings about my upcoming trip to Dallas. Deathbed scenes can be beautiful, providing an opportunity for expressions of love and final goodbyes. (Admittedly, this would be more painful if Dad were alert and active when the time came for me to return to North Carolina and my job.

Both of us would more acutely experience our final parting, the grief unassuaged by sedatives, sinking blood pressure, or woozy driftings in and out of consciousness.)

Despite the chance for last embraces and heartfelt farewells, I dreaded my trip home. I dreaded it for myself, for Mom and my sisters, and for Dad himself. He would certainly not want to put *any* of us through excessive pain and stress.

Up to this point, my thoughts had been wafting outward like incense, addressed to Dad.

But now I sent them upward, imploring heaven itself: "Please, God," I begged, "couldn't you just *take* him?"

I later discovered that at this very moment back in Dallas, Mom was sitting under a beauty-salon hair dryer, silently lifting this exact same prayer.

The phone call came less than an hour later.

Dad had been waiting for his discharge papers and for Mom to come get him. He was in a good mood and had joked to one visitor that he wanted to stop for some sodium-laden, high-fat Mexican food on the way home.

Then, while he was momentarily between visitors, someone heard a loud *thud* from behind his door.

They found him on the floor.

A cardiac monitor at the nurses' station confirmed that his death had been instantaneous. (The speed of Dad's "transition" reminded me of the obituary for one of my great-uncles back in North Carolina: "Among Herbert Moody's loves were his home, his family, rest at the end of the day, his dogs, and his grandchildren—so how fitting it was that he was surrounded by all this, there in his own backyard, when, at the close of the day, he should quietly and suddenly leave it all and step over into Eternity to be with his Lord, and join other loved ones who had already passed over.")

I arranged to fly to Dallas the following morning. I had much to do to prepare, and while I could have been with others—including my cousins or Uncle Bill, who would be traveling to Dallas on my same flight—I preferred to be alone.

Thus late that night, I lay on my living room sofa with the lights off and the television on but muted. Because of my cats, I had not put up a Christmas tree but instead had strung colored lights across a wide archway leading to the dining room. Set against swags of greenery, the acorn-shaped bulbs created familiar hues from my Christmases past: ruby red, cobalt blue, emerald green . . . It seemed that I had known these electric colors forever. Indeed, I probably first encountered them during a babyhood trip to Baytown, where I crawled beneath Grandmother Withers's Christmas tree in my flannel sleeper, enveloped by love and warmth and succulent aromas.

Now, these same colors brought comfort as I lay on the sofa, surrounded by their soft glow.

My thoughts drifted not only to Daddy but also to my birth mother, who had died forty-five years earlier. In our family, we rather freely bantered about heavenly reunions with kith and kin (Mommie Mac, we were sure, was Up There caring for all our former pets). But we never discussed—nor likely even *considered*—Daddy's first wife waiting in the wings for his celestial homecoming. Even if the thought did cross our minds, it would have felt awkward to mention it.

Nevertheless, as Dad had grown sicker during the previous year, I *had* occasionally flirted with the thought of his fast-approaching reunion with his "beloved Jean." Even so, I did not feel comfortable broaching the topic with him. The very notion was like a lovely but too intense flame that I circled at a safe distance.

On a far more mundane level, I also found it difficult to mentally reconcile the worlds of 1956 and 2001, for the former seemed part of an entirely different universe. How *does* one suddenly span the enormous gap between Mamie Eisenhower and MTV? Perry Como and the rapper Eminem? Our tiny, bare duplex on Marquita Street and the spacious, memento-filled house on Ridge Spring Drive?

The thought that such disparate worlds could ever converge was so stunning that it almost took my breath away.

All the same, I was certain of two things on that December night. First, I truly believed that the timing and manner of Daddy's passing had been a *gift* to all of us, sparing our family a drawn-out deathbed vigil. My second certainty was this: that ten hours earlier, the earthly space between five decades *had* collapsed in a heavenly nanosecond, transporting my father into an eternity where time is meaningless, where loved ones wait, and where "we *shall* know each other."

And so as I rested on the sofa, soothed by the colors of my childhood, I was numb. I was sad. But I also felt strangely peaceful, for I knew that Daddy-Boy had at last been reunited with Mother, and I strongly sensed *both* of them watching over me as they had done so many years ago.

43

Kissing Cousins

ON DECEMBER 22, 2001, my Aunt Ella deplaned in Dallas to learn that her brother had just passed away.

On the day before Dad's funeral, my Aunt Winkie and Uncle Roger rang our Ridge Spring Drive doorbell. They had driven from their home in Houston to visit a son who lived in the Dallas area. They would be leaving the following day for a trip to Europe and would thus miss Dad's memorial service. But for over an hour, Mom and I—along with Aunt Ella and Uncle Bill—visited in our living room. Because of geographical distances, my maternal and paternal relatives had not seen each other in decades. Despite the sad occasion, it was a happy reunion. Aunt Ella reminded us that during the 1950s, she and Winkie had shared maternity clothes, shipping them cross-country throughout their many pregnancies. These two aunts had also shared another bond: caring for *me* after my mother's death. On that December morning, Ella and Winkie spent a good amount of time relating anecdotes from my childhood, laughing at misadventures, and comparing the number of spankings each had doled out.

As a child, I had spent an equal amount of time with each aunt, but the situation changed once I was grown.

During the years I lived in Greensboro—both in the 1970s and after my 2000 return—Aunt Ella and Uncle Bill were like surrogate parents. Their house was never more than a couple of miles away from my own residences; as their church pianist, I saw them at least once a week and shared with them many a meal in the fellowship hall. (In 2015, I would play for Uncle Bill's funeral, jazzing up traditional hymns in the New Orleans and "swing" styles that he loved.) I also regularly crossed paths with my cousins, since Bill Jr. lived across town, and Susan and Steve often visited from their homes in nearby states.

The Brooks side of my family was just as dear to me, but through the years my visits with Aunt Winkie and Uncle Roger had been far more sporadic. In earlier decades, my uncle's job as a college administrator took the family to several Texas cities and towns before they eventually settled in Houston. (Granddaddy Withers lived with them from 1968 until his death in 1974.) After I moved to North Carolina in 1972, I was lucky to visit my maternal relatives even once a year.

Once I returned to Texas and settled in College Station, a mere 110 miles separated me from my aunt and uncle. Despite this, our mutually hectic schedules kept us from visiting as much as we would have liked. Winkie stayed busy as a speech pathologist, and she and Roger frequently traveled.

Even if the Brooks had been easier to pin down, I almost never braved Houston's nightmare traffic. I was more likely to meet my aunt and uncle at a College Station restaurant, where they occasionally stopped en route to North Texas to visit one of their sons.

Or we sometimes connected in Waco. In the 1990s, Baylor University lured Uncle Roger out of retirement to serve as director of their Armstrong Browning Library: the beautiful museum/conference center that had once been envisioned by Dr. A and completed in 1954. Thus, for much of the decade, Roger commuted to Waco each week, where he shared an apartment with his youngest son. A couple of times during my teaching career, I made the two-hour drive from College Station to attend academic symposiums held at the library. Winkie often attended these events as well, so hopping over to Waco gave me a rare chance to see both of them.

Our most memorable visit, however, took place in London. My aunt and uncle had leased a flat for six months while Roger did research at the British Library, and they invited me to spend my Spring Break as their houseguest.

After I moved back to North Carolina in 2000, I managed to fly to

Aunt Ella and me

Aunt Winkie

Houston every few years. We would have loved to make these into annual visits, but mutual complications always seemed to interfere. If Winkie and Roger had been disappointed in my choice to leave the teaching field, they did not express it; instead, they seemed more concerned that I was working too hard or under too much stress. Whenever I visited, they pampered me with both home-cooked and restaurant meals, as well as excursions to clothing boutiques, museums, or the theater.

And we always made the forty-five-minute drive to Baytown, where Aunt Winkie would point out various sites and relive her childhood memories: "Over there is the park where Jean and I played. . . . This is the sidewalk where we left the sack of groceries after we squabbled. . . ."

It seemed that every time I was with my aunt, I learned yet another fact about my birth mother. For instance, I'd had little exposure to ballet until I worked at the performing arts camp in the 1970s, and I was instantly captivated by its beauty. It would be another twenty years before Winkie told me that, as a child, Mother had studied and excelled in ballet. At the same time, I learned that my mother had also been a tomboy until she reached adolescence. In fact, she was so good at ball games that the neighborhood boys willingly let her play with them. "When Jean was seven," Winkie recounted, "Mother took her shopping for a swimsuit. Jean wanted to dress like the boys, wearing only swim trunks. When Mother told her that young ladies needed to cover their chests, she lay down on the dressing room floor and pitched a royal fit, just a-crying and screaming."

So much for the myth that my mother *never* lost her temper.

Aunt Winkie would continue to narrate as we slowly cruised through the older sections of Baytown. "Over here is where our friend Della Sue lived . . . and here is our first house. I can still hear Jean's piano music pouring through those open windows: Chopin and Mozart, and endless scales!" A few blocks later, we would come to the Lobit Street house, which Granddaddy had sold in 1968. The fig tree was now gone, as were the windows' jalousies; the new owners had enclosed the property with an ugly chain-link fence. But I recognized the small door panes where Grandmother had pointed out the devil's horns and visualized her as she sat in her antique rocker studying genealogy records. I could

*Cousins Elyse, Chelsea, and Leslie (Elyse
strongly resembles my birth mother)*

almost smell Granddaddy's chicken and dumplings and hear his merry
chuckles. I could catch the "sweethearts" and "darlings" now preserved
in Winkie's own speech.

Whenever I went to Houston, I visited with cousins Leslie, Stephen,
and Douglas, who all lived close by (Geoffrey and Eddy were raising
their families in more distant cities).

Leslie had grown up to be a spitfire maverick who questioned
traditional beliefs, championed the underdog, welcomed controversy,
and freely voiced her opinions on most any topic. In many ways, the two
of us were "soul sisters," and I could bare my innermost thoughts to her.

I once confessed to Leslie how jealous I had been of her when we were
younger. She was surprised. "But I was jealous of *you!*" she exclaimed.
"You got to go to Baytown and have Grandmother and Granddaddy all
to yourself for a whole week. Whenever I went, it was with my four little
brothers, and I didn't get all the special attention you did."

While in Houston, I sometimes crossed paths with Leslie's almost-
grown daughters. Her oldest, Chelsea, was a blue-eyed, curly headed
blond—traits that she had inherited from Granddaddy Withers and
Winkie. Elyse, on the other hand, was a *carbon copy* of my birth mother
with her dark hair, brown eyes, and deep dimples. Leslie looked nothing
like her Aunt Jean, so everyone was amazed at how the DNA had

managed to hopscotch through the family and end up in my second cousin. When Elyse and I were together, I had to apologize for staring at her.

A similar surprise had occurred with the Music gene. Although each of my cousins was blessed with unique talents, the oldest four had never shown any interest in the piano. That skill landed with Douglas, the youngest. From childhood on, Doug thrived in piano lessons and developed concert-caliber abilities. He continued his keyboard studies at Baylor but majored in the more marketable field of Speech Pathology.

I had very few chances to visit with this younger cousin, because I was in North Carolina during a good part of his childhood and youth. But many years later, I reunited with Doug in Houston, where he and Winkie worked at the same public school. Doug lived close to his parents, and he came to their house several evenings when I was there. One night after supper, the two of us sat at a baby grand piano and had a marvelous time as we tackled Mozart duets and got punch-drunk silly pounding out Scott Joplin rags. Between selections, I told my cousin about a recent and especially vivid dream in which I had traveled to heaven. There, I found myself inside an enormous rehearsal hall full of grand pianos and walls of cabinets holding all the sheet music any keyboardist could desire. Doug agreed that this was indeed a magnificent picture of eternity. And then we resumed our playing.

Douglas had been only a toddler when Grandmother Withers died: he carried no memories of her, but I recalled how proud she had been of this youngest grandchild. As Doug and I filled the room with music, I could easily imagine our grandmother sitting in a celestial rocking chair, beaming with pride and tapping along with her good foot.

We were all devastated a few years later when Doug unexpectedly died of natural causes. But in the midst of my own grief, I must admit that I was a bit jealous because my cousin had gotten the chance to play heavenly duets with my mother before *I* did.

44
Second Childhood

IN SOME WAYS, it seems an eternity since Daddy and Cousin Doug left us. At other times, I feel that the years have flown by at a dizzying rate.

On April 6, 2017, I celebrated my sixty-fifth birthday. Despite arthritic joints and henna-tinted hair, I didn't *feel* that old, and people assured me that I looked far younger than my years. But the fact remained that I now qualified for senior-citizen discounts and would soon be eligible for Medicare and Social Security.

The latter nicely supplemented my airport cashiering job, which I had held for sixteen years and intended to keep. Shortly after Dad died, the airport offered me a full-time position—still manning a parking booth but with full benefits, including health/dental insurance and retirement. I didn't exactly plan to grow up to be a parking cashier, but it worked out well for me. I not only enjoyed the work, but it was relatively stress-free, physically undemanding, and continued to provide a great deal of free time for personal writing.

During my first couple of years back in Greensboro, I taught quite a few piano students, but once the airport job and accompanist positions at *two* churches began to demand more of my time, I gradually phased out all private lessons. My churches were fairly small, but both had excellent choir directors; it was rewarding to work with them. And while I was still a loner by nature and by choice, the churches nudged me to socialize at talent shows, fundraisers, and covered-dish suppers.

Back in my bohemian days, I would never have foreseen myself toting a casserole or dessert into a church's fellowship hall. But life sometimes has a way of coming full circle.

At other times, it veers off into utterly unexpected directions. For instance, twenty years earlier, I would never have predicted that if I needed recipe advice, I would phone my mother at her home in . . . *Tennessee.*

This jaw-dropping change had been set in motion less than a year after Daddy's death, when "The Widow McIver" attended a Baptist convention. There, she met Dr. W. C. Fields, a retired pastor thirteen years her senior (he was also a truly brilliant man, who for many years served as editor for the Baptist Press). Recently widowed himself, W. C. fell hard for Mom and began wooing her long-distance from his home in Nashville. After another few months of Internet courtship and a series of plane trips, W. C. proposed, and my equally smitten mother accepted. It was decided that they would both sell their homes and Mom would move to Nashville, where they would purchase a condo.

Although the news came as a bombshell, I was thrilled for my mother, for I genuinely wanted her to be happy. In April of 2002, scores of mutual family members converged in Dallas for a wedding at Wilshire. The ceremony itself was limited to kinfolk and close friends, followed by a church-wide reception. A few weeks earlier, I had flown to Dallas to cull through special mementos that I wanted from the Ridge Spring Drive house. During that same visit, Mom and I giggled like teenagers as I helped her finalize wedding details and select a cake.

Belated as it was, that experience helped us to bond more closely than we ever had before. And our relationship was even further strengthened after Mom moved to Nashville. As a younger adult, I never imagined that a time would come when the two of us could so easily chat, chuckle, and share our feelings, free of the tensions that had once strained our relationship. I'm not sure exactly why or how this sea change came about. It was certainly connected to the silent promise I had made to Dad on the very day he died. But at the same time, I truly did *not* want to hurt Lawanna or cause her undue worry or stress, for I had come to love her "somethin' fierce."

Although Mom was now geographically closer to me than she had

With Mom and W.C. in Nashville

been in Texas, I didn't see her as often as I would have liked. For one thing, it was a hard eight-hour drive over the mountains, and I had grown near-phobic about highway driving. I preferred to fly when I did visit Nashville, and the cost of airfare limited my trips. Still, Mom and I talked by phone every week or so. We came to share many of the same interests and discussed everything from world events to best-selling books to our mutual arthritis. We exchanged household tips, reminisced about Wilshire members and other Dallas friends, and caught up on family news.

None of us McIvers ever dreamed that Dallas would no longer be our "home base," or that none of us would even *live* in Texas. My sister Shannon had lived in Calgary, Canada, for many years, while Renie and John had settled in Pennsylvania. My five nieces and nephews were scattered from New York City to Los Angeles and points between.

In 2017, Mom was eighty-two, and W. C. was ninety-five. When they married in 2003, they had asked themselves if their love was strong enough to nurse each other through long, chronic illnesses if that day came. Their answer was an unequivocal "yes." And they spent many wonderful years together, traveling the world and experiencing all manner of new adventures. W. C. treated Mom like a queen and lovingly embraced the rest of our family. But his health had been failing, necessitating a move to a small apartment in an assisted care facility. With Mom experiencing chronic health problems of her own, Shannon and her husband were planning to relocate to Nashville to be closer to her.

*   *   *

In the meantime, my mother and I tried to stay connected through our smartphones. Usually, I just wanted to check in and see how she was doing. But occasionally, I needed emergency advice.

"Mom!" I greeted her during one typical call. "For a Texas Chocolate Sheet Cake, do I use a half cup of shortening, or a half cup of buttermilk?"

"Are you using my recipe from the Wilshire cookbook?"

"No, Mom. Yours—the one here on page 136—is for a two-layer chocolate cake. I'm fixing the 'Texas Cake' over on page 143."

"Isn't that Dot Newsom's?"

"No, it's Mother Hathcox's, but there are several variations listed below."

"Well, I would just follow hers to the letter—I think it calls for *both* shortening and buttermilk. And does hers use cinnamon in the batter?"

"Yes, and pecans in the frosting."

"Well, honey, make sure that you toast the pecans first—it will give them *so* much more flavor!"

"Okay," I said. "And you think I should just stick with her recipe?"

"I absolutely would!"

From there, we segued into a discussion of our various ailments. I asked about her blood pressure, vertigo, and arthritis.

"Aunt Ella told me that you were smoking marijuana for your feet," I joked.

"No," Mom corrected, "I'm rubbing a derivative of cannabis *on* my feet. It really helps."

"Where'd you get it?" I asked.

She named a friend in California, and I teased her about transporting drugs across state lines.

Mom asked about my acid reflux and a recent bout of bronchitis that was being treated with amoxicillin.

"Make sure you don't take the antibiotics on an empty stomach," she warned. My sisters and I had been given this advice so many times that it was almost like a "family mantra" for us (in the same fashion, Daddy would always urge us to drink plenty of orange juice at the first sniffle of a cold). I didn't resent the advice. Instead, I enjoyed feeling "cared for"—even if I *was* sixty-five.

For the next few minutes, Mom and I leapfrogged through a range of topics. She updated me on several Wilshire friends with whom she had stayed in touch. I filled her in on Aunt Ella's latest gardening project (at eighty-seven, my aunt was in excellent health and still going strong). We talked about Shannon's impending move to Nashville and laughed over a couple of wacky things that had happened at the Greensboro Airport.

Mom asked me if I had been watching the Netflix series *The Crown*. Neither of us would have predicted it during our headbutting days of the 1960s, but Mom and I had come to share a passion for Great Britain and British history. Since she also had a keen interest in archaeology, we discussed the 2012 discovery of Richard III's bones under a Leicester parking lot.

"I've just finished a great book about it," I told her. "It documents the whole project and is full of photos. If I come to Nashville, I'll just bring it with me and you can have it. By the way, I still have a $95 credit on American Airlines that has to be used before November. Maybe I can plan a trip for August or September."

"No," countered Mom, "you *first* need to go to Houston and see your Aunt Winkie." I acknowledged that it had indeed been far too long since I had visited my maternal aunt and uncle.

Mom then said it was about time for her to wake W. C. from his nap so that he could get ready for a doctor's appointment. I told her that I also needed to wind up the call. "I've got a nail appointment at 2," I explained, "and then I'll go shopping for the cake ingredients."

"What color are you going to get your nails painted?" asked Mom.

"I haven't decided. Maybe lavender or aqua. Something summery— even though that's a few weeks off."

Mom said those colors sound pretty.

And then we exchanged the words that we uttered too infrequently in earlier years, but that now—like a benediction—concluded every phone conversation:

"I love you, Mom," I said.

"I love you too, honey."

After ending the call, I studied my nails for a moment and wondered which color I *would* choose today: *Tahiti Sunrise? Hyacinth Blue? Shamrock?*

I thought back to my "hippie" days, when my college wardrobe consisted of little more than patched jeans and grungy sweatshirts. Back then, the notion of a woman (a *feminist*, no less!) sashaying into a salon to "have her nails done" would have triggered the world's biggest "you have *got* to be kidding!" eye roll and smirk.

But once I began teaching piano, I quickly grew ashamed of my ragged, uneven, and badly stained nails. Then, several years ago, I went to Nashville for a big family reunion and formal banquet to celebrate W. C.'s ninetieth birthday. Having splurged on a new dress, shoes, accessories, and an extra-special haircut, I decided that my nails needed attention (the one time I had attempted my own manicure, I came *very* close to losing my Christianity). At the salon, I opted for white-coated acrylics.

The next time I had them done, I switched to red polish, which I loved for one special reason: whenever I played the piano, my hands looked exactly like my birth mother's, with their softly rounded, apple-red nails.

Then, within a few weeks, I discovered a whole kaleidoscope of additional colors: *Peppermint Whip, Key Lime, Grape Punch.*

I was hooked.

The latest trend was for shades of gray or other neutral hues. But I was having too much fun with my colors to give them up. I almost felt like a little girl again, relishing a pleasure that was not as readily available to me when I was small. In fact, it sometimes seemed as if I were going through a second childhood . . . except that I was *much* happier this time around.

45

Return To Texas

ON A SUMMER MORNING in 2018, I watched Greensboro's suburbs fall away as my American Airlines jet lifted from the runway, then banked steeply to the west, toward Texas. Although I was headed to Houston for a long-overdue visit with Aunt Winkie and Uncle Roger, the first leg of my trip would take me to Dallas for a few days. There, I planned to reunite with various friends, attend services at Wilshire, and root around in the church's Archives Room for photos to use in my almost-finished memoir.

So this was how I ended up *en route* to Big D, covering in less than two hours the same distance that had taken all day in the 1950s. Through the years, I had become quite familiar with the nonstop flight path: as always, we climbed due west over the Smoky Mountains (here, I pictured Daddy boarding a rickety Trailways bus back in 1944, heading into the unknown with his cardboard suitcase and sack of ham biscuits) . . . bisected Tennessee, passing just south of Nashville and Memphis . . . cruised high above the Mississippi River . . . angled southwest across Arkansas . . . clipped a corner of Oklahoma . . . and then, from my window seat, I easily spotted the Red River, whose rust-colored squiggles marked Texas's northeast boundary.

"Black dirt!" I whispered excitedly a moment later, when plots of green and black and tan farmland glided beneath our wing. I often joked that for much of my life, I'd had one foot in Texas's rich black soil and the other in red Carolina clay. The earth below signaled that I was returning, prodigal-like, to one of my "homes."

A few minutes later, the captain announced that we were beginning our descent into the Dallas area, seventy miles to the southwest. Soon, we were very close to Sherman, the town where I first attended college. Back in 1970, an hour's worth of prairie separated Sherman from Dallas. Now, as I watched from the window, it appeared that in 2018, towns and suburbs had coalesced to form a nearly unbroken line of sprawl.

By the time north Dallas itself came into view, we were flying at a much lower altitude and a greatly reduced speed. I tried to spot familiar landmarks but was disoriented by the tangle of expressways, malls, businesses complexes, parks, and residential areas below. I finally located White Rock Lake, which *should* have helped me to find Wilshire's steeple, Mockingbird Lane, or Baylor Hospital. But after many decades, inner Dallas was now covered with enough greenery to camouflage most neighborhoods.

A colorful Southwest Airlines jet streaked across the sky below us—a sign that we were near that airline's base at Love Field, which I had flown into and out of as a child. On this day, friends would meet me at the massive DFW airport, fifteen miles beyond the Dallas skyline that was now passing off to my left. The cityscape, dominated by the Reunion Tower's iconic sphere and the Bank of America Plaza's crisscross pattern of green lights, was quite different from the one I gazed upon from my duplex window as a young girl. For one thing, the old Republic Bank and the Magnolia Building were totally obscured by much taller skyscrapers. When I had been in Dallas a few years earlier, I visited the Magnolia, which had become a boutique hotel. Pegasus had been removed from its rooftop and was displayed in the lobby, mounted on a pedestal behind protective ropes. I could not resist reaching over the rope and gently touching one of his red forepaws.

✳ ✳ ✳

During my Dallas sojourn, I was a houseguest of Monna Brown, a longtime Wilshire member now in her eighties. While I would not have been able to recognize many of the church's newer and younger faces, there were still quite a few members for whom I would always be "the preacher's daughter." Monna arranged for me to visit with a score of these friends.

With my sweet friend, Monna Brown

I was especially happy to visit with longtime friend Dot Newsom. At ninety-two, she was one of the very few remaining people who had known my birth mother. (It was Dot's husband, Asa, whose number was listed on the telephone notepad when Mother got sick in 1956. An ob-gyn, Asa later delivered both of my sisters.) As Dot and I shared a restaurant meal one evening, I mentioned the cookout that my parents had hosted the evening before Mother took sick.

"No," Dot corrected. "That cookout was a Sunday school social held in *another* member's home."

"Are you sure?" I argued. "My Aunt Winkie always told me that the cookout was at our duplex."

"No," insisted Dot. "It was at Bob and Marvalene Landrum's house over on Swiss Avenue. I know, because I was there!"

I thanked Dot for this new information, grateful for her ironclad memory.

During my visit, Monna, whose boundless energy put mine to shame, also insisted on squiring me all over Dallas to revisit every landmark from my childhood and youth. I had already heard that our orange duplex was in a neighborhood now known as "The M Streets" (*Marquita, Mercedes, Morningside, Martel*). It was considered a quirky and quite desirable part of town, attracting young adults who renovated or completely

6005 Marquita

rebuilt many of the older homes. So when Monna and I turned onto
Marquita one morning, I was not overly surprised to see cracker-box
cottages squeezed between fortress-sized McMansions. At 6005, we
paused for a long moment. Two large trees spread over what had once
been a barren front yard, almost completely hiding the orange house
from view. But we could see that both sides of the duplex appeared to
be vacant, with bare windows, peeling trim, and a buckled and useless
driveway. We agreed that the house was likely slated for an upcoming
demolition or total overhaul.

Over on Llano Avenue, I could find no trace of Claire Ball's cozy
Craftsman-style house, which had morphed into something much larger
and more contemporary.

My old school, Robert E. Lee, still stood on Delmar Avenue, but had
been renamed "Geneva Heights Elementary."

Changes had also come to the small shopping center at Skillman and
Live Oak. The A&P grocery store now housed a wine bar, the drugstore
was a yoga studio, and Ashburn's Ice Cream was a bagel shop. A fitness
center occupied what had once been Volk Department Store—site of
my fitting-room tantrums. And when we passed a yuppie-style restaurant
that had replaced Dr. Spegal's office, I fancied that I could still hear
the screams of a thousand tortured children.

My childhood friend, Claire Ball

One place that had *not* changed was Keller's Drive-In over on Northwest Highway, and Monna and I headed there after visiting my old neighborhood. While we lunched on cheeseburgers and Tater Tots, she asked about several people from my past.

For instance, what ever happened to Annie Kaye Howard, the housekeeper who had tended me in the 1950s? I knew that after Dad's remarriage, we lost touch with her, and she fell completely off my radar. Forty years later, when I was teaching in College Station, I drove to Dallas for a weekend visit. Mom had alerted me that she was planning a "big surprise," but I couldn't imagine what it might be. Then, on Saturday evening, I answered the doorbell to find Annie Kaye and her husband, John, standing on our front porch. Mom had managed to track them down and had invited them to dinner. Annie Kaye was still beautiful, and she and I had a wonderful time reminiscing.

But none of us had been aware, until that night, that Annie Kaye also bore painful memories from her days on Marquita Street. While we lingered over coffee and dessert, she told us about the sexual harassment she had endured from a male neighbor—a confession that stunned Dad (he recalled that he had found Annie Kaye weeping one afternoon but was never able to discern the cause of her tears). She had also been subjected to racial slurs and hostile glares when she and I rode the

A surprise visit with Annie Kaye (Bowen),
who tended me when I was young

Skillman Street bus or went into other "White" venues.

Monna next asked about the Brannons, who had moved to another part of Dallas and another church in the 1960s. Through the years, my parents and I saw Myrtle and Forrest from time to time, but I did not cross paths with any of the children until 1997. Daddy had been asked to officiate at Forrest's funeral, and since I was home for a visit, I tagged along. Bo was at the funeral home with his wife and teenage children; no, he had *not* grown up to be a robber but instead was one of Dallas's top real-estate agents. Ricky and his partner owned an art museum in the upscale Turtle Creek area. Rosemary ("Sis") was there as well, along with her children.

Through the decades, Myrtle had phoned my mother once or twice a year. In 2013, Mom heard from friends that ninety-three-year-old Myrtle was in a nursing home. It occurred to me that I had never *thanked* Myrtle for all she had done for me in those four years after my birth mother died. I thus decided to write her a letter of gratitude, and was told that she was touched and pleased to receive it. When Myrtle passed away a few weeks later, Lawanna and I sent yellow roses to the funeral home.

Monna also inquired about Ruby and Sterling Ball, whom she had not known very well. I told her that when Claire and I were older grade-schoolers, the Balls had moved to Arlington, Texas, and our contacts were sporadic. In the later 1960s, they returned to Dallas and to Wilshire, where Claire and I were in the same youth program. While we still enjoyed socializing, our orbits had shifted us toward different groups of friends and different schools; thus we were not quite as close as in childhood. Through Internet research, I knew that the elder Balls were deceased and that Claire and her husband lived in Lubbock, where they had raised a son and daughter. I had recently contacted Claire with questions about my memoir. She was delighted to hear from me, and we have become Facebook friends.

A side note: I could not recall ever again seeing our little white house after we left Lubbock in 1956. I decided to locate the house on a Google satellite map. Its exact address (2318 8th Street) I found on a surviving envelope and letter that Mother had sent to Grandmother Withers in 1955. I easily located West 8th Street, but the east side had apparently fallen off the grid. Switching to a street view, I noticed that my old street had been replaced by an apartment- and condo-lined boulevard, apparently designed for Texas Tech students.

I then vaguely recalled Daddy once telling me that our neighborhood *might* have been destroyed by a tornado. A cyber search confirmed that in 1970, an area of Lubbock near the university *had* been struck by a deadly F-5 tornado. I next located a meteorological diagram that superimposed the storm's vortex "touchdowns" over a 1970 street map.

Indeed, that tornado had obliterated our neighborhood.

I could not help but remember myself as a toddler in that little white house, swaddled in a footed sleeper and curled into a deceptively snug corner of my crib. I had loved the story of the Three Little Pigs, but in retrospect I shuddered to think how easily a Big Bad Wolf—or Panhandle cyclone—could have snapped our home's thin walls like twigs. Nor did I fail to recognize that my home did "tumble down," so to speak, shortly after we moved away.

While Monna and I were still reminiscing at Keller's, I happened to mention Betty Faye Dickey, Daddy's secretary who had taken me on an outing the day my mother fell ill. A moment later, Monna had a sudden revelation. "Betty Faye Dickey?" she repeated.

"Uh-huh."

*Betty Faye
in 1952*

With Betty Faye in 2018

"Why that's Betty Faye *Taylor*! She and her husband go to Park Cities Baptist, and she once taught my granddaughter in Sunday school. Betty and I are good friends! Let me call her right now and see if we can arrange a visit."

It turned out that Betty Faye had a busy schedule that afternoon, but she arranged to meet us at a nearby Starbucks for a cup of coffee. Pressed as she was for time, she had still managed to compile a file folder of copied photos and documents from my parents' BSU days, which she brought to me. I had been unaware that Betty Faye was Dad's secretary not only in Dallas but *also* in Lubbock and in San Marcos. In fact, she had been with my mother the night I was born. She apparently had been such an excellent assistant that my father's boss asked her to accompany him from city to city.

Dad and Lawanna occasionally crossed paths with the Taylors through the years, and Betty Faye attended Dad's memorial service. But as I had no clear memory of seeing her at those times, this current reunion was special to me. Short as our time was at Starbucks, the two of us were able to compare notes from the past (it was her handwriting on the telephone pad during Mother's illness and death) and enjoyed catching up in the present.

Betty Faye asked me about Melba Brown Shelton, my mother's best friend from her Baylor days. Recently widowed, Melba had lived in Waco for several decades and was now ninety-two years old. She and her husband had stayed in touch with our family after Dad's remarriage and had befriended Lawanna. I had seen the Sheltons only sporadically until I began teaching in College Station. One day in the 1990s, I rather impulsively located Melba's telephone number and called her. She invited me to spend a weekend at her home, and the two of us had a wonderful reunion. Melba's grown daughters lived in Waco, and I had brought photos from Mother's wedding, in which their mother was a bridesmaid. Melba had also gone through some memorabilia, and she gave me several letters that Mother had written to her.

Every year since we reconnected, Melba sent me a birthday card on April 6. The gesture touched me greatly, because it almost seemed that Melba was a special messenger delivering a love-gift from heaven.

Dot Newsom. Betty Faye Taylor. Melba Shelton. I could now count on one hand those remaining friends who had once known my birth mother. I was deeply grateful for these women who were the only remaining link to that distant part of my life.

A reunion with Aunt Winkie and Melba Brown Shelton

46

The Chapel

TOWARD THE END of my Dallas sojourn, Monna and I attended Sunday-morning services at Wilshire. The church had changed a great deal through the years. Since 1966, an enormous Georgian colonial sanctuary occupied what had once been the empty field with its swing set and jungle gym. Educational buildings had been added, along with basements and third stories. Membership remained fairly constant at around 3,600, for the church had long ago run out of physical space. Pastor George Mason, with my father's encouragement and magnanimous spirit, easily transitioned into the pulpit a decade before Daddy's death. Although some members were hesitant to accept another pastor, most came to embrace George, who not only filled Daddy's shoes but went on to chart new courses. Wilshire was now considered one of the most progressive and inclusive churches in the Cooperative Baptist Fellowship. The church's values were expressed in its motto: "Baptist by heritage, Christian by faith, Ecumenical in spirit."

Wilshire's interior had been so totally altered that it was nearly impossible to find the footprint of rooms I had once prowled. The office areas had many times been gutted, enlarged, moved, renovated, and divided between two floors. The nurseries, now filling an entire wing, were protected with a high-tech security system and accessible only through keypad passwords. Yet another wing was reserved for musicians and included a one-hundred-seat choral hall. Wilshire's music was mainly traditional and of superior quality. The church had its own orchestra and brass band as well as a magnificent pipe organ.

My mother would have loved Wilshire's pipe organ!

The other facilities were equally beautiful, consisting of atria, graceful staircases, chandeliers, a fountain, gardens, and a statuary. The cinder-block-and-tile fellowship hall of the 1950s was now an elegant reception room.

Despite its high-class decor, Wilshire poured untold amounts of money and labor into helping the less fortunate, both locally and globally. The church's membership had also changed through the years, and on each return visit I recognized fewer and fewer faces. But I cherished the love and friendship of many other congregants for whom I would always be "the preacher's daughter."

* * *

On my last day in Dallas, I returned to Wilshire, where longtime friends Janice Jernberg and Max Post accompanied me to the Archives Room. I could have spent hours culling through file cabinets of old photos and church scrapbooks, but my time was limited. I had preselected some photos from Wilshire's recently published history book to include in my memoir. As a member of the History Committee, Janice gave me permission to use the pictures, and Max—the church's computer guru—transferred my selections onto a flash drive.

The other purpose of my Archives visit was to look at the bulletins from 1956, since I wanted to determine exactly *when* my parents had joined Wilshire. The bulletins filled almost seventy volumes, one for each year since the church's founding in 1951. Janice pulled the 1956 volume from a shelf and handed it to me. Wearing protective gloves, I turned to the month of July and scanned a weekly list of "New Members." I saw nothing for Sunday, July 1, nothing for the 8th, the 15th, or the 22nd. Then, on July 29, my parents' names finally appeared:

> Mr. and Mrs. Bruce McIver
> 6005 Marquita

Since the listings were for those who joined the church the previous week, my parents apparently "walked down the aisle" on Sunday the 22nd.

I knew that they had been members for only a very short time before Mother got sick (on August 12), but I had no idea that the interval had been *that* short.

Leafing through the September bulletins, I discovered a thank-you note from my father:

> August 30, 1956
>
> Dear Ralph,
>
> It would be futile to attempt fully to express my appreciation for what you and the Wilshire Church have meant to me in recent days. I shall endeavor to show my gratitude by being a better member of the church and faithful to its programs.
>
> I am most grateful for your message at the funeral. Mrs. Withers remarked that she "seemed to see Christ standing next to Ralph and speaking through him." As someone remarked, "We looked in on heaven [that day]."

I shall attempt to express my appreciation to the church
at large from time to time. However, I hope that you will pass
along my sincere gratitude to the staff, deacons, officers, and
members.

Your friend,
Bruce McIver

Janice next located an enormous ledger, an official handwritten
roster of every Wilshire member since the church's founding in 1951. To
her amazement, she discovered that my mother's name was nowhere to
be found. The only thing we could deduce was that Mother died before
the church secretary or recordkeeper had a *chance* to enter her name.
(Several months later, Janice *did* find her name on a typewritten roster.)

* * *

Before leaving the church, I had one more place I wanted to visit.
While Janice stopped in the main office to chat with staff members, I
excused myself and walked a short distance down to the north wing.
The original sanctuary where we had once worshipped had been totally

renovated in the 1990s and, over my father's protests, named "McIver Chapel."

Lining a hallway near the entrance hung studio photographs of Wilshire's four pastors: Huber Drumwright (1951–1955), Ralph Langley (1955–1958), Bruce McIver (1958–1988), and George Mason (1989–2023). In 2023 Timothy Peoples would become Wilshire's fifth pastor.

The chapel itself bore little resemblance to the place where I once slithered under pews, played hide-and-seek in the balcony, and raced pell-mell up and down aisles. For one thing, the original front doors had been bricked up, and the balcony was gone. The altar had been switched from the north to the south end, and the pews were completely reversed. The electric organ had vanished, as had the choir loft. Instead, a baby grand piano anchored one end of a rostrum. The carpet, pew cushions, and the pews themselves were new. But unchanged were the stained glass windows, whose muted tones added to the room's quiet beauty.

McIver Chapel was most often used for weddings, funerals, musical concerts, lectures, and other events.

I stood at the back (what had originally been the *front*) of the chapel, and pondered how special this place had become to our family through the decades. My birth mother's funeral was held here. This was where Daddy and Lawanna got married, and where Daddy baptized me when I was eight. When my father died in 2001, his casket reposed near the altar while hundreds of mourners filed by to pay their respects during visitation. And one of my nieces chose the chapel as the venue for her wedding. "This room," observed Pastor George Mason as he officiated at the latter occasion, "is *packed* with spirits."

Studying the renovations, I now tried to superimpose a mental image of how the chapel looked decades earlier . . . and how it must have looked at my mother's memorial service on August 22, 1956. Very few remnants of that service existed, but I had learned several details from one Mary Jo Bentley, who sent Daddy a letter in January of 1957. In the opening lines, Mrs. Bentley apologized for her delinquency in writing and hoped that the belated letter would not "reopen wounds that have begun to heal." Still, she felt compelled to tell my father how profoundly the funeral had affected her and to share some of her impressions:

After five months, the memory of that service is as fresh in my mind as if it were yesterday. The first thing I remember was the sight of all those wonderful Baylor friends, and it brought home anew to me the joy of having Christian friends who rejoice and weep with us according to life's days.

Next, I remember the sight of Jean's lovely casket, with nothing on it but a dear little pink corsage. The sweet, sweet simplicity of it, so like her own life! One of the sweetest things of all to me was that her pastor [from Baytown] called her "Mary Jean," as if she were still a little girl. Then, he referred to your victorious spirit when you acknowledged that your prayers for Jean's "complete recovery" had been answered—and all of the precious tributes from Ralph. My! I'm sure she was pleased, and that you were comforted by "the peace that passeth understanding."

I felt that it was a holy hour, Bruce.

The letter, penned on pale-blue stationery, was the very last one placed in Volume Two of the JEAN books.

I knew about the funeral's music selections only because they were listed in a memorial book provided by Restland. The choir director's wife (Mrs. David Taylor) had played the organ, and the choral anthem was "My God and I." Contralto JoAnn Shelton sang "Blessed Redeemer," a hymn that depicts Christ as He walks "up Calv'ry's mountain . . . weary and worn" to face "death on the cross." I had always thought that a song about the crucifixion was an odd choice for a funeral . . . until one day when I noticed the hymn's final verse:

> O how I love Him, Savior and Friend,
> How can my praises ever find end?
> Thro' years unnumbered on heaven's shore,
> My tongue shall praise Him forevermore!

Now, I stood quietly inside the chapel . . . waiting . . . listening. For what, I was not sure.

A faint melody echoing down through the years? ("My God and I go in the fields together/We walk and talk as good friends should and do.")

The ethereal harmonies of a heavenly choir?

The whisper of angel wings?

I had come over 1,000 miles and was reluctant to leave this place until I received some message or "sign" . . . or perhaps a lovely epiphany with which to conclude my memoir.

Suddenly, my reverie was interrupted—not by celestial music but rather by a silly Nokia tune chiming from deep inside my pocketbook. Fishing out my phone, I noted a Nashville area code on the caller ID.

"Hey, Mom!" I answered.

"Hey, Kathie!" Lawanna's voice sounded froggy as she addressed me by the name still used by family members and old friends.

"Your cold has gotten worse," I said. "Have you been to the doctor?"

"No," she croaked, "I'm just toughing it out. But I wanted to know how your trip is going."

And so for the next couple of minutes I filled her in on all the details. Most Baptists see little need to separate their sacred spaces from friendly chatter, so I felt quite comfortable standing at the back of the chapel with a phone pressed to my ear. In fact, even as Mom and I talked, a wedding consultant and bride entered the room and were conferring down near the altar.

Lowering my voice a bit, I mentioned my sister's upcoming move to Nashville (from Canada), about which Mom was tremendously excited. But while Mom was updating me on Shannon's plans, she dissolved into a fit of coughing.

"Mother," I asked when she caught her breath, "what are you taking for that?"

"Nothing, really. Just over-the-counter stuff."

"Don't you have some hydrocodone cough syrup?"

"No, they don't like to prescribe that anymore."

"They're afraid you're gonna become a junkie at eighty-three?"

We laughed, and then I said, "Look, you should at least try a hot toddy. Do you have any whiskey?"

"I don't think so."

"Well, then go get some from Alma." Alma was the ninety-year-old Jewish lady who lived on the same hall and had become very close to Mom.

I experienced a moment of cognitive dissonance when I realized that Mom, a former Baptist preacher's wife, was now best friends with a Jewish lady . . . and that we were discussing hot toddies in a chapel where a 1950s-era statement of faith had once admonished congregants to "abstain from intoxicating drinks." (For the record, Mommie Mac, who lived to be ninety-four, enjoyed a toddy every night during her twilight years. Whenever she visited us in Dallas, Daddy would fix them for her.)

Mom assured me that she would get some whiskey from Alma and go see her doctor for antibiotics.

Between Mom's cough and my needing to reconnect with Janice, we should have wound up our chat. Instead we continued to jabber like schoolgirls. Mom thanked me for the book on Richard III that I recently sent her, and I told her about the latest Philippa Gregory historical novel I was reading.

"Is that the one about Anne Boleyn's sister?" she asked.

"No, this one's called *The Last Tudor*. It's about Lady Jane Grey."

We then incongruously veered to the topic of clothes.

"Were you able to find some comfortable sandals for your trip?" Mom asked.

"Yes, I got a great pair at Shoe Market but paid a fortune for them." I told her about some casual tops I bought as well as some new earrings. "And guess what color my nails are?" I prompted.

"What?"

"Turquoise!"

"Oh, that sounds so pretty! Wish I could see . . . uh-oh!" she exclaimed mid-sentence. "I think that's my physical therapist knocking at the door. Look, I'm gonna have to go. I have an appointment and don't want to keep her waiting."

"I've gotta go too," I said. "Janice and I are meeting Monna, Ann Hill, and Dot Laux for lunch."

"Tell them I'm sending hugs from Nashville. And be sure to give Winkie and Roger my love when you see them tomorrow."

"I will," I promised. "I love you, Mom."

"I love you too, honey."

As I stowed my phone, I found myself once again feeling profoundly grateful that Mom and I had achieved not just peace in our relationship but genuine warmth, camaraderie, and deep affection. (I pictured Daddy hovering in the chapel rafters, savoring his *own* moment of relief and gratitude. For, Lord knows, there were probably countless times through the years when he wondered what on earth we McIvers had gotten ourselves into.)

In the past, I often wondered why God had given me a second mother whose temperament and style seemed so very different from the first. And Lawanna probably wondered why God had saddled *her* with such a contrary, contentious daughter. I don't pretend to know exactly why certain people and experiences come into our lives (as the old hymn assures us, "We'll understand it better by and by"). Nevertheless, I strongly believe that whatever our circumstances, they can become a catalyst for spiritual and emotional growth.

And in recent years, I had wondered whether it was perhaps divinely ordained—as opposed to being a random fluke—that Lawanna took my birth mother's place here on earth. (In retrospect, the notion reminded me of one of those "find the hidden image" drawings where the image has been hiding in plain sight all along.) But while this was a relatively new revelation for me, Lawanna had apparently accepted it long ago.

While recently sorting through boxes of old papers, I had stumbled upon a typewritten letter that I had not seen in decades. Lawanna had composed it in May of 1974, when she and Daddy attended my graduation from Guilford College. Her very heart poured forth in the opening paragraph:

> Oh God, so many things have gone through my mind on this, the college graduation day of my daughter. My feelings are kaleidoscopic! I am very proud of her and for her, very grateful to you *for* her; very apprehensive as she exchanges dependence for independence; and perhaps more protective and maternal than I've ever felt toward her before. I suppose

this is a "proxy" prayer, Lord, knowing full well that her own mother would have prayed the same kind of soul prayer on her behalf—if she could have. So accept these concerns and desires of *ours* for the daughter we've both been blessed to love.

She then beseeched the Lord to grace me with wisdom, self-acceptance, love for others, courage, faith, and inner peace.

At the end of the letter, she added a postscript:

Kathie, I realize I've taken tremendous liberties in sending you my rambling thoughts that went "all over the place" during the Commencement address. But I feel that this may be my greater "graduation gift" to you to share them—not just for this significant day, but these very same desires will be my prayer for you every day if you live to be 100! I do love you very, very much.

I remembered Lawanna giving me this letter, but I didn't recall much more about it. In 1974, I was still quite antagonistic toward my parents, God, and pretty much the whole world. Did I even truly *thank* Lawanna for taking the time to bare her soul and express her heartfelt love in the letter?

It is this letter that I was thinking of after our phone conversation. The chapel was again empty and silent, and I tried one final time to mentally transport myself back to 1956 . . . to the pink corsage on a "lovely" casket and strains of "Blessed Redeemer." But these images were elusive, vanishing like will-o'-the-wisps before I could fully grasp them.

Instead, my thoughts kept returning to Lawanna. And if I had any revelation on that August day, it was this: while my birth mother might have given me life and shaped my earliest years in immeasurable ways, Lawanna was the one who had truly "mothered" me over the past six decades.

She was the one who had prodded, affirmed, fussed, trained, nagged, defended, cheered, and loved unconditionally.

She was the one who straightened my collars, signed report cards, kept vigil over my sickbed, endured piano recitals, sat through graduations, and encouraged me to write. She loaned me shoes, taught me how to make Swiss steak, and reminded me to toast my pecans for a Texas sheet cake.

She had wept, rejoiced, and lifted countless prayers.

The fact was, if anything ever happened to Lawanna—with whom I had forged a lifetime of collective memories, private jokes, and secret signals—*she* was the one for whom I would cry buckets of tears.

If I were to say that this revelation was accompanied by trumpet fanfare or the parting of the heavens, I would be lying. As it was, I simply took a final look around the chapel, then walked out to meet my friends.

But on that Monday morning at Wilshire, the faintest outline of a vision was sketched in my subconscious mind. Over the next days and weeks, I would become gradually aware of its evolving shape—of blurry edges that sharpened, grays that morphed into colors, and details that enlivened empty space—until I could instantly conjure an image that years later still remains fresh in my mind.

The scene is a vista of heavenly clouds backlit with iridescent pinks and purples and golds. Nested within these billowy forms is the same kitchen table of my "coffee klatch" earlier dream.

My birth mother is there.

I am there.

And then—*oh, my soul!* (as Daddy would say)—here comes *Lawanna*, out of breath and running late, as usual! She approaches the table, and moments later I interrupt my own reunion to witness *both* of my mothers as they finally meet each other face-to-face. They embrace. They weep tears of joy but also of *relief*: for in raising me, they have "fought the good fight" and finished the race, coming out more or less victorious. My birth mother Jean then thanks Lawanna for standing "in her stead" to complete the task that she had begun.

Lawanna joins us at the dinette, and I listen with vicarious pleasure as the two women share anecdotes, compare battle scars, chuckle at misadventures, and roll their eyes ("Remember when she did such and such?"). Then I join in, adding my own stories. But it is not all about me. As we chat and sip coffee, we three come to better know each other as individuals. What a glorious time we have as we recall our earthly hopes and dreams, remember our proudest moments, confess our most embarrassing faux pas. We tell our funniest jokes and even swap recipes (I can almost hear Daddy groaning in the background when someone mentions "Tuna Casserole." Yes, I very much long for a heavenly reunion with my father . . . but he is going to have to wait his turn: right now, this is a "girls only" tea party!)

And how sweet it is for the three of us to laugh, reminisce, and perhaps sing some of the good old hymns as we sit through years unnumbered, enjoying each other's company like the very best of friends.

Afterword

In 2020, I completed *The Forever Staircase* and mailed a copy to Lawanna.

Deeply moved, she later phoned me in tears. "I can die happy now," she confessed.

Mom passed away in November of 2022.

Although she died in Nashville, her burial and memorial service were held in Dallas. There, I joined my two sisters, five nieces and nephews, and two great-nephews who had flown in from all over the United States and Canada. Our bittersweet reunion was filled with laughter, memories, and many "Lawanna" stories. (Ever the shopaholic, Mom had ordered a new pantsuit during the final days of her terminal illness. Spying a stack of catalogs during a recent visit, Shannon asked, "Mom, why in the world do you need *more* clothes?" Our mother explained that her recent weight loss meant she needed a new outfit to wear in the casket. She was happy when the pantsuit arrived but told Shannon that the back of the top looked better than the front. Shannon rolled her eyes. "Mother," she sighed, "we are *not* going to bury you upside down!")

Mom was buried next to Daddy, who years earlier had purchased a double plot in a newer section of Restland Cemetery (as prearranged, W. C. was laid to rest in Nashville, next to his first wife).

After the graveside rites, we drove to Wilshire for a memorial service. I had been invited to provide pre-service music on the sanctuary's beautiful Bechstein grand piano and was happy to do so. As I played lyrical arrangements of "Shall We Gather at the River?," "In the Sweet By and By," and "Blessed Assurance," the sanctuary began to fill with church members and longtime friends, including Betty Faye Taylor. And how thrilled I was to see my childhood companion, Claire Ball! Claire lived in Lubbock but had grandsons in Dallas. When she learned of Mother's death from Facebook, she decided to attend the memorial service. Sadly, Aunt Winkie and Uncle Roger had both passed away in 2021, but two of my cousins surprised me by coming to the service.

I would visit with all of these special people during the after-service reception, where I would also be introduced to a woman whom I did not recognize. Her name was Carol Valentine, and she was a relatively new member of Wilshire. The name "Valentine" rang a bell, and I finally realized that her mother, Mary Louise, had kept me during my own mother's funeral. "I used to sit in your high chair and eat banana popsicles!" I told Carol. She and I would later become close Facebook friends.

For now, though, my task was to keep my emotions in check while playing lovely arrangements of "Precious Lord, Take My Hand" and "Amazing Grace." Finally, after a duet with organist Bill Jernberg, I went down to sit with family members in the second row of pews. Accompanied by the pipe organ, the congregation rose to sing "Great Is Thy Faithfulness." Shannon then eulogized Mom, eliciting both laughter and tears. Music director Doug Haney sang "Savior, Like a Shepherd Lead Us," which had been sung at my father's funeral. Pastor George Mason had officially retired, but he graciously returned to the pulpit to bring an inspiring message.

To conclude the service, we stood for a final congregational hymn. We turned to page 149 of our hymnals, Bill played an organ introduction, and we launched into the first verse of "Blessed Redeemer":

> Up Calvry's mountain, one dreadful morn,
> Walked Christ my Savior, weary and worn.

Shannon, standing beside me, looked stunned. "It's the *wrong* hymn!" she whispered. "It's supposed to be 'Blessed Assurance'!"

"No," I told her. "It's not wrong." Since I had not studied the bulletin ahead of time, I too was surprised . . . but for an entirely different reason. Mother had planned every detail of her service and knew exactly what she was doing when she selected "Blessed Redeemer" for the concluding hymn.

She had read a draft of my memoir.

Shannon had not.

My sister continued to quietly fume through the next two stanzas. "I can't *believe* they messed this up!" she hissed. "Why would Mom have chosen *this* hymn?" The congregation possibly shared her thoughts. Considering Mom's larger-than-life personality, wouldn't it have been more fitting to conclude with a majestic "To God Be the Glory" or "Guide Me, O Thou Great Jehovah"? A rather subdued song about the crucifixion seemed a strange choice for the funeral of Lawanna McIver Fields.

"Maybe they listed the wrong page number," Shannon fretted. "Or we submitted the wrong *title!*"

"It's okay," I assured my sister as we came to the final verse. "It's the right song."

"No, it's *not!*"

> Blessed Redeemer, Savior and friend,
> How can my praises ever find end!

But of one thing I was certain: I was probably the only person in that sanctuary who *fully* understood the import of those words.

> Thro' years unnumbered, on heaven's shore,
> My tongue shall praise Him forevermore!

And I alone recognized what a special gift had been sent my way.

A Service of Celebration and
Thanksgiving for the Life of

Lawanna McIver Fields
May 13, 1935 – November 5, 2022

November 18, 2022
11:00 a.m.
Sanctuary
Wilshire Baptist Church
Dallas, Texas 75214

ACKNOWLEDGMENTS

Many people helped this memoir move from a pipe-dream to a reality.

Special thanks go to the editorial and production staff of Book Villages, LLC. and to Susan Bussard for recommending this publisher. Tia Stauffer was meticulous in her fact-checking and copy editing. Book designer Scot McDonald worked magic with my half-baked ideas, creating the memoir's beautiful cover and interior art work. Publisher Karen Pickering deserves a medal for helping me through several anxiety attacks with patience, encouragement, good humor, and long-distance hand-holding.

Scores of friends supported me through the lengthy gestation of *The Forever Staircase*. It would be impossible to mention every member of this cheering squad, but I am grateful to each of you. Special thanks go to Monna Brown, who lodged, fed, and squired me all over Dallas during my 2018 visit down "Memory Lane." I am grateful to Alan Akins for the use of several photographs, to Max Post for transmitting these images, and to Janice Jernberg for helping me navigate the Wilshire Baptist Church archives. I appreciate longtime friends Dot Newsom and Ann Hill for sharing many of their own memories. And I am grateful to Dot Laux, who threatened to kill me if I didn't complete this memoir before her 100th birthday (I did meet that deadline!). Many thanks go to Toni Austin-Allen and Jeanne Harris, who read early drafts of the book and provided feedback. And thank you to George Mason for suggesting the reference to Psalm 16:6.

I am grateful to Chelsea and Elyse Blechman for giving me permission to use a photo of themselves and their mother, Leslie, in the chapter "Kissing Cousins." Sadly, Leslie passed away just as this book was going into publication.

A couple of final notes:

First, I am grateful to the "Brannon" family for the immeasurable support they gave to my father and me after my mother's death. I regret that I do not have any photos of "Myrtle." Many of the Brannons have passed away, and I have tried unsuccessfully to contact others. I was hoping that they could provide me with photographs, and I also wanted permission to write about their family. Since I was not able to secure this, I decided to change their surname and most first names. I do hope that whether or not the Brannons get a chance to read my memoir, they will be assured of my deep gratitude for the role they played in my life.

Finally, I want to thank my five nieces and nephews for serving as an "invisible audience" for this book.

To Emily Fox (and her children Knox, River, and Baby Fox due in June), Drew Allen, Ali McCarthy, John McCarthy, and Kyle McCarthy: Aunt Kate has no money to leave you, but I can offer you a legacy of family stories. I hope that you will treasure and enjoy them!